MW01231101

# Guide
## to
## Minnesota Foundations
## and
## Corporate Giving Programs
## 1983

# Guide
## to
## Minnesota Foundations
## and
## Corporate Giving Programs
## 1983

THE
MINNESOTA COUNCIL
ON
FOUNDATIONS

University of Minnesota Press

Copyright © 1983 by the University of Minnesota
All rights reserved.
Published by the University of Minnesota Press,
2037 University Avenue Southeast, Minneapolis, MN 55414
Printed in the United States of America

**Library of Congress Cataloging in Publication Data**
Main entry under title:

Guide to Minnesota foundations
and corporate giving programs, 1983.
Includes indexes.
1. Endowments—Minnesota—Directories.
2. Corporations—Charitable contributions—Minnesota—Directories
I. Minnesota Council on Foundations.
HV98.M65G843  1983     361.7′632′025776     82-21928
ISBN 0-8166-1219-6 (pbk.)

The University of Minnesota
is an equal-opportunity educator and employer.

# Contents

# Preface

In 1977, the Minnesota Council on Foundations published its first edition of the *Guide to Minnesota Foundations*. In 1980, the council published a second edition of the *Guide*. This book, like the first two *Guides*, is designed to help individuals and organizations seeking grants as well as to aid grant makers and the general public.

Unlike the first two directories, the new *Guide* includes information about corporate giving programs as well as private, corporate, and community foundations. Of the new *Guide's* full entries, more than one-fifth represent corporate giving programs—either charitable contributions programs or corporate foundations. This third edition of the *Guide*, therefore, has a new name: *Guide to Minnesota Foundations and Corporate Giving Programs*. The 1983 directory includes new data and three indexes designed to help direct readers to appropriate Minnesota grant makers.

We owe special thanks to those foundations and corporations that responded to our questionnaire; to the council's public information committee, which served in an advisory capacity to the project; and to those who used the *Guide* in the past and, through their comments, helped to improve it.

Jacqueline Reis
*Executive Director*
*Minnesota Council on Foundations*

Humphrey Doermann
*Chairman*
*Minnesota Council on Foundations*

# Acknowledgments

Jacqueline Reis
    Executive director,
    Minnesota Council on Foundations
Roberta Berner
    Editor and project director
Gary Henrickson, Ph.D.
    Researcher
Elaine Arndt
    Administrative assistant

*Board of Directors, Minnesota Council on Foundations*

Humphrey Doermann, Chairman
Sally A. Anson
Dennis W. Dunne
Isabel C. Huizenga
Robert C. Lauppe
David M. Lilly
Michael W. McCarthy
Robin B. Nelson
Dale R. Olseth
Robert J. Reardon
Hazel H. Reinhardt
Sam Singer
Emily Anne Staples
Mary Ida Thomson, secretary

*Public Information Committee, Minnesota Council on Foundations*

John Archabal, chair
Nancy Anderson
Martha Butt
Cheryl Byers
Pat Davis
Linda Hall
Isabel Huizenga
David Nasby
Mariam Noland
Marcia Townley

# Introduction

## BEFORE YOU WRITE YOUR LETTER

Keep in mind that most proposals are sent to inappropriate funders. Use this directory to increase the chances that your needs fit a prospective grant maker's interests and are within a funder's geographic, legal, and financial limitations.

If you need more information, try to find it before making uninformed guesses. Many grant makers make available guidelines, annual reports, or application procedures. It also make sense to follow a funder's protocol.

Become familiar with other sources of information. The *Guide* is meant to serve as a first step in your reseach on prospective donors. The Foundation Center Regional Collection, Minneapolis Public Library and Information Center, and the Foundation Center Affiliate Collection, St. Paul Public Library, have many useful materials and a trained staff to help you in your search.

Remember that a mass-produced letter directed at the general audience of "Minnesota grant makers" is likely to hinder you more than help you in your search for funds. Each grant-making organization has a distinct personality, a different background, and unique requirements and interests. Take some time to learn about a funder's individuality before you write your letter.

## THE MINNESOTA COUNCIL ON FOUNDATIONS

The Minnesota Council on Foundations (MCF) is an association of private grant makers that seeks to increase the practice of responsible and informed giving for community concerns. More than 100 members represent private foundations, corporate foundations, corporations with contributions programs, operating or special interest foundations, and community foundations. Council members are identified in the *Guide* by the reference mark (●) next to their names.

The council has provided information to the public since it first was formed in 1975. The *Guide* is one effort to provide information about private grant makers to the public. The MCF also publishes *Giving Forum,* a quarterly newspaper focusing on philanthropy. The council sponsors meetings and workshops for the public and also conducts research on giving in Minnesota. One reason that the council provides information to the public is based on the belief that informed grant seekers will direct their proposals to the grant makers most able to respond to them.

The MCF provides a wide variety of services to members, including seminars, workshops, special programs, and an informal newsletter. Through its services to members, the council helps to improve communication and the sharing of information among Minnesota's grant makers.

The MCF is a nonprofit organization supported entirely by its members. It does not make grants itself, nor does it direct applicants for funds to particular foundations or promote grants to specific applicants. Member organizations review grant proposals and commit funds independently.

## THE 1983 GUIDE TO MINNESOTA FOUNDATIONS AND CORPORATE GIVING PROGRAMS

The 1983 *Guide to Minnesota Foundations and Corporate Giving Programs* includes entries for more than 420 Minnesota grant makers—private foundations, corporate foundations, corporate charitable contributions programs, and community foundations. In its appendixes, it also lists foundations that are not accepting applications, those that are presently inactive, and those that make grants exclusively to designated organizations (including scholarship funds).

Entries describe the grant makers' interests, funding limits, financial data, application procedures, and geographic orientation. In most cases, entries also include sample grants, specific examples of where a grant maker's funds went during the preceding fiscal year.

Primary research for private foundations involved collecting data from the most recent Internal Revenue Service (IRS) 990PF forms on file at the Minnesota attorney general's office. The attorney general's files on foundations also include copies of foundations' original trust instruments. The *Guide* researcher collected data from both the most recent IRS 990 and the trust instrument in order to make the entries as complete and accurate as possible. In many cases, the trust instrument provided information about the foundation's interests, limits, geographic orientation, and history.

Community foundations' tax files were examined at the Minnesota Department of Commerce, Charities Division.

A second stage in the research involved surveying grant makers. (See the surveys in Appendixes 5 and 6.) One survey went to Minnesota's private and community foundations; the other went to 200 Minnesota businesses. The foundation survey was designed to verify information collected from IRS 990PF forms and to provide more complete data about foundations' funding interests, funding limits, fields of activity, types of organizations funded, and application procedures. Of 390 foundations described in the 1983 *Guide*, 97 responded to the survey, thus ensuring that their entries are as complete and as up-to-date as possible.

Corporations that give through a charitable contributions program rather than a foundation are not legally required to make their corporate giving information public. Fifty corporations responded to the MCF survey—twenty-eight corporations with foundations, twenty-four with charitable contributions programs. Many of the corporations that responded to the questionnaire indicated whether or not they have employee matching gift programs and scholarships for children of employees in addition to answering questions asked of other grant makers.

Those foundations that did not respond to the council's request for information are described according to data from their files in the attorney general's office or the Department of Commerce. All information was updated during the week prior to final publication deadlines. The published data reflect information from 1981 or 1982, depending on when the grant maker's fiscal year ended.

Three indexes follow the directory listings. The first, an alphabetical index, directs *Guide* users to grant makers included among the directory entries and among the lists of foundations excluded from the entries. The second is an index of the types of organizations funded and is based on data from the foundation and corporate surveys. By using the second index, readers may refer to grant makers that have expressed interest in funding in a particular area. The third index lists grant makers by size, using grants paid as a gauge.

Not every organization that is legally entitled to call itself a foundation will be of interest to grant seekers. For example, operating foundations are not listed in the *Guide*. Those foundations that are inactive but that, nonetheless, register with the attorney general's office are listed in Appendix 1. Inactive foundations are defined here as those that filed tax returns showing no grants for the last three or more years. Appendix 2 lists those foundations that give to designated recipients. Such foundations make grants only to a predesignated set of recipients (most often listed in the original trust instrument). Appendix 2 also lists those foundations that exist solely to disburse scholarships to students in particular geographic areas or for particular programs. Foundations that are legally registered in Minnesota but make grants only outside the state are listed in Appendix 3. Foundations that are not soliciting and will not accept new applications are listed in Appendix 4. These four appendixes include more than 200 legally registered Minnesota foundations.

Appendix 5 reproduces the survey the MCF sent to Minnesota foundations; Appendix 6, the survey sent to Minnesota corporations.

# FOUNDATION ENTRIES

The following information is included for those foundations with complete descriptions in the *Guide*. Information for the entries came from the IRS 990PF form and from survey returns.

## FOUNDATION NAME

**Address**

**Telephone number**

**Contact person and title:** Person to whom inquiries should be directed

**Established:** Date upon which foundation was established

**Type:** Specification of whether the foundation is private, corporate, or community (or whether the entry is for a corporate charitable contributions program)

**Program's purpose:** Description of specific purpose(s) of the foundation

**Program's limits:** Description of specific limits on the foundation's grant making

**Geographic orientation:** List of areas in which foundation makes grants

**Fields of activity:** List of areas a survey respondent checked off as activities applicable to the foundation (general areas were: arts and humanities [eight specific checkoff choices]; education [six choices]; health [six choices]; religion [three choices]; science [three choices]; social sciences [three choices]; welfare/social services [seventeen choices])

**Types of organizations funded:** List of types of organizations a survey respondent checked off as funded (general areas are the same as those listed under the fields of activity section)

**Targeted population groups:** List of groups that a survey respondent indicated to be specific targets of interest

**Types of support for organizations:** List of types of financial support a respondent reportedly provides to donees (e.g., capital support, matching grants, program-related investments)

**Types of support for individuals:** List of types of financial support provided to individuals

**Sample grants:** Listing of "typical" grants (usually three), recipients, and amounts

**Financial data for year ending:** Date of end of fiscal year

**Assets**

**Grants paid**

**Number of grants**

**Largest/smallest** (grants)

**Paid professional staff:** Yes or no, as indicated by the respondent

**Contact made by:** Indication of grant maker's preference for method by which grant seeker makes contact

**Available by request:** List of information available from the grant maker (in some cases, when a respondent said that the annual report is available, the funder meant the IRS 990 rather than a published annual report; the IRS 990 would then be available in the grant maker's office)

**Proposal deadlines**

**Board meetings:** Frequency and timing of board meetings

**Applicants notified:** Indication of how long it takes for the applicant
to learn the status of the application after the grant decision
has been made

**Directors/trustees**

Grant makers that are members of the Minnesota Council on Foundations are designated by this
symbol: ●.

## CORPORATION ENTRIES

The following information is included in the entries for corporate charitable contributions programs. Information for the entries came from survey.
Unless otherwise noted, the information sought was the same as that
obtained for the foundations.

**CORPORATION NAME**

**Address**

**Telephone number**

**Contact person and title**

**Type:** Corporate charitable contributions program (rather
than foundation)

**Program's interests or purpose**

**Program's limits**

**Geographic orientation**

**Fields of activity**

**Types of organizations supported**

**Targeted population groups**

**Employee matching gift programs:** Yes or no, as indicated by the
respondent (if the corporation has such programs, the respondent
specified which types of gifts the corporation would match)

**Types of support for organizations**

**Types of support for individuals** (in corporate entries, includes
scholarship programs for children of employees)

**Sample grants**

**Financial data for year ending**

   **Contributions paid** (may be a range rather than a specific figure)

   **Number of contributions**

   **Largest/smallest** (contribution)

**Contact made by**

**Available by request**

**Proposal deadlines**

**Contributions decisions made:** Indication of frequency and
time of year

**Applicants notified**

## TYPES OF GRANT MAKERS

### Foundations and Corporate Giving Programs

A foundation is a private, nonprofit organization with funds managed by its trustees or directors. Foundations generally support social, educational, religious, cultural, or other activities serving the community, primarily through the contribution of grants. Foundations are designated as such by the Internal Revenue Service and are regulated by laws at both the federal and state levels.

A private foundation, or an independent foundation, is a grant-making organization whose assets most commonly have been the gift of an individual or a family. Many are directed by family members and are known as "family foundations." Others, which may bear the family names of the donors, are managed by independent boards of trustees and may have paid professional staffs. Examples of private foundations are the Jerome Foundation, The Phillips Foundation and the Wasie Foundation.

A corporate foundation also is classified as a private foundation under the tax laws but derives its funds from a profit-making company or corporation. In most cases, foundation income comes from annual donations from the corporation rather than from investments, and therefore, corporate foundations may have minimal assets. Although legally independent of the sponsoring company, the corporate foundation generally is governed by trustees who are also officers within the corporation. A corporate foundation often focuses its contributions in communities where the corporation operates and in program areas of interest to the corporation or its employees. Examples of corporate foundations are those of Cargill, Deluxe Check Printers, and Medtronic.

Corporate charitable contributions programs that are administered within the corporation differ from corporate foundations. Some corporations choose to contribute to community organizations exclusively through corporate giving programs; others establish both an internal giving program and a company-sponsored foundation. Charitable contributions programs do not have the same reporting requirements as foundations (and, therefore, are less easily researched). Corporate giving, however, has gained importance, exceeding foundation giving in 1979, 1980, and 1981 and appearing to have potential for continued growth in future years. Corporation staff members in such departments as community relations, personnel, public relations, and planning may administer the corporate charitable contributions program as part of their work. In many cases, charitable contributions are handled solely by the chief executive officer. Some of the larger programs have set up their own staffs, the members of which work exclusively on the corporation's philanthropic and volunteer activities in the community. A corporate contributions program frequently is governed by corporate officers. Examples of corporations that have charitable contributions programs are Data Card Corporation, Investors Diversified Services (IDS), and Northwestern National Life Insurance Company.

A community foundation is one that receives funds from many sources—including smaller family foundations, gifts and wills, corporations and private foundations—and then distributes grants to local programs according to the donors' instructions. Community foundations are required by law to have trustees representing broad community interests. Although community foundations have funds restricted to designated donees, they also have undesignated funds available for other organizations. Community funds are designated by the Internal Revenue Service as "public charities," as are churches and most other nonprofit organizations. Minnesota's active community foundations are the Eden Prairie, Minneapolis, Rochester Area, and Saint Paul Foundations.

An operating foundation is not a grant-making organization; instead, it uses its income to support the operation of one or more designated nonprofit programs. Examples are the Amherst H. Wilder and Hamm Foundations. Some private foundations, as well as some public charities, function as special purpose foundations, whose grants are restricted to one area of giving or to a specific institution. An example is the Minnesota Medical Foundation, a public charity that provides student loans and grants to the University of Minnesota medical schools. Neither operating nor special purpose foundations are included in the *Guide.*

## GRANT MAKING IN MINNESOTA

Minnesota's corporations and foundations contributed more than $154,000,000 in 1981-82. MCF data for 1979-80 showed foundation and corporate giving in excess of $112,000,000.

Of the 414 grant makers included in the 1983 *Guide,* 52 corporations contributed approximately $62,260,000; 357 private foundations granted approximately $82,830,000; and five community foundations granted $6,400,000. National figures indicate that corporate giving surpassed foundation giving in 1979, 1980, and 1981 ($3 billion to $2.62 billion in 1981), with the trend likely to continue in the future.

Minnesota has more than 600 private foundations. Nationally, approximately 22,500 foundations exist. Most foundations—in Minnesota and across the country—are rather small, with assets under $150,000 and grants of less than $25,000 per year. Few corporations give more than 1 percent of pretax income, although they are allowed to deduct up to 10 percent of pretax income from federal income taxes according to 1982 law.

The Greater Minneapolis and the St. Paul Area Chambers of Commerce recognize area businesses for contributions of more than 2 percent of their domestic pretax taxable income for charitable and community purposes. In 1982, the Chambers recognized sixty-two companies for contributions that made them eligible for the "Minnesota Business Community 5% Investment Club" (companies that contributed 5 percent of their domestic pretax taxable income). Twenty-one additional companies were recognized for giving between 2 percent and 5 percent of their domestic pretax taxable income. The list of "Minnesota Business Community Partnership Award" winners and "Minnesota Business Community 5% Investment Club" members is on pages xviii and xix of the 1983 *Guide.*

Data collected for the 1983 *Guide* indicate that forty-four Minnesota foundations and corporations contributed in excess of $500,000 in 1981-82. Although these grant makers represent only 7 percent of the total number of Minnesota donors, they account for 80 percent of total giving by corporations and foundations in Minnesota. Of Minnesota's largest private grant makers, twenty-four are private foundations, two are community foundations, and the remainder are corporate foundations and charitable contributions programs (see list on pages xvii and xviii).

Most Minnesota grant makers are located in the Twin Cities area, although many of them support programs throughout Minnesota and in other states. Many corporations that have contributions programs give not only to organizations located in the vicinity of their headquarters but also to programs located in areas where they have facilities, plants, or business activities.

Less than a quarter of the grant makers described in this *Guide* employ a staff to review proposals and assist in the decision-making process. Most foundations continue to be managed entirely by their directors and officers, often with the assistance of a bank's trust department.

In the recent past, a third of the grants made by Minnesota foundations and corporations have supported education. Social services traditionally have received approximately 25 percent of private grant makers' support. Arts have received approximately 20 percent. Health, religion, community affairs, and other fields of activity together have received less than 20 percent of the grant makers' contributions. Among smaller foundations, gifts to religious organizations and institutions traditionally have tended to predominate. Education and social services receive stronger support from the larger giving programs. United Ways have tended to receive a large portion of dollars allocated to social services. The MCF's 1979-1980 figures showed that United Ways received 36 percent of the funds within the social services category from the state's largest grant makers.

The MCF does not collect data on giving by individuals or from bequests, which together comprise approximately 90 percent of total gifts to philanthropy nationally, according to information published in *Giving U.S.A.* by the American Association of Fund Raising Counsel. National data show that religious institutions and organizations are the recipients of most individual donations.

## NATIONAL GRANT MAKERS
## GIVE TO MINNESOTA ORGANIZATIONS

How many grants come into Minnesota from foundations located outside the state? Late in 1981, the MCF ordered a COMSEARCH printout of grants to Minnesota nonprofit organizations in 1980. The printouts, published by The Foundation Center, are computer-produced guides to foundation grants of $5,000 or more awarded by more than 400 major foundations throughout the country.

The printout of grants to Minnesota in 1980 showed that 51 out-of-state foundations made 119 grants to the state's nonprofit organizations. The grants totaled $6,353,850. Because the computer search covered only the 400 major American foundations and included only their grants of $5,000 or more, it is probably somewhat incomplete.

Research and educational organizations received the largest numbers of grants from foundations outside of Minnesota. Grants to Minnesota social services tended to support community United Way drives, capital campaigns, or special projects. Grants to the arts and humanities also tended to go toward support for special projects or capital expenditures.

An informal analysis of the printout indicated that most of the out-of-state foundations that made grants to Minnesota organizations had very specific interests that matched the organizations' needs precisely.

Grant seekers might also note that corporations based outside of Minnesota but with large Minnesota-based plants or constituencies may be willing to consider making grants to Minnesota organizations.

**Minnesota's Largest Grant Makers, Identified by Grants Paid in Fiscal Year 1981 or 1982 (the Latest Figures Available as the 1983 *Guide* Went to Press)**

| Grant Maker | Grants Paid | Fiscal Year |
| --- | --- | --- |
| The McKnight Foundation | $24,796,148 | 1981 |
| The Bush Foundation | $12,256,713 | 1981 |
| 3M Foundation and Corporation[a] | $10,317,111 | 1981 |
| Dayton Hudson Foundation | $ 7,141,648 | 1982 |
| Northwest Area Foundation | $ 5,870,135 | 1982 |
| General Mills Foundation | $ 5,658,663 | 1982 |
| Honeywell Foundation | $ 4,500,581 | 1981 |
| Blandin Foundation | $ 4,136,956 | 1981 |
| The Saint Paul Foundation | $ 3,939,632 | 1981 |
| First Bank System Foundation and affiliates[b] | $ 3,851,250 | 1981 |
| Consolidated Northwest Bancorporation/ Northwest Bancorporation Foundation and subsidiaries[c] | $ 3,187,311 | 1981 |
| The Saint Paul Companies, Inc. | $ 3,056,759 | 1982 |
| Charles and Ellora Alliss Educational Foundation | $ 2,877,400 | 1981 |
| Phillips Foundation | $ 2,740,363 | 1981 |
| The Pillsbury Company Foundation | $ 2,613,370 | 1982 |
| The Minneapolis Foundation | $ 2,417,664 | 1982 |
| Otto Bremer Foundation | $ 2,361,403 | 1982 |
| Deluxe Check Printers Foundation and Corporation | $ 1,668,110 | 1981 |
| Northern States Power Company | $ 1,400,000 | 1981 |
| I. A. O'Shaughnessy Foundation | $ 1,371,100 | 1981 |
| Cargill Foundation | $ 1,251,963 | 1981 |
| Jerome Foundation | $ 1,094,002 | 1982 |
| Benjamin A. Miller Family Foundation | $ 1,029,000 | 1981 |

## Minnesota's Largest Grant Makers, Identified by Grants Paid in Fiscal Year 1981 or 1982 (the Latest Figures Available as the 1983 *Guide* Went to Press) (*continued*)

| Grant Maker | Grants Paid | Fiscal Year |
|---|---|---|
| Northwestern Bell[d] | $ 1,000,000 or more | 1982 |
| The Andreas Foundation | $ 988,681 | 1981 |
| General Service Foundation | $ 977,526 | 1981 |
| F. R. Bigelow Foundation | $ 820,205 | 1981 |
| Fingerhut Foundation | $ 802,408 | 1981 |
| Frederick and Margaret L. Weyerhaeuser Foundation | $ 783,500 | 1981 |
| The Medtronic Foundation | $ 756,337 | 1982 |
| IDS Corporation | $ 750,000 | 1982 |
| Jostens Foundation | $ 709,900 | 1981 |
| Jostens Corporation | | 1982 |
| Tozer Foundation | $ 702,569 | 1981 |
| The Andersen Foundation | $ 646,696 | 1981 |
| Mardag Foundation | $ 634,822 | 1981 |
| H. B. Fuller Company | $ 582,854 | 1981 |
| Carolyn Foundation | $ 565,864 | 1981 |
| Edwin W. and Catherine M. Davis Foundation | $ 558,680 | 1981 |
| Bemis Company Foundation | $ 549,442 | 1981 |
| Bayport Foundation | $ 538,648 | 1981 |
| Mary Livingston Griggs and Mary Griggs Burke Foundation | $ 518,032 | 1981 |
| The Wasie Foundation | $ 515,283 | 1981 |
| Edwards Memorial Trust | $ 505,100 | 1981 |

[a.] Data on grants paid by the 3M Foundation and Corporation come from research conducted by the MCF in the winter of 1982. The 1983 *Guide* includes an entry for the 3M Foundation only.

[b.] Data on contributions made by the First Bank System Foundation and affiliates come from First Bank System's publication, "Grants Program for 1981." The *Guide* includes entries for the First Bank System Foundation, the First National Bank of Minneapolis Foundation, and First Bank St. Paul.

[c.] Data on grants paid by the Consolidated Northwest Bancorporation/Northwest Bancorporation Foundation and subsidiaries come from research conducted by the MCF in the winter of 1982. The 1983 *Guide* includes entries for the Northwestern Bancorporation Foundation and the Northwestern National Bank of Minneapolis.

[d.] Corporations with internal giving programs, rather than foundations, are not legally required to make public their contributions record. Northwestern Bell replied to the 1983 *Guide*'s corporate questionnaire and gave the MCF the figure of "more than $1,000,000" for its contributions paid in 1982.

## MINNESOTA BUSINESS COMMUNITY PARTNERSHIP AWARD WINNERS, 1982

Companies that gave between 2 percent and 5 percent of their domestic pretax taxable income for charitable and community purposes in 1981.

Bachman's, Inc.
Bemis Company, Inc.*
Brown Photo Company*
Campbell-Mithun, Inc.
Conwed Corporation
General Mills, Inc.
Honeywell Inc.*
International Multifoods
Juster's*
Least Moore Equipment Inc. and Subsidiary*

Litton Microwave Cooking Products
Medtronic, Inc.
Peavey Company
The Pillsbury Company
Quantum Group, Inc.*
Road Machinery & Supplies Company*
Robins, Zelle, Larson & Kaplan*
Sharpe Manufacturing Company, Inc.
WCCO AM/FM/TV*
The Webb Company
Willows Convalescent Centers, Inc.*

*New members

## MINNESOTA BUSINESS COMMUNITY 5 PERCENT INVESTMENT CLUB MEMBERS, 1982

Companies that gave at least 5 percent of their domestic pretax taxable income for charitable and community purposes in 1981

Anderson's China Shop
Animal Fair, Inc.*
Arthur Andersen & Company
Arthur Young & Company*
Bolger Publications/Creative Printing
Brum & Anderson Public Relations, Inc.*
Business Incentives, Inc.*
Carlson Companies Inc.
Carousel Snack Bars of Minnesota, Inc.*
Century Manufacturing Company
Custom Business Forms
Dayton Hudson Corporation
Deferred Compensation Administrators
Deloitte Haskins & Sells*
dor and associates, inc.*
Ellerbe, Inc.*
Ernst & Whinney
First Bank Minneapolis
H. B. Fuller Company
Gabberts Inc.
General Office Products Company
Grace-Lee Products, Inc.*
Graco Inc.
Harold Chevrolet, Inc.
Harold Corporation*
The Hartfiel Company
Hartzell Corporation
Hoffmann Electric Company and
   Nucomp Systems Inc.
The Holes-Webway Company*
Insty-Prints, Inc.
Inter-Regional Financial Group, Inc.

The Jefferson Company
Jennings Agency
Juhl Brokerage Incorporated
Lamperts, Inc.
Laventhol & Horwath
Leslie Paper Company
Mackay/Minnesota Envelope
Marco Business Products
Maxim's Beauty Salons, Inc.*
Minneapolis Star and Tribune Company
MSI Insurance
Sam Miller Bag Company
Munsingwear, Inc.
Northwestern National Bank
   of Minneapolis
Northwestern National Bank of Saint Paul
Old Peoria Company, Inc.
Owens Services Corporation*
Padilla and Speer, Inc.
Peat, Marwick, Mitchell & Company
Piper, Jaffray & Hopwood Incorporated
Price Waterhouse
Rauenhorst Corporation
Republic Acceptance Corporation
Schaak Electronics, Inc.*
Schmitt Music Company
Sell Publishing Company
R. J. Steichen & Company
Thorpe Brothers., Inc.*
Touche Ross & Company
Twin City Die Castings Company*
Ziegler, Inc.

*New member

## RESEARCH ON GRANT MAKERS

Early in the fund-raising process, a grant seeker must select appropriate funders to approach. The *Guide to Minnesota Foundations and Corporate Giving Programs* is one tool for use in the preliminary research on grant makers. To determine which grant makers may be interested in considering a specific grant proposal, the grant seeker might review the *Guide* with the following questions in mind:

Which funders make grants in the general program area of the proposal?

Do any of these have geographic or other restrictions that make the proposal ineligible for consideration?

Can the grant request fit into the funding cycle of those grant makers that seem most appropriate?

How do each of the grant makers selected as potential funders wish to be contacted?

Which of these grant makers will send further information, such as a published annual report, guidelines, or application procedures?

It may be helpful to seek more specific information about grant makers initially identified as potential funders. Reviewing the complete list of grants made by a funder during the past year can give a clear picture of its funding patterns and interests. Such information usually is included in a grant maker's annual report, if one is published and is required as part of a private foundation's 990 report filed with the Internal Revenue Service. (See the section on the 990AR and 990PF forms to find out how to obtain the reports.)

One's research, then, may include one or all of the following steps.

1. Request an annual report, guidelines, and/or application procedures from a grant maker if the *Guide* indicates that such materials are available.
2. Review the form 990 tax report of a foundation.
3. Look at the Minnesota-oriented materials at the Foundation Center Regional Collection and Foundation Center Affiliate Collection. (See the section below on this topic.) The collections include the grant makers' publications (for example, annual reports and newsletters), and the *Minnesota Foundation Directory*, a detailed listing of Minnesota foundations.
4. Communicate directly with the grant maker about the proposal, either by telephone or letter. Many funders welcome such initial inquiries. Communicating with a grant maker before submitting a proposal can

help determine the grant maker's interest in the proposal and its capacity for funding the project. Some funders can provide suggestions for developing the proposal. Although preliminary contact with a funder can be helpful, typically it is not necessary. Smaller, unstaffed programs may not have the ability to guide prospective grant seekers through the process. In most cases, complete proposals that fit within a grant maker's guidelines can be submitted without prior contact with the grant maker.

## MINNESOTA'S FOUNDATION CENTER COLLECTIONS

The Twin Cities' two downtown city libraries house collections connected with the New York-based Foundation Center: The Foundation Center Regional Collection, Sociology Department, Minneapolis Public Library and Information Center, and The Foundation Center Affiliate Collection, Reference Department, St. Paul Public Library. The Foundation Center is a national service organization founded and supported by foundations to provide a single authoritative source of information on foundation giving. Almost 100 library collections throughout the United States are affiliated with The Foundation Center and make the center's books and directories available to the public.

The Foundation Center Regional Collection in Minneapolis is the older of the Twin Cities' collections. It includes national, regional, and state directories of grant makers; sources of information on proposal writing, corporate giving, philanthropy in general, and giving to individuals; and publications, including annual reports, of specific grant makers. The regional collection also includes the most recent 990AR and 990PF Internal Revenue Service reports filed by private foundations in Minnesota, North Dakota, and South Dakota.

The Foundation Center Affiliate Collection in St. Paul was formed in 1982 and includes the basic Foundation Center directories and more than 50 additional books on grantsmanship. The affiliate collection will continue to build its holdings in the St. Paul Public Library Reference Department. Although it does not have available the IRS 990 reports, the affiliate collection does include the same basic types of material as the regional collection: national, regional, and state directories of grant makers; books on proposal writing and philanthropy; and grant makers' publications, such as annual reports.

Both collections can perform computer searches for people conducting research on grant makers. In both collections, the first eight minutes of computer search are free.

Among the directories each collection includes are the following.

*The National Data Book*, a Foundation Center publication that profiles all of the country's 22,535 grant making foundations.

*Source Book Profiles,* a Foundation Center publication that describes in detail the 1,000 largest American foundations.

*The Foundation Directory,* a Foundation Center publication that provides current fiscal and program information on the 3,363 largest American foundations.

*The Foundation Grants Index,* a Foundation Center publication that reports on and describes foundation grants and giving interests.

*Corporate Foundation Profiles,* a Foundation Center directory that includes analyses of more than 200 of the largest company-sponsored foundations and summary data for more than 300 additional corporate foundations

*Minnesota Foundation Directory,* a Foundation Data Center publication that provides a detailed list of all Minnesota foundations, including information on their contributions, gifts, and grants.

*Guide to Minnesota Foundations and Corporate Giving Programs, 1983,* Minnesota Council on Foundations.

Directories and books within the Foundation Center Regional and Affiliate Collections are available for use only within the library. The collections contribute a column to the MCF's newspaper, *Giving Forum,* detailing recent acquisitions.

Grantsmanship journals available in the library collections or by subscription include the following.

*Foundation News,* a bimonthly magazine published by the national Council on Foundations, 1828 L Street Northwest, Washington, D.C. 20036 ($24 per year), which includes articles on foundation grant making, administration, and proposal writing.

*Grantsmanship Center News,* a bimonthly magazine published by the Grantsmanship Center, 1031 South Grand Avenue, Los Angeles, CA 90015 ($28 per year), which includes articles about developments in public and private funding, planning programs, writing proposals, managing nonprofit programs, and fund raising. Reprints of specific articles are available.

## THE FOUNDATION'S INTERNAL REVENUE SERVICE REPORTS—990AR and 990PF

One of the best sources of information about private foundations is the informational return they are required to file annually with the Internal Revenue Service. Federal law requires that foundations' returns, unlike personal tax returns, be made available to the public by both the Internal Revenue Service and the foundations themselves. This means that for all foundations, regardless of size, there is a public record available that provides basic facts about their operations and grants. For the smaller foundations, these reports are often the only available records of their activities. For larger foundations, the forms provide data that supplement other available information, generally with more detail about investments and assets than is provided in published sources.

Key pieces of information you should be able to find on a foundation's return are: Name and address; assets at market value; gross contributions, gifts, and grants of $5,000 or more received by the foundation during the year; contributions, gifts, or grants paid by the foundation; and names of principal foundation officer and other officers, trustees, directors, and foundation managers.

The three ways to obtain a foundation Internal Revenue Service return are contacting the foundation itself, using The Foundation Center's services, or ordering information through the Internal Revenue Service.

The Internal Revenue Service requires that foundations make copies of their 990ARs available in their principal office for public inspection for 180 days after filing. The filing date is four and a half months after the end of the foundation's fiscal year.

The Foundation Center Regional Collection, Minnesota Public Library, makes available the Internal Revenue Service returns of Minnesota and Dakota foundations. Each of the forms is on an aperture card, a computer card with a small window in which a reproduction of the 990 form in film is mounted for use through a microfiche viewing machine. Each foundation has at least two aperture cards, one each for the 990AR and the 990PF; each card contains up to fourteen pages of information.

In 1982-1983 The Foundation Center initiated an experimental program to test the public's need for access to key pages from foundations' returns. The Foundation Center offers key pages from returns for $2 per foundation. Copies are made of the return for any foundation that does not publish an annual report. To use the service, you should contact The Foundation Center at 888 Seventh Avenue, New York, NY 10106, by submitting a letter with the names of the foundations for which returns are desired, their city and state location, and the date of the return requested. You may order up to six returns in a single request; the payment of $2 per foundation must accompany the order.

This section is based upon "How to Obtain Information about Foundations," published by The Foundation Center in 1982.

Free inspection of any foundation's return can be arranged in any of nineteen Internal Revenue Service district offices by writing to the district office and requesting that it obtain copies of specific returns.

Copies of individual foundations' returns can be ordered from the Internal Revenue Service for a fee. The cost of this service differs, depending on whether you order copies on aperture cards or on paper. Send orders to Mid-Atlantic Service Centers, Internal Revenue Service, Box 245, Bensalem, PA 19020, Attention: Public Inspection Drop Point 536. In ordering Internal Revenue Service returns, you should include the following information for each foundation requested: full name, city and state location, desired year of return, and, if available, the employer identification number (EIN). This number may be found for all foundations in The Foundation Center's *National Data Book* and on Internal Revenue Service returns for previous years. The Internal Revenue Service will send a bill when the order is completed.

# Directory Listings

# Directory Listings

## ADDUCCI FAMILY FOUNDATION

107 West Pleasant Lake Road
North Oaks, MN 55110
(612) 482-8192

**Contact Person:** Anthony J. Adducci, president

**Established:** December 1981

**Type:** Private foundation

**Program's Purpose:** To make grants for charitable, medical, and educational purposes

**Program's Limitations:** Foundation receiving no requests for grants until January 1984

**Geographic Orientation:** National

**Fields of Activity:** Music/opera; religion; religious education; medical missions; family services

**Types of Organizations Funded:** Colleges; universities; religious service groups; religious colleges; centers for children; homes serving victims of child abuse

**Targeted Population Groups:** Aged; children/youth; handicapped

**Types of Support for Organizations:** Not yet determined

**Types of Support for Individuals:** Not yet determined

**Financial Data for Year Ending June 30, 1982:**
Assets: $52,373
Grants Paid: None to date

**Paid Professional Staff:** No

**Contact Made by:** Letter of inquiry after January 1984

**Board Meetings:** Biannual

**Directors/Trustees:** Anthony J. Adducci, president; Sandra R. Adducci, vice-president; Thomas Dougherty, secretary; Annette Adducci Schmit, director

## ADLER FOUNDATION

1311 Hillcrest Avenue
St. Paul, MN 55116

**Established:** December 1964

**Type:** Private foundation

**Geographic Orientation:** Minnesota

**Sample Grants:**
Mount Zion Hebrew Congregation—$1,200
KTCA—$100
University of Denver—$100

**Financial Data for Year Ending January 31, 1982:**
Assets: $32,844
Grants Paid: $3,750
Number of Grants: 38
Largest/Smallest: $1,200/$10

**Paid Professional Staff:** No

**Directors/Trustees:** John W. Adler; Sally F. Adler; Eugene Heck

## ALEXANDRA FOUNDATION

2200 First National Bank Building
St. Paul, MN 55101

**Established:** March 1963

**Type:** Private foundation

**Geographic Orientation:** National

**Sample Grants:**
Massachusetts Institute of Technology—$2,000
New York Foundling Hospital—$500
Corpus Christi Monastery—$50

**Financial Data for Year Ending December 31, 1981:**
Assets: $245,817
Grants Paid: $15,375
Number of Grants: 31
Largest/Smallest: $2,000/$50

**Paid Professional Staff:** No

**Directors:** C. A. Kalman, president; Diana J. Kalman, vice-president; H. B. Thielbar, treasurer; Cole Oehler, secretary

## • CHARLES AND ELLORA ALLISS EDUCATIONAL FOUNDATION

c/o First Trust Company of St. Paul
W-555 First National Bank Building
St. Paul, MN 55101
(612) 291-5114

**Contact Person:** Jeffrey T. Peterson, secretary

**Established:** July 1958

**Type:** Private foundation

**Program's Purpose:** To support scholarships for students pursuing secondary and higher education

**Program's Limits:** Grants made to Minnesota colleges, universities, and secondary schools in support of scholarship programs administered by their student-aid offices; no direct grants to individuals

**Geographic Orientation:** Minnesota

**Fields of Activity:** Secondary education; higher education

**Types of Organizations Supported:** Secondary schools; colleges; universities; scholarship funds

**Type of Support for Organizations:** Continuing support

**Sample Grants:**
   University of Minnesota (Scholarships)—$404,400
   Minnesota Independent School Fund (Scholarships)—$325,000
   Saint John's University (Scholarships)—$122,050

**Financial Data for Year Ending December 31, 1981:**
   Assets: $31,873,111
   Grants Paid: $2,877,400
   Number of Grants: 22
   Largest/Smallest: $404,400/$20,000

**Paid Professional Staff:** No

**Contact Made by:** Complete proposal

**Available by Request:** Application procedures

**Board Meetings:** Quarterly—March, June, September, December

**Applicants Notified:** Within 12 weeks of decision

**Directors/Trustees:** Harry L. Holtz; Elmer L. Andersen; Sidney Barrows; Richard Gunderson; Frank Hammond

## AMERICAN HOIST AND DERRICK FOUNDATION

63 South Robert Street
St. Paul, MN 55107

**Type:** Corporate foundation

**Geographic Orientation:** National

**Sample Grants:**
   East/West Foundation—$25,000
   University of California—$10,000
   Cleveland United Fund—$1,000

**Financial Data for Year Ending December 31, 1981:**
   Assets: $62,438
   Grants Paid: $122,075
   Number of Grants: 41
   Largest/Smallest: $25,000/$539

**Paid Professional Staff:** No

**Directors/Trustees:** Robert P. Fox, chairman; William B. Faulkner, president; Dennis L. Nordstrand, secretary-treasurer

## ANDERSEN FOUNDATION

Bayport, MN 55003

**Established:** November 1959

**Type:** Corporate foundation

**Geographic Orientation:** Minnesota

**Sample Grants:**
   Mayo Foundation—$302,820 (stock)
   Washington County Association for Senior Citizens—$146,160 (stock)
   Lakeview Memorial Hospital—$41,738 (stock)

**Financial Data for Year Ending December 31, 1981:**
   Assets: $30,864,598
   Grants Paid: $490,718 (stock FMV); $155,978 (cost)
   Number of Grants: 4
   Largest/Smallest: $302,820 (stock FMV)/$41,738 (stock FMV)

**Paid Professional Staff:** No

**Directors/Trustees:** Katherine B. Andersen, president; Earl C. Swanson, vice-president/secretary; Roy H. Sakrison; Leonard W. Kedrowski, assistant treasurer; Keith R. Clements

## ● ELMER L. AND ELEANOR J. ANDERSEN FOUNDATION

800 Rosedale Towers
Roseville, MN 55113

**Established:** November 30, 1957

**Type:** Private foundation

**Geographic Orientation:** Minnesota

**Sample Grants:**
   Minnesota Public Radio—$40,000
   University of Minnesota Foundation—$10,000
   People—$750

**Financial Data for Year Ending November 30, 1981:**
   Assets: $1,686,736
   Grants Paid: $147,481
   Number of Grants: 21
   Largest/Smallest: $40,000/$200

**Paid Professional Staff:** No

**Directors/Trustees:** Elmer L. Andersen, president; Eleanor J. Andersen, vice-president; Samuel H. Morgan, secretary; Barbara B. Miller

## HUGH J. ANDERSEN FOUNDATION

Bayport, MN 55003

**Established:** March 1962

**Type:** Private foundation

**Geographic Orientation:** Minnesota; national

**Sample Grants:**
   Croixdale—$30,000
   American Cancer Society—$10,000
   Ducks Unlimited—$200

**Financial Data for Year Ending February 28, 1982:**
Assets: $1,887,451
Grants Paid: $112,285
Number of Grants: 39
Largest/Smallest: $30,000/$10

**Paid Professional Staff:** No

**Directors/Trustees:** Carol F. Andersen, president; Sarah J. Andersen, vice-president; Christine E. Andersen, treasurer; A. D. Hulings, secretary

## THE ANDREAS FOUNDATION

Box 728
Mankato, MN 56001

**Established:** March 1945

**Type:** Private foundation

**Geographic Orientation:** National

**Sample Grants:**
American University, Washington, D.C.—$100,000
United Cerebral Palsy Fund—$2,000
Youth for Christ in Mankato—$1,000

**Financial Data for Year Ending December 31, 1981:**
Assets: $2,712,388
Grants Paid: $988,681
Number of Grants: 109
Largest/Smallest: $100,000/$25

**Paid Professional Staff:** No

**Directors/Trustees:** Dwayne O. Andreas, president; Lowell W. Andreas, vice-president/treasurer; Michael D. Andreas, vice-president/secretary; Sandra Andreas McMurtrie; Dorothy Inez Andreas; Terry Lynn Bevis

## • THE ANKENY FOUNDATION

930 Dain Tower
Minneapolis, MN 55402
(612) 338-3872

**Contact Person:** Donald K. Morrison

**Established:** February 1963

**Type:** Private foundation

**Types of Organizations Supported:** Theaters/dance groups; music/opera groups; public television/radio; arts councils; secondary schools; colleges; universities; hospitals; churches/synagogues; environmental agencies; United Way; organizations for youth

**Sample Grants:**
KTCA—$220
Minnesota Orchestra—$150
YMCA—$125

**Financial Data for Year Ending March 31, 1982:**
Assets: $407,810
Grants Paid: $72,012
Number of Grants: 63
Largest/Smallest: $51,500/$25

**Paid Professional Staff:** No

**Contact Made by:** Letter of inquiry

**Board Meetings:** Monthly

**Directors/Trustees:** DeWalt H. Ankeny, Jr., president; Sally A. Anson, vice-president; Kendall A. Mix, secretary; Michael Ankeny, treasurer

## • APACHE FOUNDATION

1700 Foshay Tower
Minneapolis, MN 55402

**Established:** December 29, 1960

**Type:** Corporate foundation

**Geographic Orientation:** Twin Cities; national

**Sample Grants:**
United Way of Minneapolis—$18,500
Boys' Clubs of Minneapolis—$5,950
American Refugee Committee—$500

**Financial Data for Year Ending December 31, 1981:**
Assets: $41,026
Grants Paid: $122,296
Number of Grants: 105
Largest/Smallest: $18,500/$25

**Paid Professional Staff:** No

**Directors/Trustees:** Raymond Plank, chairman of the board; Dean G. Newman, president; Beatrice L. Huston, vice-president/secretary; William N. Lundberg, treasurer/assistant secretary

## ARCHER-DANIELS-MIDLAND FOUNDATION

4666 Faries Parkway
Box 1470
Decatur, IL 62525

**Established:** December 1953

**Type:** Corporate foundation

**Sample Grants:**
University of Minnesota, Humphrey Institute—$100,000
O'Neill Fund for Ireland—$25,000
Decatur Audubon Society—$500

**Financial Data for Year Ending June 30, 1981:**
Assets: $4,540,777 (net worth)
Grants Paid: $858,313
Number of Grants: 133
Largest/Smallest: $100,000/$75

**Paid Professional Staff:** No

**Directors/Trustees:** Richard E. Burket, manager; L. W. Andreas, president; R. L. Erickson, secretary; D. P. Poboisk, treasurer

# MARK L. AREND FOUNDATION

668 Woodridge Drive
St. Paul, MN 55118

**Established:** November 1966

**Type:** Private foundation

**Sample Grants:**
St. Leo's Church—$200
St. Louis Church—$200
Multiple Sclerosis Society—$100

**Financial Data for Year Ending December 31, 1981:**
Assets: $19,112
Grants Paid: $500
Number of Grants: 3
Largest/Smallest: $200/$100

**Paid Professional Staff:** No

**Directors/Trustees:** Mark L. Arend; Michael W. Arend; Matthew J. Levitt

# • ATHWIN FOUNDATION

901 Midwest Plaza East
Minneapolis, MN 55402
(612) 340-3616

**Contact Person:** Atherton Bean, trustee

**Established:** March 1956

**Type:** Private foundation

**Program's Purpose:** To contribute to primarily local educational, cultural, religious, and community-welfare programs

**Program's Limits:** No grants to individuals or for scholarships or fellowships; no loans

**Geographic Orientation:** Twin Cities; Minnesota; Phoenix-Claremont area

**Fields of Activity:** Arts/architecture; music/opera; theater/dance; arts education; medical research; medical/health education

**Types of Organizations Funded:** Museums/historical societies; music/opera groups; secondary schools; colleges; medical schools; medical research groups; clinics; United Way; organizations for the elderly; day-care centers; United Fund

**Types of Support for Organizations:** Capital support; continuing support; general operating support; matching grants; research

**Sample Grants:**
Science Museum of Minnesota—$35,000
Blake Schools—$15,000
Minneapolis Society of Fine Arts—$10,000

**Financial Data for Year Ending December 31, 1981:**
Assets: $3,380,585
Grants Paid: $208,118
Number of Grants: 36
Largest/Smallest: $35,000/$100

**Paid Professional Staff:** No

**Contact Made by:** Letter of inquiry

**Available by Request:** Annual report

**Board Meetings:** Whenever the volume of applications demands it

**Trustees:** Atherton Bean; Winifred W. Bean; Bruce W. Bean; Mary F. Bean; Eleanor Nolan

# BERNARD AND FERN BADZIN FOUNDATION

2855 Eagandale Boulevard
St. Paul, MN 55121

**Established:** December 1968

**Type:** Private foundation

**Sample Grants:**
Minneapolis Federation for Jewish Service—$29,100
Beth El Synagogue—$7,155
Minnesota Orchestra Association—$100

**Financial Data for Year Ending December 31, 1981:**
Assets: $88,940
Grants Paid: $39,508
Number of Grants: 25
Largest/Smallest: $29,100/$10

**Paid Professional Staff:** No

**Directors/Trustees:** Bernard Badzin; Fern Badzin

# • BAKER FOUNDATION

4900 IDS Center
Minneapolis, MN 55402

**Established:** February 1954

**Type:** Private foundation

**Geographic Orientation:** Twin Cities; national

**Fields of Activity:** Arts/architecture; music/opera; theater/dance; higher education; medical research; medical care/treatment; community affairs; welfare/social services

**Types of Organizations Funded:** Museums/historical societies; theaters/dance groups; music/opera groups; public television/radio; colleges; universities; scholarship funds; hospitals; medical schools; medical research groups; conservation groups; United Way; organizations for youth

**Types of Support for Organizations:** Capital support; general operating support

**Sample Grants:**
Mount Holyoke College—$150,000
Boys' Clubs of Minneapolis—$10,000
Ocean Reef Medical Center—$100

**Financial Data for Year Ending December 31, 1981:**
  Assets: $1,449,874
  Grants Paid: $288,534
  Number of Grants: 46
  Largest/Smallest: $150,000/$100

**Paid Professional Staff:** No

**Directors:** William M. Baker, president; Roger L. Baker, vice-president; David C. Sherman, vice-president; Mary J. Bierman, secretary; James W. Peter, treasurer

# MR. AND MRS. EDWARD F. BAKER FOUNDATION

301 Chamber of Commerce Building
Minneapolis, MN 55402
(612) 339-8601

**Contact Person:** J. M. Nimmerfroh, secretary to director

**Established:** October 1972

**Type:** Private foundation

**Program's Purpose:** To make donations to religious, charitable, scientific, and educational organizations

**Geographic Orientation:** Twin Cities

**Fields of Activity:** Arts/architecture; media/communications; music/opera; theater/dance; arts education; medical care/treatment

**Types of Organizations Funded:** Museums/historical societies; theater/dance groups; music/opera groups; public television/radio; Children's Heart Fund

**Type of Support for Organizations:** Capital support

**Sample Grants:**
  Minneapolis Federation for Jewish Service—$21,002
  Minnesota Dance Theater—$5,000
  Sister Kenny Institute—$1,000

**Financial Data for Year Ending August 31, 1981:**
  Assets: $46,885
  Grants Paid: $29,462
  Number of Grants: 9
  Largest/Smallest: $21,002/$10

**Paid Professional Staff:** No

**Contact Made by:** Letter of inquiry

**Available by Request:** Annual report

**Board Meetings:** Monthly

**Applicants Notified:** Within four weeks of decision

**Director:** Edward F. Baker, principal manager

# BARATZ FAMILY FOUNDATION

6005 Wayzata Boulevard
St. Louis Park, MN 55416

**Established:** December 1976

**Type:** Private foundation

**Geographic Orientation:** Twin Cities

**Sample Grants:**
  Talmud Torah of Minneapolis—$5,000
  Jewish Theological Seminary—$1,000
  United Way—$200

**Financial Data for Year Ending December 31, 1981:**
  Assets: $106,486
  Grants Paid: $6,200
  Number of Grants: 3
  Largest/Smallest: $5,000/$200

**Paid Professional Staff:** No

**Directors/Trustees:** Maurice L. Baratz, president; Ida Baratz; Zollie Baratz

# BAYPORT FOUNDATION

Bayport, MN 55003

**Established:** December 1941

**Type:** Private foundation

**Sample Grants:**
  Washington County Association for Senior Citizens—$100,000
  Mayo Medical School—$50,000
  First Baptist Church, Hudson, WI—$500

**Financial Data for Year Ending November 30, 1981:**
  Assets: $6,529,389
  Grants Paid: $538,648
  Number of Grants: 114
  Largest/Smallest: $100,000/$200

**Paid Professional Staff:** No

**Directors/Trustees:** W. A. Wellman, president; M. A. Hulings, vice-president; A. D. Hulings, vice-president; H. C. Meissner, vice-president; L. R. Croone, secretary/treasurer

# THE BEIM FOUNDATION

6750 France Avenue South
Minneapolis, MN 55435
(612) 920-1556

**Contact Person:** William H. Beim, president

**Established:** February 1957

**Type:** Private foundation

**Program's Purpose:** To make grants for capital expenditures to Minneapolis-area organizations

**Geographic Orientation:** Twin Cities; Minnesota

**Fields of Activity:** Higher education; medical research; religion; business/economic education

**Types of Organizations Funded:** Public television/radio; universities; medical research groups; churches/synagogues

**Type of Support for Organizations:** Capital support

**Sample Grants:**
  YMCA of Minneapolis—$15,000
  KTCA—$5,000
  Science Museum of Minnesota—$2,500

**Financial Data for Year Ending December 31, 1981:**
  Assets: $2,396,919
  Grants Paid: $125,000
  Number of Grants: 41
  Largest/Smallest: $20,000/$500

**Paid Professional Staff:** No

**Directors/Trustees:** W. H. Beim, president; R. N. Beim, vice-president; W. H. Beim, Jr., secretary-treasurer; Judith McKim, director

## DAVID WINTON BELL FOUNDATION

Suite 450
10,000 Highway 55 West
Minneapolis, MN 55441

**Established:** December 1955

**Type:** Private foundation

**Geographic Orientation:** National

**Sample Grants:**
  Trinity Films—$5,000
  Washburn Child Guidance Center—$1,500
  United Negro College Fund—$500

**Financial Data for Year Ending December 31, 1981:**
  Assets: $507,694
  Grants Paid: $24,500
  Number of Grants: 12
  Largest/Smallest: $5,000/$400

**Paid Professional Staff:** No

**Directors/Trustees:** Charles H. Bell; Lucy Winton Bell; Lucy Bell Hartwell; L. L. Arnevik

## GINGER AND MARTIN BELL FOUNDATION

2229 Edgewood Avenue South
St. Louis Park, MN 55426

**Established:** December 1980

**Type:** Private foundation

**Geographic Orientation:** Twin Cities

**Sample Grants:**
  Minneapolis Federation for Jewish Service—$3,000
  Juvenile Diabetes Foundation—$100
  Ronnie Greenhouse Blood Research Fund—$25

**Financial Data for Year Ending November 30, 1981:**
  Assets: $40,372
  Grants Paid: $4,225
  Number of Grants: 5
  Largest/Smallest: $3,000/$25

**Paid Professional Staff:** No

**Directors/Trustees:** Ginger Bell; Martin Bell; Leland Gottstein

## JAMES F. BELL FOUNDATION

Suite 450
10,000 Highway 55 West
Minneapolis, MN 55441

**Established:** February 1955

**Type:** Private foundation

**Geographic Orientation:** Twin Cities; national

**Sample Grants:**
  University of Minnesota, James F. Bell Library—$36,148
  YMCA of Minneapolis—$12,000
  Ruffed Grouse Society—$650

**Financial Data for Year Ending December 31, 1981:**
  Assets: $3,918,179
  Grants Paid: $177,413
  Number of Grants: 41
  Largest/Smallest: $36,148/$500

**Paid Professional Staff:** No

**Directors/Trustees:** Samuel H. Bell; Charles H. Bell; Ford W. Bell; L. L. Arnevik

## BELZER FOUNDATION

4370 Brookside Court
Minneapolis, MN 55436

**Type:** Private foundation

**Geographic Orientation:** Minnesota; national

**Sample Grants:**
  American Cancer Society—$5,325
  Minneapolis Federation for Jewish Service—$1,000
  Minnesota Medical Foundation—$500

**Financial Data for Year Ending December 31, 1981:**
  Assets: $67,980
  Grants Paid: $8,325
  Number of Grants: 5
  Largest/Smallest: $5,325/$500

**Paid Professional Staff:** No

**Director/Trustee:** Kathleen Belzer

## • BEMIS COMPANY FOUNDATION

800 Northstar Center
Minneapolis, MN 55402
(612) 340-6018

**Contact Person:** Thomas E. Davies, executive director

**Established:** December 1959

**Type:** Corporate foundation

**Program's Purpose:** To match foundation funds with public, company, and employee needs

**Program's Limits:** No grants to individuals, to organizations for religious or political purposes, educational capital fund programs, or endowment purposes or for trips or tours

**Geographic Orientation:** Communities in which the Bemis Company operates

**Types of Organizations Funded:** Museums/historical societies; theaters/dance groups; music/opera groups; zoos; public television/radio; vocational schools; colleges; universities; junior colleges; hospitals; clinics; chemical dependency services; counseling services; United Way; legal aid; multiservice centers; organizations for the elderly; organizations for the handicapped; organizations for women; organizations for youth; centers for children; organizations for minorities; neighborhood agencies

**Types of Support for Organizations:** Continuing support; general operating support; federated fund drives

**Sample Grants:**
United Way of St. Louis, MO—$11,000
Center for the Performing Arts, Grand Rapids, MI—$2,500
Courage Center, Golden Valley, MN—$2,500

**Financial Data for Year Ending December 31, 1981:**
Assets: $357,656
Grants Paid: $549,442
Number of Grants: 180
Largest/Smallest: $25,000/$500

**Paid Professional Staff:** No

**Contact Made by:** Letter of inquiry

**Available by Request:** Application procedures

**Board Meetings:** Quarterly, in mid-February, June, September, and December

**Applicants notified:** Within one week of decision

**Directors/Trustees:** Al Park, vice-president of personnel and industrial relations; Ben Field, vice-president and treasurer; Thomas E. Davies, executive director

# WILLIAM J. BENFIELD TESTAMENTARY TRUST

c/o Gordon E. Mills
Route 4, Lake Pulaski
Buffalo, MN 55313

**Established:** February 1974

**Type:** Private foundation

**Geographic Orientation:** Minnesota

**Sample Grants:**
American Cancer Society, Minnesota Division—$5,000
Crime Stoppers of Buffalo—$1,000
Church of St. Francis—$500

**Financial Data for Year Ending December 31, 1981:**
Assets: $232,373
Grants Paid: $18,000
Number of Grants: 10
Largest/Smallest: $5,000/$500

**Paid Professional Staff:** No

**Directors/Trustees:** Gordon E. Mills; Ethel M. Mills

# THE BENTSON FOUNDATION

Suite 900
Foshay Tower
Minneapolis, MN 55402

**Established:** October 1956

**Type:** Private foundation

**Sample Grants:**
United Jewish Fund—$15,200
Variety Heart Association—$1,410
Ducks Unlimited—$15

**Financial Data for Year Ending October 31, 1981:**
Assets: $169,994
Grants Paid: $29,373
Number of Grants: 36
Largest/Smallest: $15,200/$10

**Paid Professional Staff:** No

**Director/Trustee:** N. L. Bentson, president

# GEORGE AND LOUISE BENZ FOUNDATION

2104 American National Bank Building
St. Paul, MN 55101

**Established:** July 1960

**Type:** Private foundation

**Geographic Orientation:** Twin Cities

**Sample Grants:**
Courage Center—$2,000
Landmark Center—$1,000
Family Service of the Greater St. Paul Area—$500

**Financial Data for Year Ending December 31, 1981:**
Assets: $220,895
Grants Paid: $8,500
Number of Grants: 6
Largest/Smallest: $2,000/$500

**Paid Professional Staff:** No

**Director/Trustee:** Louise B. Benz

# SVEN AND C. EMIL BERGLUND FOUNDATION

1578 University Avenue
St. Paul, MN 55104

**Established:** November 1974

**Type:** Private foundation

**Geographic Orientation:** Twin Cities

**Sample Grants:**
KTCA—$7,000
Gustavus Adolphus College—$4,000
United Hospitals of St. Paul—$1,000

**Financial Data for Year Ending November 30, 1981:**
  Assets: $293,712
  Grants Paid: $27,380
  Number of Grants: 11
  Largest/Smallest: $7,000/$480

**Paid Professional Staff:** No

**Directors/Trustees:** A. A. Heckman; Lilliam Wright; James A. Polzak; Bernice Jensen

# BIG GAME CLUB SPECIAL PROJECTS FOUNDATION

4900 IDS Center
Minneapolis, MN 55402

**Established:** January 1968

**Type:** Private foundation

**Program's Purpose:** To promote conservation, protection, and preservation of forests, wild animals, birds, and fishes

**Geographic Orientation:** National

**Financial Data for Year Ending December 31, 1981:**
  Assets: $4,935
  Grants Paid: $0

**Paid Professional Staff:** No

**Directors/Trustees:** Wallace C. Dayton, president; John D. Chandler, secretary; Anthony Bechik, treasurer; Michael Bechik, vice-president

# • F. R. BIGELOW FOUNDATION

1120 Northwestern National Bank Building
St. Paul, MN 55101
(612) 224-5463

**Contact Person:** Paul A. Verret, secretary

**Established:** 1946

**Type:** Private foundation

**Program's Limits:** Generally limited to the greater St. Paul metropolitan area; no grants to individuals; generally no grants for endowment funds

**Geographic Orientation:** Twin Cities

**Fields of Activity:** Arts/architecture; history/preservation; language/literature; media/communications; music/opera; theater/dance; arts education; elementary/secondary education; vocational education; higher education; adult/continuing education; medical care/treatment; medical/health education; public health; business/economic education; community affairs; crime/law enforcement; drug-abuse programs; economic development; employment/job training; environment/energy; family services; welfare

**Types of Organizations Funded:** Museums/historical societies; theaters/dance groups; music/opera groups; libraries; zoos; public television/radio; arts councils;

historic preservation organizations; other arts and humanities organizations; elementary schools; secondary schools; vocational schools; colleges; universities; educational councils; scholarship funds; special education; adult education; junior colleges; libraries; other educational organizations; hospitals; clinics; chemical dependency services; counseling services; other health organizations; environmental agencies; energy agencies; conservation groups; United Way; multiservice centers; organizations for the elderly; organizations for the handicapped; organizations for drug abusers; organizations for youth; centers for children; housing agencies; organizations for offenders; organizations for minority groups; neighborhood agencies; day-care centers; community centers; other welfare and social services organizations

**Types of Support for Organizations:** Capital support; matching grants; program development; federated fund drives; other

**Sample Grants:**
  The Saint Paul Foundation, for the Minority Student Education Project—$25,000
  Courage Center Attendant Care Program—$15,000
  Natural History Society, *Naturalist Magazine*—$1,000

**Financial Data for Year Ending December 31, 1981:**
  Assets: $23,018,688
  Grants Paid: $820,205
  Number of Grants: 50
  Largest/Smallest: $250,000/$500

**Paid Professional Staff:** Yes

**Contact Made by:** Request for guidelines

**Available by Request:** Proposal guidelines; application procedures; annual report

**Proposal Deadlines:** At least two months prior to board meeting

**Board Meetings:** Biannual, early June and early December

**Applicants Notified:** Within two weeks of decision

**Directors/Trustees:** Ronald M. Hubbs, chairman; Carl B. Drake, Jr., vice-chairman; Richard L. Gunderson; Malcolm W. McDonald; Roger B. Shepard, Jr.

# BING FOUNDATION

Box 2336, Loop Station
Minneapolis, MN 55402

**Established:** May 1960

**Type:** Private foundation

**Program's Purpose:** To support primarily educational/cultural programs with emphasis on human consciousness and human potential

**Geographic Orientation:** National

**Sample Grant:**
 Cross Cultural Studies Program, Kansas—$400

**Financial Data for Year Ending December 31, 1981:**
 Assets: $13,608
 Grants Paid: $400
 Number of Grants: 1

**Paid Professional Staff:** No

**Contact Made by:** Letter of inquiry

**Proposal Deadlines:** None

**Directors/Trustees:** Robert M. O'Connor, president; Michael E. LaBrosse, treasurer; Louise Stout, secretary; Peggy Peterson, vice-president

# ● C. K. BLANDIN FOUNDATION

Box 630
Grand Rapids, MN 55744
(218) 326-0523

**Contact Person:** Paul M. Olson, executive director

**Type:** Private foundation

**Program's Purpose:** To support education, arts and humanities, recreation, human services, and economic development

**Program's Limits:** In the Grand Rapids, MN, area projects funded "that seek to raise the quality of life without displacing the functions of local government or other civic groups"; funds not used to supplant tax dollars for services generally considered to be the responsibility of governmental units; in northeastern/north-central Minnesota, funds for projects likely to have a broad impact on the region; projects that serve only a few communities not funded unless they constitute a demonstration project with wide-ranging implications; statewide organizations and programs funded only if they offer direct or indirect benefit to residents of northeastern Minnesota

**Geographic Orientation:** Grand Rapids; northeastern/north-central Minnesota

**Fields of Activity:** Media/communications; music/opera; theater/dance; arts education; technical assistance in the arts and humanities; elementary/secondary education; vocational education; higher education; adult/continuing education; public health; mental health; social sciences; advocacy; business/economic education; drug-abuse programs; economic development; environment/energy; family services; recreation; special population groups

**Types of Organizations Funded:** Museums/historical societies; theaters/dance groups; music/opera groups; public television/radio; arts councils; elementary schools; secondary schools; vocational schools; colleges; universities; educational councils; scholarship funds; special education; adult education; junior colleges; chemical dependency services; counseling services; research/study institutes; environmental agencies; United Way; multiservice centers; organizations for the elderly; organizations for the handicapped; organizations for women; organizations for drug abusers; organizations for youth; organizations for minorities; day-care centers; community centers

**Types of Support for Organizations:** Matching grants; program development, program-related investments

**Type of Support for Individuals:** Scholarships

**Sample Grants:**
 Itasca Development Corporation (to develop economic opportunities in Itasca County)—$430,800 (over five years)
 Science Museum of Minnesota, Opportunities in Science Program—$327,000 (over three years)
 College of Saint Scholastica (feasibility study for a baccalaureate program in long-term-care administration for northeastern Minnesota—$41,850

**Financial Data for Year Ending December 31, 1981:**
 Assets: $8,385,162
 Grants Paid: $4,136,956
 Number of Grants: 433 scholarships; 75 grants to organizations
 Largest/Smallest: $616,423/$440

**Paid Professional Staff:** Yes

**Contact Made by:** Letter of inquiry

**Available by Request:** Proposal guidelines; application procedures; annual report

**Board Meetings:** Quarterly

**Applicants Notified:** Within one to two weeks of decision

**Trustees:** James R. Oppenheimer, chairman; Lois Gildemeister; Margaret M. Matalamaki; Harold Zigmund; George Rossman; Warren Anderson; Eugene Rothstein; William G. King; C. A. Akre; Robert L. Bullard; Russ Virden; Henry Doerr; Peter Heegaard; Paul M. Olson, executive director

# THE BONHOMIE FOUNDATION

Box 128
Waverly, MN 55390

**Established:** December 1965

**Type:** Private foundation

**Geographic Orientation:** National

**Sample Grants:**
 Church of St. John the Evangelist, Hopkins—$2,864
 Our Lady of Good Counsel Cancer Home, St. Paul—$500
 Waverly United Fund—$20

**Financial Data for Year Ending December 31, 1981:**
Assets: $102,099
Grants Paid: $5,709
Number of Grants: 16
Largest/Smallest: $2,864/$10

**Paid Professional Staff:** No

**Directors/Trustees:** Mark L. Graham; Marjorie Q. Graham

# WILLIAM BOSS FOUNDATION

2356 University Avenue
St. Paul, MN 55114

**Established:** January 1956

**Type:** Private foundation

**Geographic Orientation:** Twin Cities

**Sample Grants:**
House of Hope Youth Project—$5,951
Minnesota Dance Theater and School—$3,500
William Mitchell College of Law—$250

**Financial Data for Year Ending June 30, 1981:**
Assets: $221,674
Grants Paid: $19,191
Number of Grants: 19
Largest/Smallest: $5,951/$100

**Paid Professional Staff:** No

**Directors/Trustees:** Harlan D. Boss, chairman; Nancy B. Sandberg, president; John P. Vitko, secretary; Albert D. Sandberg, treasurer

# • OTTO BREMER FOUNDATION

700 Northwestern National Bank Building
St. Paul, MN 55101
(612) 227-8036

**Contact Person:** John Kostishack, grants administrator

**Established:** May 1944

**Type:** Private foundation

**Program's Purpose:** To make grants in the areas of community affairs, higher education, health and human services

**Program's Limits:** Grant making limited to organizations serving communities in Minnesota, North Dakota, and Wisconsin where Bremer banks are located and to programs for relieving poverty in the city of St. Paul; support to higher education limited to institutions in Minnesota; no grants to individuals

**Geographic Orientation:** Communities in Minnesota, North Dakota, and Wisconsin where Bremer banks are located and the city of St. Paul

**Fields of Activity:** Arts/architecture; history/preservation; language/literature; media/communications; music/opera; theater/dance; arts education; vocational education; higher education; adult/continuing education; medical care/treatment; medical/health education; public health; mental health; religion; advocacy; business/economic education; community affairs; crime/law enforcement; drug-abuse programs; economic development; employment/job training; environment/energy; equal rights/legal aid; disaster relief; family services; recreation; safety; special population groups; welfare; consumer interests; rural development

**Types of Organizations Funded:** Museums/historical societies; theaters/dance groups; music/opera groups; libraries; public television/radio; arts councils; historical preservation; cultural centers; vocational schools; colleges; universities; scholarship funds; special education; adult education; junior colleges; libraries; hospitals; medical schools; clinics; chemical dependency services; family-planning agencies; counseling services; churches/synagogues; religious service groups; religious colleges; environmental agencies; conservation groups; United Way; legal aid; multiservice centers; organizations for the elderly; organizations for the handicapped; organizations for women; organizations for veterans; organizations for drug abusers; organizations for youth; centers for children; housing agencies; organizations for offenders; organizations for minorities; neighborhood agencies; day-care centers; community centers

**Targeted Population Groups:** Children/youth; women/girls; refugees; Asian Americans; blacks; Hispanics; native Americans

**Types of Support for Organizations:** Capital support; continuing support; general operating support; matching grants; program development; federated fund drives

**Types of Support for Individuals:** Scholarships; loans for education

**Sample Grants:**
Centro Legal, St. Paul (for start-up funds for a bilingual, bicultural legal services program to serve the Hispanic community)—$25,000
Luther-Northwestern Theological Seminary, St. Paul (to increase participation of women in the faculty)—$10,000
Quad County Community Action Agency, Grand Forks, ND (to support the development of a food cooperative in the rural community of Grafton)—$1,250

**Financial Data for Year Ending June 30, 1982:**
Assets: $42,409,740
Grants Paid: $2,361,403
Number of Grants: 386
Largest/Smallest: $80,000/$200

**Paid Professional Staff:** Yes

**Contact Made by:** Telephone inquiry or complete proposal

**Available by Request:** Annual report

**Board Meetings:** Monthly

**Applicants Notified:** Within one week of decision

**Directors/Trustees:** William Lipschultz; Robert Reardon; Gordon Shepard

# BRIN FOUNDATION

2861 Burnham Boulevard
Minneapolis, MN 55416
(612) 377-3887

**Contact Person:** Howard B. Brin, president

**Established:** November 1956

**Type:** Private foundation

**Program's Purpose:** To make contributions or to lend financial aid to religious, charitable, scientific, and educational institutions

**Geographic Orientation:** Twin Cities; Minnesota; national

**Fields of Activity:** Music/opera; theater/dance; arts education; adult/continuing education; medical care/treatment; medical/health education; religion; religious education; community affairs; environment/energy; equal rights/legal aid; family services; recreation; welfare; consumer interests

**Types of Organizations Funded:** Museums/historical societies; theaters/dance groups; music/opera groups; public television/radio; arts councils; cultural centers; colleges; universities; scholarship funds; other educational organizations; hospitals; family-planning agencies; other health organizations; churches/synagogues; religious service groups; religious colleges; United Way; multiservice centers; organizations for the elderly; organizations for women; organizations for youth; organizations for minorities; community centers

**Types of Support for Organizations:** Capital support; continuing support; general operating support; federated fund drives

**Sample Grants:**
Jewish Community Center of Greater Minneapolis—$5,335
Minneapolis Society for Fine Arts—$100
United Negro College Fund—$50

**Financial Data for Year Ending December 31, 1981:**
Assets: $10,860
Grants Paid: $7,202
Number of Grants: 31
Largest/Smallest: $5,335/$10

**Paid Professional Staff:** No

**Contact Made by:** Letter of inquiry

**Available by Request:** Application procedures

**Board Meetings:** Biannual

**Applicants Notified:** Within one week of decision

**Directors/Trustees:** Howard B. Brin, president and treasurer; Jerome B. Ingber, vice-president; Ruth F. Brin, secretary

# THE BROMS FAMILY FOUNDATION

2515 Twenty-fourth Avenue South
Minneapolis, MN 55406

**Established:** December 1979

**Type:** Private foundation

**Geographic Orientation:** Twin Cities

**Sample Grants:**
Minneapolis Federation for Jewish Service—$7,000
Paul Salloway Camp Scholarship Fund—$250
March of Dimes—$15

**Financial Data for Year Ending March 31, 1982:**
Assets: $47,224
Grants Paid: $8,156
Number of Grants: 18
Largest/Smallest: $7,000/$15

**Paid Professional Staff:** No

**Directors/Trustees:** Mathew Broms, president; Evelyn Broms, secretary-treasurer; Richard Broms, vice-president

# BRONSTIEN FAMILY FOUNDATION

Box 217
Chaska, MN 55318

**Established:** December 1946

**Type:** Private foundation

**Geographic Orientation:** Twin Cities

**Sample Grants:**
St. Paul United Jewish Fund and Council—$31,600
MIT Alumni Foundation—$400
National Council of Christians and Jews—$100

**Financial Data for Year Ending December 31, 1981:**
Assets: $22,441
Grants Paid: $33,700
Number of Grants: 7
Largest/Smallest: $31,600/$100

**Paid Professional Staff:** No

**Directors/Trustees:** E. L. Bronstien, Jr., foundation manager; Donald M. Fahrenkamp, assistant secretary

# THE SAM AND IRMA BROWN FAMILY FOUNDATION

1250 Builders Exchange Building
Minneapolis, MN 55402

**Established:** November 1970

**Type:** Private foundation

**Geographic Orientation:** Twin Cities

**Sample Grants:**
    Minneapolis Federation for Jewish Service—$15,600
    Merkos Lubovitch Association—$4,100

**Financial Data for Year Ending July 31, 1981:**
    Assets: $31,906
    Grants Paid: $19,700
    Number of Grants: 2
    Largest/Smallest: $15,600/$4,100

**Paid Professional Staff:** No

**Directors/Trustees:** Eugene Brown; Alvin S. Malmon

## BUCKBEE-MEARS FOUNDATION

1150 American National Bank Building
St. Paul, MN 55101

**Type:** Corporate foundation

**Geographic Orientation:** National

**Sample Grants:**
    United Way of the St. Paul Area—$21,683
    Guthrie Theater—$1,500
    Northwestern University—$100

**Financial Data for Year Ending December 31, 1981:**
    Assets: $173,247
    Grants Paid: $37,933
    Number of Grants: 27
    Largest/Smallest: $21,683/$25

**Paid Professional Staff:** No

**Contact Made by:** Request for guidelines

**Directors/Trustees:** E. F. Carter, president; A. P. Witt, vice-president; C. M. Lund, vice-president; S. K. Richardson, treasurer; G. J. Reichow, secretary

## ● BURDICK GRAIN COMPANY CHARITABLE FOUNDATION

375 Grain Exchange
Box 15306
Minneapolis, MN 55415
(612) 339-6811

**Contact Person:** Allan L. Burdick

**Established:** June 1974

**Type:** Corporate foundation

**Program's Limits:** Grants usually restricted to $1,000 or less

**Geographic Orientation:** Minnesota

**Fields of Activity:** Music/opera; theater/dance; higher education; medical research; medical care/treatment

**Types of Organizations Funded:** Theaters/dance groups; music/opera groups; colleges; hospitals; medical research groups

**Type of Support for Organizations:** Continuing support

**Sample Grants:**
    Minnesota Orchestra—$500
    United Negro College Fund—$200
    Courage Center—$200

**Financial Data for Year Ending February 28, 1982:**
    Assets: $125,000
    Grants Paid: $17,665
    Number of Grants: 37
    Largest/Smallest: $1,740/$100

**Paid Professional Staff:** No

**Contact Made by:** Letter of inquiry

**Available by Request:** Application procedures; annual report

**Board Meetings:** Infrequent

**Directors/Trustees:** Allan L. Burdick; W. Brooks Fields; Otto W. Seiderberg; R. J. Currier

## BURLINGTON NORTHERN FOUNDATION

1111 Third Avenue
Seattle, WA 98101
(206) 625-6794

**Established:** May 1970

**Type:** Corporate foundation

**Geographic Orientation:** National

**Sample Grants:**
    University of Nebraska—$251,810
    United Way of the Ozarks—$19,000
    Junior Achievement of Billings—$350

**Financial Data for Year Ending December 31, 1981:**
    Assets: $3,655,879
    Grants Paid: $2,646,176
    Number of Grants: 464
    Largest/Smallest: $251,810/$25

**Paid Professional Staff:** No

**Director:** Donald K. North, executive director

## W. R. BUSCH FOUNDATION

803 Degree of Honor Building
St. Paul, MN 55101

**Established:** December 1968

**Type:** Private foundation

**Geographic Orientation:** Twin Cities

**Sample Grants:**
    College of Saint Thomas (scholarships)—$15,500
    Cretin High School (scholarships)—$2,500
    Little Sisters of the Poor—$2,400

**Financial Data for Year Ending December 31, 1981:**
    Assets: $142,174
    Grants Paid: $20,400
    Number of Grants: 3
    Largest/Smallest: $15,500/$2,400

**Paid Professional Staff:** No

**Director/Trustee:** William R. Busch

## ● THE BUSH FOUNDATION

E-900 First National Bank Building
St. Paul, MN 55101
(612) 227-0891

**Contact Person:** Humphrey Doermann, president

**Established:** February 1953

**Type:** Private foundation

**Program's Purpose:** To support primarily higher
    education; performing arts and humanities; delivery
    of health care; social service agencies; and fellowship
    programs in Minnesota, North Dakota, and South
    Dakota

**Geographic Orientation:** Minnesota; North Dakota;
    South Dakota

**Fields of Activity:** Arts/architecture; history/preservation;
    media/communications; music/opera; theater/dance;
    elementary/secondary education; higher education;
    adult/continuing education; medical/health education;
    mental health; other health activities;
    business/economic education; crime/law enforcement;
    drug-abuse programs; employment/job training,
    environment/energy; family services; recreation; special
    population groups

**Types of Organizations Funded:** Arts and humanities
    organizations; educational organizations; health
    services; welfare/social services

**Targeted Population Groups:** Children/youth; minorities

**Types of Support for Organizations:** Capital support;
    continuing support; endowment; matching grants;
    program development

**Type of Support for Individuals:** Fellowships

**Sample Grants:**
    Augustana College Faculty Development
    Program—$180,000
    Minnesota Orchestral Association (support for 1981-
    1982 season)—$165,000
    Domestic Abuse Project (treatment program for
    violent men and their families)—$60,000

**Financial Data for Year Ending November 30, 1981:**
    Assets: $232,555,444
    Grants Paid: $12,256,713
    Number of Grants: 104
    Largest/Smallest: $1,000,000/$5,125

**Paid Professional Staff:** Yes

**Contact Made by:** Letter of inquiry or telephone
    inquiry

**Available by Request:** Proposal guidelines; application
    procedures; annual report

**Board Meetings:** Quarterly—February 1983, April 1983,
    June 1983, October 1983

**Applicants Notified:** Within one week of decision

**Directors/Trustees:** Thomas J. Clifford, chairman; Harriet
    B. Medlin, secretary; George C. Power, Jr., treasurer;
    Humphrey Doermann, president; Waverly G. Smith,
    first vice-chairman; John A. McHugh, second vice-
    chairman; Ellen Z. Green; Hess Kline; Phyllis B.
    France; Thomas E. Holloran; Herbert
    E. Longenecker; Diana E. Murphy; John F. Nash;
    James P. Shannon; Harry P. Sweitzer; Frank B.
    Wilderson, Jr.

## BUSINESS INCENTIVES FOUNDATION

Box 1610
Minneapolis, MN 55440

**Established:** October 1979

**Type:** Corporate foundation

**Geographic Orientation:** Twin Cities

**Sample Grants:**
    College of Saint Thomas—$88,000
    Hospitality House—$1,800
    American Heart Association—$75

**Financial Data for Year Ending September 30, 1981:**
    Assets: $1,709
    Grants Paid: $96,550
    Number of Grants: 12
    Largest/Smallest: $88,000/$25

**Paid Professional Staff:** No

**Directors/Trustees:** L. Guy Schoenecker,
    president/treasurer; Lila M. Johnson, vice-
    president/secretary; James E. O'Brien

## ● PATRICK AND AIMEE BUTLER FAMILY FOUNDATION

W-1380 First National Bank Building
St. Paul, MN 55101
(612) 222-2565

**Contact Person:** Peter M. Butler, vice-president

**Established:** November 1951

**Type:** Private foundation

**Program's Purpose:** To direct resources to organizations
    in the St. Paul area; primary emphasis on Catholic
    activities and institutions; additional emphasis on
    education, cultural programs, chemical dependency
    programs, community-based programs, public health,
    and women's needs

**Program's Limits:** Does not make loans and does not provide grants to individuals

**Geographic Orientation:** St. Paul area

**Fields of Activity:** Arts/architecture; secondary education; higher education; public health; religion; drug-abuse programs; equal rights/legal aid; family services

**Types of Organizations Funded:** Museums/historical societies; theaters/dance groups; music/opera groups; public television/radio; historic preservation; cultural centers; secondary schools; colleges; universities; clinics; chemical dependency services; churches/synagogues; religious colleges; United Way; organizations for women; organizations for drug abusers

**Types of Support for Organizations:** Capital support; continuing support; endowment; general operating support

**Sample Grants:**
Film in the Cities (for Agent Orange Film Project)—$1,000
New Connection Program (services for chemically dependent children)—$1,000
Little Sisters of the Poor (holiday meals contribution)—$400

**Financial Data for Year Ending December 31, 1981:**
Assets: $3,474,531
Grants Paid: $151,790
Number of Grants: 94
Largest/Smallest: $10,000/$250

**Paid Professional Staff:** No

**Contact Made by:** Letter of inquiry

**Proposal Deadlines:** February 1; July 1; November 1

**Board Meetings:** As required

**Applicants Notified:** Within four weeks of decision

**Directors/Trustees:** Patrick Butler, president; Peter M. Butler, vice-president; Aimee Mott Butler; Patrick Butler, Jr.; Kate Butler Peterson; Sandra K. Butler

## CAMPBELL CHARITABLE TRUST

North City National Bank Trust Department
Duluth, MN 55801

**Established:** November 1950

**Type:** Private foundation

**Sample Grants:**
United Way of Greater Duluth—$6,777
Duluth-Superior Symphony Association—$1,290
Youth for Christ—$323

**Financial Data for Year Ending December 31, 1981:**
Assets: $139,350
Grants Paid: $12,909
Number of Grants: 10
Largest/Smallest: $6,777/$322

**Paid Professional Staff:** No

## • MARTIN AND ESTHER CAPP FOUNDATION

8151 Bridge Road
Bloomington, MN 55437
(612) 835-3577

**Contact Person:** Leonard Horowitz, director and secretary-treasurer

**Established:** 1961

**Type:** Private foundation

**Geographic Orientation:** National

**Fields of Activity:** Arts/architecture; history/preservation; music/opera; arts education; research; medical research; medical care/treatment; medical/health education; religion; religious education; life sciences; physical sciences; legal education; business/economic education; crime/law enforcement; employment/job training; environment/energy; equal rights/legal aid; family services; recreation

**Types of Organizations Funded:** Museums/historical societies; theaters/dance groups; music/opera groups; libraries; zoos; public television/radio; arts councils; historic preservation; cultural centers; universities; hospitals; medical schools; medical research groups; family-planning agencies; churches/synagogues; religious service groups; religious schools; religious colleges; research/study institutes; environmental agencies; energy agencies; conservation groups; United Way; legal aid; multiservice centers; organizations for the elderly; organizations for the handicapped; organizations for women; organizations for veterans; organizations for drug abusers; organizations for youth; organizations for men; centers for children; community centers; animal centers

**Types of Support for Organizations:** Capital support; continuing support; general operating support; research

**Type of Support for Individuals:** Research grants

**Sample Grants:**
St. Paul United Jewish Fund and Council—$18,000
United Way—$1,016
Greenpeace-Save the Whales—$50

**Financial Data for Year Ending December 31, 1981:**
Assets: $146,872
Grants Paid: $45,093
Number of Grants: 41
Largest/Smallest: $18,000/$5

**Paid Professional Staff:** No

**Contact Made by:** Letter of inquiry

**Available by Request:** Annual report

**Board Meetings:** Annual

**Directors:** Martin Capp; Esther Capp; Leonard Horowitz; Robert Brin; Burton Ross

## THE CARGILL FAMILY FUND

c/o D. E. Billbe
Department 28, Box 9300
Minneapolis, MN 55440

**Established:** October 1967

**Type:** Private foundation

**Sample Grants:**
Minnesota Medical Foundation—$5,000
Ducks Unlimited—-$250
Trout Unlimited—$250

**Financial Data for Year Ending December 31, 1981:**
Assets: $45,248
Grants Paid: $5,500
Number of Grants: 3

**Paid Professional Staff:** No

## • THE CARGILL FOUNDATION

Box 9300
Minneapolis, MN 55440
(612) 475-6122

**Contact Person:** Calvin J. Anderson, executive director

**Established:** December 1951

**Type:** Corporate foundation

**Program's Limits:** No grants to individuals or to religious organizations for religious purposes

**Geographic Orientation:** Twin Cities

**Fields of Activity:** Music; higher education; medical research; mental health; business/economic education; drug-abuse programs; equal rights/legal aid; family services

**Types of Organizations Funded:** Museums/historical societies; music groups; public television/radio; secondary schools; colleges; universities; medical schools; medical research groups; chemical dependency services; family-planning agencies; counseling services; United Way; legal aid

**Types of Support for Organizations:** Continuing support; general operating support

**Financial Data for Year Ending December 31, 1981:**
Assets: $13,997,529
Grants Paid: $1,251,963
Number of Grants: 81
Largest/Smallest: $325,000/$500

**Paid Professional Staff:** Yes

**Contact Made by:** Telephone inquiry or letter of inquiry

**Proposal Deadlines:** One month before board meeting

**Board Meetings:** Quarterly

**Applicants Notified:** Within two weeks of decision

**Directors:** H. Robert Diercks, president; Cargill MacMillan, Jr., vice-president; J. R. Cargill, vice-president; Peter Dorsey, vice-president; Clinton Morrison, vice-president; Calvin J. Anderson, secretary-treasurer; Dwane E. Billbe, assistant secretary-treasurer

## CARIDAD GIFT TRUST

c/o Trust Department
First National Bank of Duluth
Duluth, MN 55801

**Established:** December 1952

**Type:** Private foundation

**Geographic Orientation:** Minnesota; national

**Sample Grants:**
College of Saint Scholastica—$50,000
United Negro College Fund—$1,000
American Indian Fund Association—$500

**Financial Data for Year Ending December 31, 1981:**
Assets: $759,810
Grants Paid: $76,900
Number of Grants: 15
Largest/Smallest: $50,000/$200

**Paid Professional Staff:** No

**Directors/Trustees:** Caroline Marshall; Newell Marshall

## CURTIS L. CARLSON FOUNDATION

12755 B State Highway 55
Minneapolis, MN 55441

**Established:** December 1959

**Type:** Private foundation

**Geographic Orientation:** Minnesota; national

**Sample Grants:**
Minneapolis Housing and Redevelopment—$100,000
Salem Academy and College—$12,500
Nature Conservancy—$50

**Financial Data for Year Ending December 31, 1981:**
Assets: $461,528
Grants Paid: $337,507
Number of Grants: 69
Largest/Smallest: $100,000/$25

**Paid Professional Staff:** No

**Directors/Trustees:** Curtis L. Carlson; Arleen E. Carlson; Chester C. Krause

## • CAROLYN FOUNDATION

1600 First Bank Place West
Minneapolis, MN 55402
(612) 339-7101

**Contact Person:** Robert B. Diercks, executive director

**Established:** 1964

**Type:** Private foundation

**Program's Purpose:** To support general-purpose organizations, with principal interests in education, culture, health and welfare, environment, and aid to the disadvantaged

**Program's Limits:** No grants to religious organizations for religious purposes, to individuals, for annual fund drives, or to cover deficits already incurred

**Geographic Orientation:** Twin Cities metropolitan area; New Haven, CT

**Fields of Activity:** Arts/architecture; history/preservation; media/communications; music/opera; theater/dance; arts education; elementary/secondary education; vocational education; higher education; medical care/treatment; mental health; community affairs; drug-abuse programs; employment/job training; environment/energy; equal rights/legal aid; family services; recreation; special population groups; welfare

**Types of Organizations Funded:** Museums/historical societies; theaters/dance groups; music/opera groups; libraries; public television/radio; historic preservation; cultural centers; elementary schools; secondary schools; vocational schools; colleges; universities; scholarship funds; special education; libraries; hospitals; chemical dependency services; family-planning agencies; counseling services; environmental agencies; energy agencies; conservation groups; legal aid; multiservice centers; organizations for the handicapped; organizations for youth; centers for children; neighborhood agencies; community centers

**Types of Support for Organizations:** Capital support; endowment; general operating support; matching grants; program development; research

**Financial Data for Year Ending December 31, 1981:**
Assets: $9,123,612
Grants Paid: $565,864
Number of Grants: 30
Largest/Smallest: $100,000/$1,000

**Paid Professional Staff:** No

**Contact Made by:** Request for guidelines

**Available by Request:** Proposal guidelines; application procedures

**Proposal Deadlines:** Grants under $10,000—April 1; grants of more than $10,000—September 15

**Board Meetings:** Biannual, in late May or early June and early December (although the full board meets biannually, it makes major grants only once a year, at the December meeting; a distribution committee meets several times during the first five months of the year to make minor grants)

**Trustees:** Olive C. Brown, chairman; Guido Calabresi, vice-chairman; Robert B. Diercks, executive director; C. John Kirsch, secretary-treasurer; Beatrice C. Booth; Edwin L. Crosby; Franklin M. Crosby III; G. Christian Crosby; Lucy C. Mitchell; Sumner McK. Crosby, Jr.; Thomas M. Crosby, Jr.; Susan W. Crosby

# CENEX FOUNDATION

5600 Cenex Drive
Inver Grove Heights, MN 55075

**Established:** December 5, 1947

**Type:** Corporate foundation

**Geographic Orientation:** National

**Sample Grants:**
Southwest State University, Marshall, MN—$25,000
Dakota Boys Ranch, Minot, ND—$2,000
Manderson (WY) Volunteer Fire Department—$100

**Financial Data for Year Ending November 30, 1981:**
Assets: $2,565,036
Grants Paid: $251,100
Number of Grants: 161
Largest/Smallest: $25,000/$25

**Paid Professional Staff:** No

# CENTRAL LIVESTOCK FOUNDATION

Exchange Building
South St. Paul, MN 55075

**Established:** December 1958

**Type:** Corporate foundation

**Geographic Orientation:** Minnesota

**Sample Grants:**
United Way—$300
United Arts Fund—$120
Future Farmers of America—$100

**Financial Data for Year Ending December 31, 1981:**
Assets: $10,076
Grants Paid: $673
Number of Grants: 5
Largest/Smallest: $300/$53

**Paid Professional Staff:** No

**Directors/Trustees:** Gail Tritle, president; Bernard Palman, manager; David M. Farrand, controller

# ● CHADWICK FOUNDATION

4900 IDS Center
Minneapolis, MN 55402

**Established:** November 1967

**Type:** Private foundation

**Geographic Orientation:** Minnesota; national

**Sample Grants:**
Minneapolis YMCA—$48,000
Westminster Presbyterian Church—$9,000
Aspen County Day School—$1,000

**Financial Data for Year Ending December 31, 1981:**
Assets: $3,052,888
Grants Paid: $146,080
Number of Grants: 48
Largest/Smallest: $48,000/$100

**Paid Professional Staff:** No

**Directors/Trustees:** Donald C. Dayton, president/treasurer; Lucy J. Dayton, secretary; Edward N. Dayton, vice-president; Robert J. Dayton, vice-president; John W. Dayton, vice-president

## CHANCERY LANE FOUNDATION

W-2200 First National Bank Building
St. Paul, MN 55101

**Established:** December 1960

**Type:** Private foundation

**Geographic Orientation:** Twin Cities

**Sample Grants:**
College of Saint Thomas—$1,000
Minnesota Historical Society—$100

**Financial Data for Year Ending June 30, 1982:**
Assets: $1,046
Grants Paid: $1,100
Number of Grants: 2

**Paid Professional Staff:** No

**Directors/Trustees:** Richard E. Kyle, president; J. Neil Morton, vice-president; Frank J. Hammond, vice-president; Agnes Gerlach, secretary-treasurer

## CHARITY INC.

7350 Commerce Lane
Fridley, MN 55432

**Established:** February 1962

**Type:** Private foundation

**Geographic Orientation:** Minnesota; international

**Sample Grants:**
New Covenant Fellowship—$38,000
North Memorial Hospital—$15,000
Catholic Deaf Committee—$1,000

**Financial Data for Year Ending February 28, 1982:**
Assets: $842,682
Grants Paid: $245,978
Number of Grants: 64
Largest/Smallest: $38,000/$500

**Paid Professional Staff:** No

**Directors/Trustees:** Rose W. Totino, president-treasurer; Joanne Elwell, vice-president; Leonard Addington, secretary

## CHAR-LYNN FOUNDATION

Box 299, Lake Zumbra
Excelsior, MN 55331

**Established:** February 1967

**Type:** Private foundation

**Geographic Orientation:** Twin Cities

**Financial Data for Year Ending January 31, 1982:**
Assets: $74,932
Grants Paid: $0

**Paid Professional Staff:** No

**Directors/Trustees:** Lynn L. Charlson, president-treasurer; Beverly G. Charlson, vice-president/secretary; Hans A. Nathan

## THE CHELGREN-HAVILAND FOUNDATION

5616 Olson Memorial Highway
Minneapolis, MN 55422

**Established:** November 1963

**Type:** Private foundation

**Geographic Orientation:** Twin Cities

**Sample Grants:**
Gustavus Adolphus College—$1,000
Gethsemane Lutheran Church—$600
KTCA—$50

**Financial Data for Year Ending December 31, 1981:**
Assets: $39,884
Grants Paid: $2,625
Number of Grants: 12
Largest/Smallest: $1,000/$25

**Paid Professional Staff:** No

**Directors/Trustees:** Paul Chelgren; Mary Chelgren

## THE CHERNE FOUNDATION

Box 975
Minneapolis, MN 55440

**Established:** January 1968

**Type:** Corporate foundation

**Geographic Orientation:** Minnesota; national

**Sample Grants:**
St. Stephen Church, Edina—$4,000
William Penn College—$1,500
DAR—$75

**Financial Data for Year Ending December 31, 1981:**
Assets: $1,014,964
Grants Paid: $52,931
Number of Grants: 87
Largest/Smallest: $4,000/$25

**Paid Professional Staff:** No

**Director/Trustee:** A. W. Cherne

## CHILDREN'S HAVEN

615 Centennial Drive
Kenyon, MN 55946

**Established:** May 1978

**Type:** Private foundation

**Sample Grant:**
 TeCate Mission—$5,000

**Financial Data for Year Ending December 31, 1981:**
 Assets: $85,150
 Grants Paid: $5,000
 Number of Grants: 1

**Paid Professional Staff:** No

**Directors/Trustees:** Harold A. Nielson; Louis V. Nielson; Richard Nielson

## CHURCHMEN'S FELLOWSHIP OF PEACE UNITED CHURCH OF CHRIST

1503 Northeast Second Avenue
Rochester, MN 55901

**Established:** March 1976

**Type:** Private foundation

**Program's Limits:** Scholarships for students in nursing and religion only

**Geographic Orientation:** Rochester

**Sample Grant:**
 Bethany Samaritan—$31,500

**Financial Data for Year Ending December 31, 1981:**
 Assets: $443,899
 Grants Paid: $37,500
 Number of Grants: 1 grant/10 scholarships
 Largest/Smallest: $31,500/$250

**Paid Professional Staff:** No

## F. B. CLEMENTS FOUNDATION

1815 Madison Avenue
Mankato, MN 56001

**Contact Person:** C. R. Butler, president

**Established:** 1970

**Type:** Corporate foundation

**Geographic Orientation:** Mankato and Rochester areas

**Fields of Activity:** Music/opera; higher education; welfare/social services

**Types of Organizations Funded:** Music/opera groups; colleges; United Way; organizations for youth; community centers

**Types of Support for Organizations:** Capital support; general operating support

**Sample Grants:**
 Mankato United Way—$1,000
 Rochester United Way—$500
 Rochester YMCA Building Fund—$200

**Financial Data for Year Ending December 31, 1981:**
 Assets: $2,310
 Grants Paid: $2,875
 Number of Grants: 11
 Largest/Smallest: $1,000/$25

**Paid Professional Staff:** No

**Board Meetings:** Annually, in January

**Directors/Trustees:** C. R. Butler, president, J. F. Madden, vice-president; D.F. Clements, vice-president; C. C. Butler, secretary-treasurer; R. L. Butler, assistant secretary-treasurer

## LOUIS M. AND TESS COHEN FAMILY FOUNDATION

7402 Oaklawn Avenue
Minneapolis, MN 55435

**Type:** Private foundation

**Geographic Orientation:** Twin Cities; national

**Sample Grants:**
 United Way of St. Paul—$5,000
 United Jewish Appeal—$2,500
 KTCA—$60

**Financial Data for Year Ending June 30, 1981:**
 Assets: $92,272
 Grants Paid: $11,990
 Number of Grants: 10
 Largest/Smallest: $5,000/$60

**Paid Professional Staff:** No

**Directors/Trustees:** Louis M. Cohen, president; Tess E. Cohen, vice-president; Burton D. Cohen, treasurer; Marjorie J. Zats, secretary

## SAMUEL COHEN AND ESTHER COHEN FOUNDATION

3916 Basswood Road
Minneapolis, MN 55416

**Established:** February 1967

**Type:** Private foundation

**Geographic Orientation:** Twin Cities; national

**Sample Grants:**
 Shelbank Community Center—$5,000
 Temple Israel—$852
 Courage Center—$150

**Financial Data for Year Ending July 31, 1981:**
 Assets: $154,514
 Grants Paid: $14,617
 Number of Grants: 36
 Largest/Smallest: $5,000/$20

**Paid Professional Staff:** No

**Director:** Sidney R. Cohen, president

# MARY ETHEL COMFORT FOUNDATION

162 York Avenue
St. Paul, MN 55117

**Established:** August 1952

**Type:** Private foundation

**Geographic Orientation:** Minnesota

**Sample Grants:**
United Way of St. Paul Area—$1,500

**Financial Data for Year Ending December 31, 1981:**
Assets: $2,197
Grants Paid: $1,500
Number of Grants: 1

**Paid Professional Staff:** No

**Directors/Trustees:** James O. Comfort, president; Robert R. Clemens, vice-president; Gilbert B. Malm, secretary-treasurer

# EDWARD C. CONGDON MEMORIAL TRUST

807 Lonsdale Building
Duluth, MN 55802

**Established:** January 1946

**Type:** Private foundation

**Geographic Orientation:** National

**Sample Grants:**
Duluth Public Library—$33,586
Sonora Desert Museum, Tucson, AZ—$33,500
Northland College, Ashland, WI—$13,000

**Financial Data for Year Ending December 31, 1981:**
Assets: $172,525
Grants Paid: $80,087
Number of Grants: 3
Largest/Smallest: $33,586/$13,000

**Paid Professional Staff:** No

**Directors/Trustees:** Mary C. Van Evera; Thomas E. Congdon

# • CONWED FOUNDATION

444 Cedar Street
Box 43237
St. Paul, MN 55164
(612) 221-1131

**Contact Person:** D. Q. Harayda, vice-president, director—administration

**Established:** November 1952

**Type:** Corporate foundation

**Program's Limits:** Generally no contributions to organizations engaged in direct patient care, to religious or political organizations, or to national health or disease organizations; no advertising in benefit or dinner publications; no direct grants to individuals

**Geographic Orientation:** Where Conwed has major facilities

**Fields of Activity:** Arts/architecture; media/communications; music/opera; theater/dance; elementary/secondary education; higher education; business/economic education; community affairs; crime/law enforcement; employment/job training; environment/energy; family services; special population groups

**Types of Organizations Funded:** Museums/historical societies; theaters/dance groups; music/opera groups; public television/radio; arts councils; historic preservation; secondary schools; colleges; universities; educational councils; libraries; hospitals (capital campaigns); family-planning agencies; conservation groups; United Way; multiservice centers; organizations for the elderly; organizations for the handicapped; organizations for drug abusers; organizations for youth; organizations for offenders; organizations for minorities; day-care centers

**Types of Support for Organizations:** Capital support; continuing support; general operating support; matching grants; federated fund drives

**Sample Grants:**
Minnesota Private College Fund—$4,000
Science Museum of Minnesota—$1,700
MEDA—$1,500

**Financial Data for Year Ending November 30, 1981:**
Assets: $639,103
Grants Paid: $148,990
Number of Grants: 29
Largest/Smallest: $40,000/$150

**Paid Professional Staff:** No

**Contact Made by:** Letter of inquiry or complete proposal

**Board Meetings:** Annual

**Applicants Notified:** Within two weeks of decision

**Directors/Trustees:** F. T. Weyerhaeuser, president; H. E. Walter, vice-president; D. E. Hinton, secretary-treasurer

# • THE COOPERATIVE FOUNDATION

1821 University Avenue
St. Paul, MN 55104

**Contact Person:** Thomas F. Ellerbe, Jr., president

**Established:** 1945

**Type:** Private foundation

**Program's Purpose:** To focus support for cooperative and mutual organizations primarily in the broad categories of research, experimentation, and education; special interest in projects that have social or economic "leverage"

**Program's Limits:** No grants to individuals, for operating budgets, for annual campaigns, for duplication of existing services, for capital funds or machinery, or to religiously oriented programs

**Geographic Orientation:** National

**Fields of Activity:** Cooperative housing; cooperative education and training; cooperative finance; cooperative development; cooperative health care; cooperative information

**Types of Support for Organizations:** Program development; research; program-related investments; educational project contracts

**Sample Grants:**
National Citizens Committee for Broadcasting—$3,700
University of Wisconsin Center for Cooperatives—$14,000
Park College, Kansas City, MO—$25,000

**Financial Data for Year Ending December 31, 1981:**
Assets: $1,358,000
Grants Paid: $55,000
Number of Grants: 9
Largest/Smallest: $25,000/$3,000

**Paid Professional Staff:** Yes

**Contact Made by:** Letter of inquiry

**Available by Request:** Application procedures

**Board Meetings:** Annual; executive committee "on call"

**Directors/Trustees:** Francis L. Lair, chairman of the board; Thomas F. Ellerbe, Jr., president; Edward E. Slettom, secretary; E. H. Sands, treasurer

# ARTHUR AND DAVID COSGROVE MEMORIAL FUND

228 South Main
Le Sueur, MN 56058

**Established:** November 1946

**Type:** Private foundation

**Geographic Orientation:** Le Sueur

**Sample Grants:**
Swimming Pool (Le Sueur)—$10,000
Bishop Whipple Schools—$2,500
United Way—$300

**Financial Data for Year Ending December 31, 1981:**
Assets: $513,218
Grants Paid: $24,969
Number of Grants: 10
Largest/Smallest: $10,000/$200

**Directors/Trustees:** R. C. Cosgrove, chairman; N. R. Morem; C. B. Way; L. C. Volling; Mrs. Dale K. Warner; Dodd Cosgrove

# COTE FOUNDATION

c/o First National Bank of Minneapolis
120 South Sixth Street
Minneapolis, MN 55450

**Established:** March 1961

**Type:** Private foundation

**Geographic Orientation:** Twin Cities

**Sample Grant:**
United Way of the Minneapolis Area—$1,100

**Financial Data for Year Ending February 28, 1982:**
Assets: $241,651
Grants Paid: $1,100
Number of Grants: 1

**Paid Professional Staff:** No

**Trustee:** First National Bank of Minneapolis

# • JOHN AND ELIZABETH BATES COWLES FOUNDATION

425 Portland Avenue
Minneapolis, MN 55488
(612) 372-4116

**Contact Person:** Norton L. Armour, vice-president and secretary

**Established:** December 1954

**Type:** Private foundation

**Geographic Orientation:** Minnesota

**Fields of Activity:** Arts/architecture; music/opera; theater/dance; higher education; community affairs; equal rights/legal aid; special population groups

**Types of Organizations Funded:** Museums/historical societies; theaters/dance groups; music/opera groups; universities; hospitals; family-planning agencies; counseling services; United Way; organizations for women; neighborhood agencies; community centers

**Type of Support for Organizations:** Matching grants

**Sample Grants:**
United Way of Minneapolis Area—$10,000
United Negro College Fund—$1,000
Planned Parenthood Federation of America—$1,000

**Financial Data for Year Ending February 28, 1982:**
Assets: $502,578
Grants Paid: $78,900
Number of Grants: 11
Largest/Smallest: $50,000/$100

**Paid Professional Staff:** No

**Contact Made by:** Letter of inquiry; complete proposal

**Available by Request:** Inspection of IRS 990AR

**Board Meetings:** Quarterly

# ● CRAY RESEARCH

608 Second Avenue South
Minneapolis, MN 55402
(612) 333-5889

**Contact Person:** William Scholer, manager, corporate contributions

**Established:** 1978

**Type:** Charitable contributions program

**Program's Interests:** Higher education, particularly in the fields of science and technology

**Program's Limits:** No grants to individuals; the company makes relatively few grants each year (ten to fifteen) and most grants are under $5,000

**Geographic Orientation:** Twin Cities; Chippewa Falls, WI

**Fields of Activity:** Arts and humanities; higher education; education

**Types of Organizations Funded:** Theaters/dance groups; music/opera groups; public television/radio; arts councils; secondary schools; vocational schools; colleges; universities; scholarship funds; United Way; organizations for minorities

**Targeted Population Groups:** Minorities

**Employee Matching Gift Programs:** Higher education; elementary/secondary education; any nonprofit organization (with the exceptions of religious or political organizations)

**Types of Support for Organizations:** Capital support; continuing support; endowment; general operating support; matching grants; program development; federated fund drives

**Type of Support for Individuals:** Scholarships for children of employees

**Financial Data for Year Ending December 31, 1981:**
Contributions Paid: $100,000
Largest/Smallest: $58,000/$10

**Contact Made by:** Telephone inquiry

**Applicants Notified:** Within two weeks of decision

# ALBERT B. CUPPAGE CHARITABLE FOUNDATION

222 East Main Street
Albert Lea, MN 56007

**Established:** August 1976

**Type:** Private foundation

**Geographic Orientation:** Albert Lea

**Sample Grants:**
YMCA—$10,000
Albert Lea Community Theater—$1,000
Lutheran Social Service—$500

**Financial Data for Year Ending December 31, 1981:**
Assets: $238,962
Grants Paid: $17,500
Number of Grants: 11
Largest/Smallest: $10,000/$500

**Paid Professional Staff:** No

**Directors/Trustees:** Clarence Schroeder; Larry Offenbecker; Henry J. Savelkoul

# ● DATA CARD CORPORATION

11111 Bren Road West
Minnetonka, MN 55343
(612) 933-1223

**Contact Person:** Tom Lindquist, manager, community relations

**Type:** Charitable contributions program

**Geographic Orientation:** Minnesota

**Fields of Activity:** Arts and humanities; history/preservation; media/communications; education; health; medical research; welfare/social services; business/economic education; economic development

**Types of Organizations Funded:** Museums/historical societies; public television/radio; historic preservation; secondary schools; colleges; universities; medical research groups; other health organizations; United Way; organizations for the handicapped; organizations for youth

**Targeted Population Groups:** Children/youth; handicapped

**Employee Matching Gift Programs:** No

**Types of Support for Organizations:** Capital support; general operating support; research

**Type of Support for Individuals:** Scholarship program for children of employees

**Financial Data for Year Ending March 31, 1981:**
Contributions Paid: $90,000
Number of Contributions: 80
Largest/Smallest: $10,000/$50

**Contact Made by:** Letter of inquiry

**Available by Request:** Proposal guidelines; application procedures

**Contributions Decisions Made:** Quarterly

**Applicants Notified:** Within two weeks of decision

# • EDWIN W. AND CATHERINE M. DAVIS FOUNDATION

2100 First National Bank Building
St. Paul, MN 55101
(612) 228-0935

**Contact Person:** Frederick W. Davis, president

**Established:** December 1956

**Type:** Private foundation

**Geographic Orientation:** Twin Cities; national

**Sample Grants:**
National Medical Fellowships, New York—$30,000
Twin Cities Chapter of Young Audiences—$15,000
Young Life, Seattle—$5,000

**Financial Data for Year Ending December 31, 1981:**
Assets:   $4,538,465
Grants Paid:   $558,680
Number of Grants:   75
Largest/Smallest:   $75,000/$500

**Paid Professional Staff:** No

**Contact Made by:** Letter of inquiry

**Available by Request:** Proposal guidelines; annual report

**Board Meetings:** Annual, in May or June

**Applicants Notified:** Within two to three weeks of decision

**Directors:** Frederick W. Davis, president; Bette D. Moorman, vice-president; Mary E. Davis, secretary; Albert J. Moorman, treasurer; J. S. Micallef, assistant secretary; Gordon E. Hed, assistant treasurer

# • DAYTON HUDSON FOUNDATION

777 Nicollet Mall
Minneapolis, MN 55402
(612) 370-6553

**Contact Person:** Vivian Stuck, administrative officer

**Established:** Founded in 1917 as Dayton Foundation

**Type:** Corporate foundation

**Program's Purpose:** To enhance the quality of life in Dayton Hudson communities, with a particular focus on the central city; priority areas: support for community-based social action institutions, organizations and programs that assist disadvantaged people to overcome barriers to self-sufficiency (40 percent of funding), and community-based arts institutions, organizations, and programs that interpret American artistic heritage or encourage contemporary artistic expression (40 percent of funding); 20 percent of funds to projects identified as critical by the foundation

**Program's Limits:** Few grants to national organizations; no grants to religious organizations for religious purposes; no grants to individuals; few grants for first-year operations; no grants for endowments; few grants to health, educational, advocacy, or research organizations or to activities identified by the foundation as the full responsibility of the government (e.g., maintenance programs for food, clothing, shelter)

**Geographic Orientation:** Minnesota; communities where the corporation has retail interests

**Fields of Activity:** Arts; language/literature; media/communications; music/opera; theater/dance; other arts and humanities activities; community affairs; employment/job training; family services; special population groups; welfare

**Types of Organizations Funded:** Museums; theaters/dance groups; music/opera groups; libraries; public television/radio; arts councils; cultural centers; libraries; United Way; multiservice centers; organizations for women; organizations for youth; centers for children; housing agencies; organizations for offenders; organizations for minorities; neighborhood agencies; community centers

**Targeted Population Groups:** Children/youth; women/girls; blacks; Hispanics; native Americans

**Types of Support for Organizations:** Capital support; general operating support; matching grants; program development; federated fund drives; other

**Sample Grants:**
United Way of Minneapolis Area (general support)—$383,000
Oakland (CA) Symphony (general support)—$20,000
Valle Del Sol (AZ) (to train potential high school dropouts for employment)—$6,000

**Financial Data for Year Ending January 31, 1982:**
Assets:   $7,762,862
Grants Paid:   $7,141,648
Number of Grants:   521
Largest/Smallest:   $383,000/$200

**Paid Professional Staff:** Yes

**Contact Made by:** Letter of inquiry, request for guidelines, or complete proposal

**Available by Request:** Proposal guidelines; application procedures; annual report

**Board Meetings:** Quarterly, in February, June, September, and December

**Applicants Notified:** Within eight weeks of decision

**Officers:** Peter C. Hutchinson, chairman; William E. Harder, secretary; Michael J. Wahlig, assistant secretary; Willard C. Shull III, vice-president/treasurer

## ROGER L. AND AGNES C. DELL CHARITABLE TRUST I

c/o First Trust Company of St. Paul
W-555 First National Bank Building
St. Paul, MN 55101

**Established:** December 1964

**Type:** Private foundation

**Geographic Orientation:** Minnesota

**Sample Grants:**
Lake Region Memorial Hospital—$10,000
St. James Episcopal Church—$5,000
Christian Children's Fund—$120

**Financial Data for Year Ending November 30, 1981:**
Assets: $287,964
Grants Paid: $15,120
Number of Grants: 3
Largest/Smallest: $10,000/$120

**Paid Professional Staff:** No

**Directors/Trustees:** Honorable Chester G. Rosengren;
First Trust Company of St. Paul

## ROGER L. AND AGNES C. DELL CHARITABLE TRUST II

c/o First Trust Company of St. Paul
W-555 First National Bank Building
St. Paul, MN 55101

**Established:** February 1966

**Type:** Private foundation

**Geographic Orientation:** Minnesota

**Sample Grants:**
Fergus Falls Public Library—$10,000
William Mitchell College of Law—$5,000
American Cancer Society—$1,000

**Financial Data for Year Ending July 31, 1981:**
Assets: $829,288
Grants Paid: $59,500
Number of Grants: 12
Largest/Smallest: $10,000/$500

**Paid Professional Staff:** No

**Directors/Trustees:** Honorable Chester G. Rosengren;
Gerald S. Rufer; Mrs. Richard C. Hefte

## • DELLWOOD FOUNDATION

1000 Pioneer Building
St. Paul, MN 55101
(612) 224-1841

**Contact Person:** J. G. Ordway, Jr., president

**Established:** December 1958

**Type:** Private foundation

**Program's Limits:** No grants to individuals or for travel

**Geographic Orientation:** Twin Cities; Minnesota

**Fields of Activity:** Arts/architecture; music/opera;
theater/dance; elementary/secondary education; higher
education; medical research; religion;
business/economic education; drug-abuse programs

**Types of Organizations Funded:** Museums/historical
societies; theaters/dance groups; music/opera groups;
public television/radio; arts councils; secondary
schools; colleges; universities; chemical dependency
services; churches/synagogues; United Way;
organizations for drug abusers

**Types of Support for Organizations:** Capital support;
continuing support; endowment; general operating
support

**Sample Grants:**
St. Paul Chamber Orchestra—$5,000
Johnson Institute—$3,000
Guthrie Theater Foundation—$1,500

**Financial Data for Year Ending December 31, 1981:**
Assets: $900,000
Grants Paid: $80,100
Number of Grants: 32
Largest/Smallest: $15,000/$100

**Paid Professional Staff:** No

**Contact Made by:** Letter of inquiry; complete proposal

**Board Meetings:** Biannual

**Directors/Trustees:** J. G. Ordway, Jr.,
president/treasurer; Margaret M. Ordway, vice-
president; J. C. Foote, secretary

## • DELUXE CHECK PRINTERS

Box 43399
St. Paul, MN 55164
(612) 483-7111 or 483-7233

**Contact Persons:** John R. Cross, treasurer; Donald W.
Steinkraus, assistant secretary-treasurer

**Established:** 1952

**Type:** Charitable contributions program

**Program's Interests:** Youth organizations; social welfare
agencies; civic groups; cultural organizations

**Program's Limits:** Generally limited to sustaining
support or special project funds

**Geographic Orientation:** Twin Cities; Minnesota;
national

**Fields of Activity:** History/preservation;
language/literature; media/communications;
music/opera; theater/dance; arts education;
elementary/secondary education; vocational education;
higher education; research; medical research; medical
care/treatment; medical/health education; mental
health; legal education; advocacy; business/economic

education; community affairs; crime/law enforcement; drug-abuse programs; economic development; employment/job training; equal rights/legal aid; family services; recreation; safety; welfare

**Types of Organizations Funded:** Museums/historical societies; theaters/dance groups; music/opera groups; libraries; zoos; public television/radio; arts councils; historic preservation; cultural centers; vocational schools; colleges; universities; educational councils; scholarship funds; junior colleges; libraries; hospitals; medical schools; medical research groups; clinics; chemical dependency services; family-planning agencies; counseling services; conservation groups; United Way; legal aid; organizations for the elderly; organizations for the handicapped; organizations for women; organizations for drug abusers; organizations for youth; centers for children; organizations for offenders; organizations for minorities; neighborhood agencies; day-care centers; community centers; animal centers

**Employee Matching Gift Programs:** Higher education; cultural organizations

**Types of Support for Organizations:** Capital support; continuing support; general operating support; matching grants

**Types of Support for Individuals:** Scholarships; scholarship program for children of employees (W. R. Hotchkiss Foundation)

**Sample Grants:**
Indianhead Council, BSA—$2,000
Minnesota Crime Prevention Clinic—$1,000
Minnesota Historical Society—$500

**Financial Data for Year Ending December 31, 1981:**
Contributions Paid:  $362,556
Largest/Smallest:  $35,000/$50

**Contact Made by:** Letter of inquiry or telephone inquiry

**Available by Request:** Proposal guidelines; application procedures

**Contributions Decisions Made:** Bimonthly

## • DELUXE CHECK PRINTERS FOUNDATION

Box 43399
St. Paul, MN 55164
(612) 483-7111 or (612) 483-7233

**Contact Person:** Donald W. Steinkraus, secretary and administrator

**Established:** 1952

**Type:** Corporate foundation

**Program's Purpose:** To make grants to organizations and institutions located in those areas where Deluxe Check Printers, Inc., has production facilities and where its employees live

**Program's Limits:** No grants to individuals, religious organizations, or primary and secondary schools; nor to non-tax-exempt organizations or propagandizing organizations; no duplication of recurring contributions, such as those made to United Way, which are made annually by the company at the local level

**Geographic Orientation:** Twin Cities; Minnesota; national

**Fields of Activity:** History/preservation; language/literature; media/communications; music/opera; theater/dance; arts education; vocational education; higher education; research; medical research; medical care/treatment; medical/health education; mental health; legal education; advocacy; business/economic education; community affairs; crime/law enforcement; drug-abuse programs; economic development; employment/job training; equal rights/legal aid; family services; recreation; safety; welfare

**Types of Organizations Funded:** Museums/historical societies; theaters/dance groups; music/opera groups; libraries; zoos; public television/radio; arts councils; historic preservation; cultural centers; vocational schools; colleges; universities; educational councils; scholarship funds; junior colleges; libraries; hospitals; medical schools; medical research groups; clinics; chemical dependency services; family-planning agencies; counseling services; conservation groups; United Way; legal aid; organizations for the elderly; organizations for the handicapped; organizations for women; organizations for drug abusers; organizations for youth; centers for children; organizations for offenders; organizations for minorities; neighborhood agencies; day-care centers; community centers; animal centers

**Types of Support for Organizations:** Capital support; continuing support; general operating support; matching grants

**Type of Support for Individuals:** Scholarships

**Sample Grants:**
Foundation for Independent Colleges of Pennsylvania—$19,400
Art Center of Minnesota—$5,000
Youth Consultation Service, West Caldwell, NJ—$5,000

**Financial Data for Year Ending December 31, 1981:**
Assets:  $2,005,499
Grants Paid:  $1,305,554
Number of Grants:  293
Largest/Smallest:  $25,000/$500

**Paid Professional Staff:** Yes

**Contact Made by:** Telephone inquiry or letter of inquiry

**Available by Request:** Proposal guidelines; application procedures; annual report

**Board Meetings:** Annual; bimonthly grants committee meetings

**Trustees:** R. L. Jensen, president; L. J. Sawicki, vice-president; F. H. Cloutier, treasurer; D. W. Steinkraus, secretary and administrator; D. N. Peters; M. F. Reeves; J. A. Black; L. B. Boyum; R. S. Hall; C. N. Herman; E. R. Olson; H. V. Haverty; J. R. Cross

## DEUBENER-JUENEMANN FOUNDATION

c/o First Trust Company of St. Paul
W-555 First National Bank Building
St. Paul, MN 55101
(612) 291-5140

**Contact Person:** Rodney T. Thein

**Established:** February 1954

**Type:** Private foundation

**Program's Purpose:** To make grants exclusively to 45 specific organizations

**Sample Grants:**
United Way of the St. Paul Area—$14,000
Hamline University—$10,000
Sholom Home Auxiliary—$150

**Financial Data for Year Ending January 31, 1982:**
Assets: $1,412,556
Grants Paid: $80,150
Number of Grants: 10
Largest/Smallest: $14,000/$150

**Paid Professional Staff:** No

**Contact Made by:** Letter of inquiry

**Proposal Deadlines:** None

**Trustee:** First Trust Company of St. Paul

## DELORES G. DIETRICH MEMORIAL FOUNDATION

108 South Main Street
Le Sueur, MN 56058
(612) 665-3349

**Contact Person:** Arthur E. Anderson, secretary

**Established:** August 1960

**Type:** Private foundation

**Program's Purpose:** To promote and develop the Minnesota River Valley and adjacent areas as conservation and recreation areas

**Program's Limits:** Program basically limited to Minnesota River Valley area, particularly the area between St. Peter and the Twin Cities

**Geographic Orientation:** Minnesota River Valley

**Fields of Activity:** Music/opera; higher education; other educational activities; medical research; medical care/treatment; recreation

**Types of Organizations Funded:** Music/opera groups; libraries; historic preservation; scholarship funds; libraries; hospitals; medical research groups; research/study institutes; conservation groups

**Type of Support for Organizations:** General operating support

**Types of Support for Individuals:** Scholarships; loans for education; research support

**Sample Grants:**
Le Sueur Public Schools Scholarship Fund—$900
AFS—$900
Le Sueur Concert Association—$200

**Financial Data for Year Ending June 30, 1982:**
Assets: $40,000
Grants Paid: $4,000
Number of Grants: 8
Largest/Smallest: $1,000/$200

**Paid Professional Staff:** No

**Contact Made by:** Letter of inquiry

**Board Meetings:** Annual, in July

**Applicants Notified:** Within two weeks of decision

**Directors:** D. McQuarrie; W. C. Dietrich; M. F. Noack; G. McQuarrie; A. E. Anderson

## DOERR FAMILY FUND

4200 IDS Center
Minneapolis, MN 55402

**Established:** January 1961

**Type:** Private foundation

**Geographic Orientation:** National

**Sample Grants:**
La Jolla Presbyterian Church—$1,200
Smith College—$200
Minnesota Public Radio—$60

**Financial Data for Year Ending December 31, 1981:**
Assets: $53,864
Grants Paid: $8,423
Number of Grants: 53
Largest/Smallest: $1,200/$10

**Paid Professional Staff:** No

**Directors/Trustees:** Charles D. Doerr; George V. Doerr; Chloe D. Ackman; Caroline D. Carse

## DOHERTY, RUMBLE & BUTLER FOUNDATION

E-1500 First National Bank Building
St. Paul, MN 55101
(612) 291-9333

**Contact Person:** Jerome Halloran, secretary

**Established:** May 1979

**Type:** Corporate foundation

**Program's Limits:** Usually, no grants in excess of $1,000 nor grants to other than cultural organizations or organizations involved in the performing arts

**Geographic Orientation:** Twin Cities

**Types of Organizations Funded:** Museums/historical societies; theaters/dance groups; music/opera groups; public television/radio; arts councils; cultural centers

**Types of Support for Organizations:** Capital support; continuing support; general operating support

**Sample Grants:**
Minneapolis Society of Fine Arts—$750
St. Paul Chamber Orchestra Society—$750
Minnesota Opera Company—$500

**Financial Data for Year Ending December 31, 1981:**
Assets: $1,272.71
Grants Paid: $32,850
Number of Grants: 32
Largest/Smallest: $15,000/$50

**Paid Professional Staff:** No

**Contact Made by:** Complete proposal

**Available by Request:** Proposal guidelines; application procedures; annual report

**Board Meetings:** At least once every three months

**Applicants Notified:** Within three weeks of decision

**Directors:** Pierce Butler; Jerome Halloran; Cynthia R. Rosenblatt; Timothy R. Quinn; James K. Wittenberg

## • THE DONALDSON FOUNDATION

Box 1299
Minneapolis, MN 55440
(612) 887-3007

**Contact Person:** Robert Schweitzer, president

**Established:** July 1966

**Type:** Corporate foundation

**Program's Purpose:** To support the needs and interests of Donaldson employees by supporting the communities in which they live and work

**Program's Limits:** No contributions to national drives, to individuals, to religious organizations, to advocacy groups, to political campaigns, or to non-501c-3 organizations

**Geographic Orientation:** Locations of Donaldson facilities

**Fields of Activity:** Vocational education; higher education; business/economic education; community affairs; employment/job training; environment/energy; family services; welfare; arts

**Types of Organizations Funded:** Museums; theaters; music; public television/radio; elementary schools; secondary schools; vocational schools; colleges; universities; scholarship funds; junior colleges; family-planning agencies; conservation groups; United Way; day-care centers

**Types of Support for Organizations:** Continuing support; general operating support; matching grants; federated fund drives

**Sample Grants:**
Minneapolis United Way—$45,000
St. Paul United Way—$18,500
TCOIC—$5,000

**Financial Data for Year Ending July 31, 1982:**
Assets: $600,000
Grants Paid: $300,000
Number of Grants: 80
Largest/Smallest: $40,000/$400

**Paid Professional Staff:** No

**Contact Made by:** Telephone inquiry

**Available by Request:** Proposal guidelines; application procedures; annual report

**Board Meetings:** Quarterly, in October, January, April, and July

**Applicants Notified:** Within two weeks of decision

**Directors/Trustees:** Erland Anderson; Frank Donaldson; Betsy Lund; W. L. Johnson; Arlene Louton; Dean McNeal; Kenneth Riesberg; Robert Schweitzer; Ray Vodovnik, secretary; William West

## VERN DONNAY FOUNDATION

2704 Ensign Avenue North
Minneapolis, MN 55427

**Established:** December 1960

**Type:** Private foundation

**Geographic Orientation:** Twin Cities

**Sample Grants:**
Church of Our Lady of Grace—$600
United Cerebral Palsy—$100
Disabled American Vets—$50

**Financial Data for Year Ending December 31, 1981:**
Assets: $7,416
Grants Paid: $850
Number of Grants: 5
Largest/Smallest: $600/$50

**Paid Professional Staff:** No

**Directors/Trustees:** L. A. Donnay, president; H. B. Strong, vice-president (according to 1980 990-AR)

## GEORGE DONOVAN FOUNDATION

1080 Montreal Avenue
St. Paul, MN 55102

**Established:** December 1962

**Type:** Private foundation

**Geographic Orientation:** Twin Cities

**Sample Grants:**
Project Life—$650
St. Paul Seminary—$450
Minnesota Public Radio—$300

**Financial Data for Year Ending December 31, 1981:**
Assets: $56,746
Grants Paid: $5,739
Number of Grants: 17
Largest/Smallest: $650/$100

**Paid Professional Staff:** No

**Directors/Trustees:** George Donovan, president; Richard Donovan, vice-president; John Donovan, secretary; Robert M. Bussen, treasurer

## PETER M. DOUGALL TRUST

Northwestern National Bank of Minneapolis
Minneapolis, MN 55479

**Established:** November 1967

**Type:** Private foundation

**Geographic Orientation:** Twin Cities

**Sample Grants:**
Mayo Foundation—$482
Walker Art Center—$482
Campus Crusade for Christ—$482

**Financial Data for Year Ending December 31, 1981:**
Assets: $90,299
Grants Paid: $4,822
Number of Grants: 10
Largest/Smallest: $482/$482

**Paid Professional Staff:** No

**Directors/Trustees:** Northwestern National Bank of Minneapolis; Mark J. Dougall

## DOUGLAS FOUNDATION

620 Twelfth Avenue South
Minneapolis, MN 55415
(612) 333-8911

**Contact Person:** C. T. Skanse, vice-president

**Established:** August 1980

**Type:** Corporate foundation

**Geographic Orientation:** National

**Fields of Activity:** Elementary/secondary education; higher education; medical research; religious education; community affairs; disaster relief; recreation; welfare

**Types of Organizations Funded:** Secondary schools; colleges; medical research groups; churches/synagogues; religious schools; religious colleges; United Way; organizations for the handicapped; organizations for youth; organizations for minorities; neighborhood agencies; day-care centers

**Targeted Population Groups:** Children/youth; blacks

**Types of Support for Organizations:** Capital support; general operating support; research

**Type of Support for Individuals:** Aid to needy persons

**Sample Grants:**
Gustavus Adolphus College—$3,000
N.A.E. World Relief, Wheaton, IL—$1,000
Metropolitan Medical Foundation—$1,000

**Financial Data for Year Ending September 30, 1981:**
Assets: $45,230
Grants Paid: $14,550
Number of Grants: 32
Largest/Smallest: $3,000/$50

**Paid Professional Staff:** No

**Directors/Trustees:** Douglas R. Skanse, president; C. T. Skanse, vice-president; Norman Kuehne, secretary

## • THE ELIZA A. DREW MEMORIAL FUND

Twin City Federal Tower
121 South Eighth Street
Minneapolis, MN 55402

**Established:** December 1934

**Type:** Private foundation

**Geographic Orientation:** Twin Cities

**Sample Grants:**
Hamline University—$19,480
Minnetonka Little League—$300
World Concern—$100

**Financial Data for Year Ending December 31, 1981:**
Assets: $892,767
Grants Paid: $53,036
Number of Grants: 15
Largest/Smallest: $19,480/$100

**Paid Professional Staff:** Yes

**Director/Trustee:** Gordon B. Sanders, president/secretary

## • THE DRISCOLL FOUNDATION

2100 First National Bank Building
St. Paul, MN 55101
(612) 228-0935

**Contact Person:** W. John Driscoll, president

**Established:** March 1962

**Type:** Private foundation

**Geographic Orientation:** Twin Cities; San Francisco

**Sample Grants:**
Peninsula Children's Center, Palo Alto, CA—$7,133
Minneapolis Society of Fine Arts—$5,000
St. Paul-Ramsey Arts and Science Council—$1,000

**Financial Data for Year Ending February 28, 1981:**
Assets: $906,340
Grants Paid: $84,032
Number of Grants: 16
Largest/Smallest: $15,000/$500

**Paid Professional Staff:** No

**Contact Made by:** Letter of inquiry

**Available by Request:** Proposal guidelines; annual report

**Board Meetings:** Annual in May or June, and on an ongoing basis to consider proposals

**Applicants Notified:** Within two to three weeks of decision

**Directors:** W. John Driscoll, president; Rudolph W. Driscoll, vice-president; Elizabeth S. Driscoll; Margot H. Driscoll; J. S. Micallef, secretary; Gordon E. Hed, treasurer

## C. J. DUFFEY PAPER COMPANY CHARITABLE TRUST FUND

c/o A. C. Reger
528 Washington Avenue North
Minneapolis, MN 55401

**Established:** December 1953

**Type:** Corporate foundation

**Geographic Orientation:** Minnesota

**Sample Grants:**
St. Therese Home—$525
House of Charity—$300
Minneapolis League of Catholic Women—$125

**Financial Data for Year Ending December 31, 1981:**
Assets: $26,989
Grants Paid: $3,570
Number of Grants: 11
Largest/Smallest: $525/$120

**Paid Professional Staff:** No

## JOSEPH C. AND LILLIAN A. DUKE FOUNDATION

c/o First Trust Company of St. Paul
W-555 First National Bank Building
St. Paul, MN 55101
(612) 291-5061

**Contact Person:** Thomas H. Patterson

**Established:** November 1963

**Type:** Private foundation

**Program's Purpose:** To provide grants to educational, cultural, youth, and community-support organizations in Minnesota

**Program's Limits:** No grants to individuals or to organizations that require expenditure responsibility

**Geographic Orientation:** Minnesota

**Sample Grants:**
St. Paul Area YMCA—$6,000
United Way of the St. Paul Area—$2,500
Indianhead Council, BSA—$1,000

**Financial Data for Year Ending December 31, 1981:**
Assets: $293,785
Grants Paid: $17,650
Number of Grants: 5
Largest/Smallest: $6,000/$1,000

**Paid Professional Staff:** No

**Contact Made by:** Letter of inquiry

**Directors/Trustees:** Lillian A. Duke, president; Joseph C. Duke, vice-president; Thomas H. Patterson, secretary-treasurer

## DULUTH BENEVOLENCE FOUNDATION

2129 West Superior Street
Duluth, MN 55806

**Established:** February 1955

**Type:** Independent foundation

**Geographic Orientation:** Duluth

**Sample Grants:**
Lakeview Covenant Church, Duluth—$10,000
First Covenant Church, Home Missions—$2,050
Morning Chapel Hour—$50

**Financial Data for Year Ending December 31, 1981:**
Assets: $34,441
Grants Paid: $16,624
Number of Grants: 21
Largest/Smallest: $10,000/$50

**Paid Professional Staff:** No

**Director/Trustee:** Robert T. Lundberg

## DULUTH CLINIC EDUCATION AND RESEARCH FOUNDATION

400 East Third Street
Duluth, MN 55805

**Established:** February 1977

**Type:** Corporate foundation

**Program's Purpose:** Medical research and education

**Geographic Orientation:** Minnesota

**Sample Grants:**
College of Saint Scholastica—$4,269
Duluth YMCA—$2,300
University of Minnesota-Duluth—$1,405

**Financial Data for Year Ending June 30, 1981:**
Assets: $104,067
Grants Paid: $10,899
Number of Grants: 4
Largest/Smallest: $4,269/$1,405

**Paid Professional Staff:** No

**Directors/Trustees:** W. T. Slack, chairman; R. P. Hood, vice-chairman; W. H. Goodnow, secretary-treasurer

# DULUTH IMPROVEMENT TRUST

c/o First National Bank of Duluth Trust Department
Duluth, MN 55802

**Established:** October 1966

**Type:** Private foundation

**Geographic Orientation:** Northern Minnesota

**Sample Grants:**
Bayfront Park Development Association—$7,000
A. M. Chisholm Museum—$4,000
Duluth Women's Club—$250

**Financial Data for Year Ending December 31, 1981:**
Assets: $675,954
Grants Paid: $13,250
Largest/Smallest: $7,000/$250

**Paid Professional Staff:** No

**Directors/Trustees:** Newell Marshall; Caroline Marshall

# • THE DYCO FOUNDATION

1100 Shelard Tower
Minneapolis, MN 55426
(612) 545-2828

**Contact Person:** Alicia Gehring, foundation manager

**Established:** December 1977

**Type:** Corporate foundation

**Program's Limits:** No grants to individuals, sectarian organizations whose services are limited to one religious group,or partisan political organizations or for lobbying efforts, purchase of tickets or subscriptions/advertising

**Geographic Orientation:** Twin Cities; Minnesota; Oklahoma; Denver

**Fields of Activity:** Arts/architecture; music/opera; theater/dance; higher education; medical research; medical care/treatment; business/economic education; crime/law enforcement; drug-abuse programs; disaster relief; family services

**Types of Organizations Funded:** Museums/historical societies; theaters/dance groups; music/opera groups; arts councils; cultural centers; colleges; universities; hospitals; medical research groups; medical societies; research/study institutes; conservation groups; United Way; organizations for the handicapped; organizations for women; organizations for drug abusers; organizations for youth; centers for children

**Types of Support for Organizations:** Capital support; continuing support; general operating support; research; federated fund drives (United Way only)

**Sample Grants:**
Children's Heart Fund—$25,000 (over five years)
Guthrie Theater—$1,000
Hospitality House—$500

**Financial Data for Year Ending December 31, 1981:**
Assets: $400,501
Grants Paid: $31,566
Number of Grants: 83
Largest/Smallest: $4,000/$20

**Paid Professional Staff:** Yes

**Contact Made by:** Written request for guidelines

**Available by Request:** Proposal guidelines; application procedures; annual report

**Applicants Notified:** Within two weeks of decision

**Directors/Trustees:** Jaye F. Dyer; N. Bud Grossman; Ronald G. Wade; Lendell Z. Williams; Wayne O. Podratz

# DYE FAMILY FOUNDATION TRUST

c/o First National Bank of Minneapolis
120 South Sixth Street
Minneapolis, MN 55480

**Established:** October 1958

**Type:** Private foundation

**Geographic Orientation:** National

**Sample Grants:**
Wayland Academy—$30,000
American Conservatory Theater—$3,000
American Indian Opportunities—$500

**Financial Data for Year Ending December 31, 1981:**
Assets: $5,740,741
Grants Paid: $190,000
Number of Grants: 77
Largest/Smallest: $30,000/$100

**Paid Professional Staff:** Yes

**Directors/Trustees:** Charles B. Woehrle, director; First National Bank of Minneapolis

# DYSON FAMILY FOUNDATION

1191 Ashland Avenue
St. Paul, MN 55104

**Established:** November 1970

**Type:** Private foundation

**Geographic Orientation:** National

**Sample Grants:**
Order Ecumenical, St. Louis—$8,400
Seattle Tenants' Union—$6,000

**Financial Data for Year Ending December 31, 1981:**
Assets: $54,743
Grants Paid: $14,400
Number of Grants: 2
Largest/Smallest: $8,400/$6,000

**Paid Professional Staff:** No

**Directors/Trustees:** Frank Dyson, president; David Dyson, secretary

# EDELSTEIN FAMILY FOUNDATION

c/o Northwestern National Bank of Minneapolis
Seventh and Marquette
Minneapolis, MN 55479

**Established:** January 1955

**Type:** Private foundation

**Geographic Orientation:** National

**Sample Grants:**
Mount Sinai Hospital Association—$3,738
University of Minnesota—$1,869
Order of the Eastern Star—$187

**Financial Data for Year Ending October 31, 1981:**
Assets: $314,311
Grants Paid: $18,692
Number of Grants: 11
Largest/Smallest: $3,738/$187

**Paid Professional Staff:** No

**Directors/Trustees:** Northwestern National Bank of Minneapolis; Thomas A. Keller III

# EDEN PRAIRIE FOUNDATION

8455 Flying Cloud Drive
Eden Prairie, MN 55344
(612) 944-2830

**Contact Person:** Roy Terwilliger, president (phone: 612-941-7100)

**Established:** April 1981

**Type:** Community foundation

**Program's Purpose:** To provide a central place for donations and bequests from residents and businesses of Eden Prairie (and elsewhere) to make grants in support of community service projects

**Program's Limits:** Local, capital requests

**Geographic Orientation:** Eden Prairie

**Fields of Activity:** Arts/architecture; history/preservation; theater/dance; arts education; elementary/secondary education; vocational education; medical care/treatment; medical/health education; public health; mental health; community affairs; crime/law enforcement; drug-abuse programs; family services; recreation; safety

**Types of Organizations Funded:** Museums/historical societies; historic preservation; cultural centers; organizations for the handicapped; organizations for drug abusers

**Sample Grants:**
Grill House Restoration (windows)—$3,000
Fraser Home (files, recreation articles)—$2,000

**Financial Data for Year Ending April 30, 1982:**
Assets: $9,000
Grants Paid: $5,000
Number of Grants: 2
Largest/Smallest: $3,000/$2,000

**Paid Professional Staff:** No

**Contact Made by:** Letter of inquiry

**Available by Request:** Proposal guidelines; application procedures; annual report

**Board Meetings:** Monthly

**Applicants Notified:** Within eight weeks of decision

**Directors/Trustees:** Billy Bye, chairman; Roy Terwilliger, president; Duane Pidcock, vice-president; Ruth Hustad, secretary; Bob Hanson, treasurer; Dean Edstrom; Helen Anderson; Gerald McCoy; Sidney Pauly; Paul Redpath; Roger Ulstad; Marge Friederichs, executive secretary

# EDWARDS MEMORIAL TRUST

c/o First Trust Company of St. Paul
W-555 First National Bank Building
St. Paul, MN 55101
(612) 291-5140

**Contact Person:** Rodney T. Thein

**Established:** July 1961

**Type:** Private foundation

**Program's Purpose:** Primarily to provide grants in the area of health care

**Geographic Orientation:** Minnesota

**Sample Grants:**
United Way of the St. Paul Area—$42,200
St. Mary's Rehabilitation Center—$12,500
Twin Cities Opera Guild—$4,000

**Financial Data for Year Ending December 31, 1981:**
Assets: $6,709,094
Grants Paid: $505,100
Number of Grants: 44
Largest/Smallest: $42,200/$1,000

**Paid Professional Staff:** No

**Contact Made by:** Letter of inquiry

**Trustee:** First Trust Company of St. Paul

# WILLIAM SAWYER AND BETTY S. EISENSTADT FOUNDATION

1 Red Cedar Lane
Minneapolis, MN 55410

**Type:** Private foundation

**Geographic Orientation:** National

**Sample Grants:**
  Minneapolis Federation for Jewish Service—$4,000
  Adath Jeshurun Congregation—$1,000
  Hamline University Law School—$100

**Financial Data for Year Ending November 30, 1981:**
  Assets:  $94,341
  Grants Paid:  $8,350
  Number of Grants:  14
  Largest/Smallest:  $4,000/$100

**Paid Professional Staff:** No

**Director/Trustee:** W. S. Eisenstadt, president

# ELLIOTT FOUNDATION

621 Tenth Avenue Southeast
Rochester, MN 55901

**Type:** Private foundation

**Geographic Orientation:** National; international

**Sample Grants:**
  St. Francis Church, Rochester, MN—$3,654
  Mother Teresa, India—$250
  March of Dimes—$10

**Financial Data for Year Ending December 31, 1981:**
  Assets:  $51,512
  Grants Paid:  $5,065
  Number of Grants:  30
  Largest/Smallest:  $3,654/$1

**Paid Professional Staff:** No

**Directors/Trustees:** Virgil M. Elliott, president; Marie K. Elliott, secretary; Konrad J. Elliott, vice-president

# ALFRED W. ERICKSON FOUNDATION

Box 1224
Minneapolis, MN 55440

**Established:** December 1964

**Type:** Private foundation

**Program's Purpose:** To provide "general purpose contributions to well established religious, education and charitable organizations which are publicly supported"

**Geographic Orientation:** Upper Midwest

**Sample Grants:**
  Blake Schools—$6,000
  Mount Olivet Lutheran Church—$1,500
  Planned Parenthood of Minnesota—$250

**Financial Data for Year Ending December 31, 1981:**
  Assets:  $35,102
  Grants Paid:  $21,923
  Number of Grants:  27
  Largest/Smallest:  $6,000/$98

**Paid Professional Staff:** No

**Directors/Trustees:** Ronald A. Erickson; Donovan A. Erickson; Neal D. Erickson

# ARTHUR T. ERICKSON FOUNDATION

Box 1224
Minneapolis, MN 55440

**Established:** December 1964

**Type:** Private foundation

**Program's Purpose:** To provide "grants to well established religious, education and charitable organizations which are publicly supported"

**Geographic Orientation:** Upper Midwest

**Sample Grants:**
  Mount Olivet Lutheran Church—$6,600
  Gustavus Adolphus College—$1,300
  Cricket Theatre—$100

**Financial Data for Year Ending December 31, 1981:**
  Assets:  $9,044
  Grants Paid:  $16,950
  Number of Grants:  23
  Largest/Smallest:  $6,600/$100

**Paid Professional Staff:** No

**Directors/Trustees:** Gerald A. Erickson; Marjorie J. Pihl

# FAIRMONT RAILWAY MOTORS FOUNDATION

415 North Main Street
Fairmont, MN 56031

**Established:** January 1963

**Type:** Private foundation

**Financial Data for Year Ending December 31, 1981:**
  Assets:  $32,333
  Grants Paid:  $1,500

**Paid Professional Staff:** No

**Directors/Trustees:** R. G. Wade, president; F. W. Kasper, vice-president

# CLARE AND ROLAND FARICY FOUNDATION

c/o Moore, Costello & Hart
1400 Northwestern Bank Building
St. Paul, MN 55101
(612) 227-0655

**Contact Person:** Richard T. Faricy, director and president

**Established:** August 1962

**Type:** Private foundation

**Geographic Orientation:** National

**Types of Organizations Funded:** Museums/historical societies; theaters/dance groups; music/opera groups; arts councils; historic preservation; cultural centers; elementary schools; secondary schools; colleges; universities; churches/synagogues; religious service groups; religious schools; religious colleges; other religious organizations

**Type of Support for Organizations:** Capital support

**Sample Grants:**
   William Mitchell College of Law—$250
   Immaculate Heart of Mary Parish and Missions,
   Pagosa Springs, CA—$200
   Minnesota Museum of Arts—$100

**Financial Data for Year Ending December 31, 1981:**
   Assets: $26,670
   Grants Paid: $3,050
   Number of Grants: 13
   Largest/Smallest: $500/$100

**Paid Professional Staff:** No

**Contact Made by:** Letter of inquiry

**Available by Request:** Annual report

**Directors/Trustees:** Richard T. Faricy, president; Clare S. Faricy, vice-president; Roland J. Faricy, secretary-treasurer; John H. Faricy

## FEDERATED INSURANCE FOUNDATION

129 East Broadway
Owatonna, MN 55060

**Established:** April 1972

**Type:** Corporate foundation

**Geographic Orientation:** Owatonna; Minnesota

**Sample Grants:**
   Owatonna Foundation—$34,200
   United Way of Steele County—$6,700
   Minnesota Pheasants—$75

**Financial Data for Year Ending December 31, 1981:**
   Assets: $104,995
   Grants Paid: $57,227
   Number of Grants: 38
   Largest/Smallest: $34,200/$50

**Paid Professional Staff:** No

## FERNDALE FOUNDATION

c/o First Trust Company of St. Paul
W-555 First National Bank Building
St. Paul, MN 55101

**Contact Person:** Paul J. Kelly, secretary-treasurer

**Established:** July 1966

**Type:** Private foundation

**Geographic Orientation:** Minnesota

**Sample Grants:**
   Abbott-Northwestern Hospital, Minneapolis—$75,000
   Wellesley College—$1,000
   Planned Parenthood of Minneapolis—$1,000

**Financial Data for Year Ending December 31, 1981:**
   Assets: $10,145
   Grants Paid: $175,106
   Number of Grants: 21
   Largest/Smallest: $75,000/$500

**Paid Professional Staff:** No

**Contact Made by:** Letter of inquiry

**Directors/Trustees:** Theodora H. Lang, president; A. Scheffer Lang, vice-president; Paul Kelly, secretary-treasurer

## ADOLPH AND MILDRED FINE FUND

Suite 601
4601 Excelsior Boulevard
Minneapolis, MN 55416

**Established:** November 1958

**Type:** Private foundation

**Geographic Orientation:** National

**Sample Grants:**
   Palm Springs Desert Museum—$2,600
   Temple Israel—$1,815
   Women's American ORT—$55

**Financial Data for Year Ending December 31, 1981:**
   Assets: $120,872
   Grants Paid: $11,207
   Number of Grants: 50
   Largest/Smallest: $2,600/$10

**Paid Professional Staff:** No

**Director:** Adolph Fine, president (from 1980 990-AR)

## THE FINGERHUT FOUNDATION

5354 Parkdale Drive
Minneapolis, MN 55416

**Established:** August 1960

**Type:** Private foundation

**Geographic Orientation:** National

**Sample Grants:**
   Minneapolis Federation for Jewish Service—$405,000
   American Cancer Society—$10,000
   Cricket Theatre—$1,000

**Financial Data for Year Ending August 31, 1981:**
   Assets: $1,894,836
   Grants Paid: $802,408
   Number of Grants: 76
   Largest/Smallest: $405,000/$100

**Paid Professional Staff:** No

**Directors/Trustees:** Manny Fingerhut, president; Rose Fingerhut, vice-president; Ronald Fingerhut, vice-president; Stanley Nemer, secretary-treasurer; Beverly Deikel

# JOHN J. FINN FOUNDATION

Suite 450
10,000 Highway 55 West
Minneapolis, MN 55441

**Established:** December 1968

**Type:** Private foundation

**Geographic Orientation:** Minnesota

**Sample Grants:**
Minnesota Foundation—$1,000
Plymouth Congregational Church—$1,000
Meals-On-Wheels—$500

**Financial Data for Year Ending December 31, 1981:**
Assets: $39,511
Grants Paid: $4,000
Number of Grants: 5
Largest/Smallest: $1,000/$500

**Paid Professional Staff:** No

**Directors/Trustees:** John F. Finn, Jr., president; T. R. Anderson, secretary

# FIRST BANK ST. PAUL

332 Minnesota Street
St. Paul, MN 55101
(612) 291-5440

**Contact Person:** Mary Ida Thomson, assistant vice-president, public affairs

**Type:** Charitable contributions program

**Program's Limits:** No grants to individuals

**Geographic Orientation:** Twin Cities; Minnesota; Wisconsin; North Dakota; South Dakota; Montana

**Fields of Activity:** Arts and humanities; education; health; welfare/social services

**Types of Organizations Funded:** Museums/historical societies; theaters/dance groups; music/opera groups; zoos; public television/radio; arts councils; cultural centers; vocational schools; colleges; universities; scholarship funds; hospitals; clinics; chemical dependency services; family-planning agencies; counseling services; religious colleges; conservation groups; United Way; organizations for the handicapped; organizations for women; organizations for drug abusers; organizations for youth; organizations for men; centers for children; organizations for minorities; neighborhood agencies; community centers

**Employee Matching Gift Programs:** Higher education; private secondary education

**Types of Support for Organizations:** Capital support; general operating support; matching grants; program development; federated fund drives

**Type of Support for Individuals:** Scholarship program for children of employees and customers

**Sample Grants:**
United Way of the St. Paul Area (annual campaign)—$224,000
United Arts Fund—$30,000
Twin Cities Neighborhood Housing Services—$21,000

**Financial Data for Year Ending December 31, 1981:**
Contributions Paid: $947,000
Number of Contributions: 66
Largest/Smallest: $224,000/$500

**Contact Made by:** Complete proposal

**Available by Request:** Application procedures

# • FIRST BANK SYSTEM FOUNDATION

1300 First Bank Place East
Minneapolis, MN 55402
(612) 370-5080

**Contact Persons:** Donna F. Carlson, grants administrator; Lloyd L. Brandt, president

**Type:** Corporate foundation

**Program's Interests:** Highest priority to social welfare and civic programs (received 38.2 percent of funds in 1981); education (34 percent of 1981 grants); visual and performing arts (20.9 percent); preservation and environment projects (5.4 percent); and health programs, usually related to research (1.5 percent)

**Program's Limits:** No grants to political or religious organizations; to individuals; to endowment funds; for trips or tours, tickets or tables for benefit purposes, advertising for benefit purposes; very low priority to single disease research programs or programs that function primarily within small geographical limits (e.g., neighborhood organizations)

**Geographic Orientation:** Areas served by First Bank System affiliates—Twin Cities; Minnesota; Montana; Wisconsin; North Dakota; South Dakota

**Fields of Activity:** Arts; history/preservation; media/communications; music/opera; theater/dance; higher education; medical research; mental health; advocacy; business/economic education; community affairs; crime/law enforcement; drug-abuse programs; employment/job training; environment; disaster relief; family services; safety; special population groups

**Types of Organizations Funded:** Museums/historical societies; theaters/dance groups; music/opera groups; public television/radio; historic preservation; cultural centers; colleges; universities; educational councils; scholarship funds; special education; medical research groups; chemical dependency services; counseling services; conservation groups; United Way; legal aid; organizations for the handicapped; organizations for women; organizations for drug abusers; organizations for youth; organizations for offenders

**Targeted Population Groups:** Substance abusers; children/youth; criminal offenders/ex-offenders; handicapped; women/girls; refugees; minorities

**Employee Matching Gift Programs:** Higher education

**Types of Support for Organizations:** Capital support; continuing support; general operating support; matching grants; program development; research (limited); federated fund drives

**Type of Support for Individuals:** Scholarships; scholarships for children of employees

**Sample Grants:**
Minnesota Private College Fund—$89,000
Employment Resources—$7,500
Actors Theatre of St. Paul—$4,000

**Financial Data for Year Ending December 31, 1981:**
Grants Paid: $1,909,773
Number of Grants: 190
Largest/Smallest: $89,000/$500

**Paid Professional Staff:** Yes

**Contact Made by:** Letter of inquiry

**Available by Request:** Proposal guidelines; application procedures; annual report

**Proposal Deadlines:** Three months prior to meetings of charitable contributions committee for larger requests; staff review smaller requests throughout the year

**Charitable Contributions Committee Meetings:** Quarterly, in February, May, September, and December

# ● FIRST FEDERAL SAVINGS OF MINNEAPOLIS

77 South Seventh Street
Minneapolis, MN 55402
(612) 371-3700

**Contact Person:** Diane Schuck, assistant vice-president for community affairs

**Established:** July 1978

**Type:** Charitable contributions program

**Program's Interests:** Health and welfare, education, culture and art, civic and social

**Program's Limits:** No applicants who do not meet standards of the Minnesota Charities Review Council; no political, religious, union organizations; no telephone solicitations; no form letters that are not personally signed or addressed

**Geographic Orientation:** Minnesota

**Fields of Activity:** Arts/architecture; history/preservation; media/communications; music/opera; theater/dance; arts education; elementary/secondary education; vocational education; higher education; adult/continuing education; research; medical research; medical/health education; mental health; advocacy; business/economic education; community affairs; crime/law enforcement; drug-abuse programs; economic development; employment/job training; equal rights/legal aid; family services; special population groups; consumer interests

**Types of Organizations Funded:** Museums/historical societies; theaters/dance groups; music/opera groups; libraries; public television/radio; arts councils; historic preservation; cultural centers; secondary schools; vocational schools; colleges; universities; scholarship funds; special education; libraries; hospitals; medical schools; medical research groups; medical societies; chemical dependency services; family-planning agencies; counseling services; religious service groups; United Way; multiservice centers; organizations for the elderly; organizations for the handicapped; organizations for women; organizations for drug abusers; organizations for youth; centers for children; housing agencies; organizations for offenders; organizations for minorities; neighborhood agencies; day-care centers; community centers

**Employee Matching Gift Program:** No

**Types of Support for Organizations:** Capital support; continuing support; general operating support; federated fund drives

**Sample Grants:**
Twin Cities Neighborhood Housing Services—$19,200
Minneapolis Girls' Club—$250
Neighborhood Center—$100

**Financial Data for Year Ending December 31, 1981:**
Contributions Paid: $58,088
Number of Contributions: 103
Largest/Smallest: $19,200/$20

**Contact Made by:** Letter of inquiry; request for guidelines

**Available by Request:** Proposal guidelines; annual report on contributions

**Contributions Decisions Made:** Monthly

**Applicants Notified:** Within one week of decision

## FIRST MINNESOTA FOUNDATION

160 Second Avenue Southwest
Milaca, MN 56353

**Established:** July 1952

**Type:** Corporate foundation

**Geographic Orientation:** Minnesota

**Sample Grants:**
Central Minnesota Council, BSA—$500
Red Cross Bloodmobile—$290
Rum River Concert Association—$75

**Financial Data for Year Ending October 31, 1981:**
Assets: $17,095
Grants Paid: $2,815
Largest/Smallest: $500/$75

**Paid Professional Staff:** No

**Directors/Trustees:** Edward M. Olsen, president; B. P. Allen, Jr.

# FIRST NATIONAL BANK OF MINNEAPOLIS FOUNDATION

First Bank Place
Minneapolis, MN 55480
(612) 370-4099

**Contact Person:** James L. Hetland, Jr., senior vice-president

**Established:** August 1969

**Type:** Corporate foundation

**Program's Purpose:** To provide "manpower" and financial assistance to social action, health, education, cultural, or recreational organizations located within or directly benefiting people living in the greater Minneapolis area or that foster an improved climate for the bank's trade area

**Geographic Orientation:** Twin Cities

**Fields of Activity:** Media/communications; music/opera; theater/dance; arts education; elementary/secondary education; vocational education; higher education; adult/continuing education; research; other educational activities; medical research; medical care/treatment; medical/health education; public health; mental health; advocacy; business/economic education; community affairs; crime/law enforcement; drug-abuse programs; economic development; employment/job training; environment/energy; equal rights/legal aid; family services; recreation; safety; special population groups; consumer interests

**Types of Organizations Funded:** Museums/historical societies; theaters/dance groups; music/opera groups; libraries; zoos; public television/radio; arts councils; cultural centers; elementary schools; secondary schools; vocational schools; colleges; universities; special education; adult education; hospitals; medical schools; medical research groups; clinics; chemical dependency services; family-planning agencies; counseling services; religious service groups; conservation groups; United Way; legal aid; multiservice centers; organizations for the elderly; organizations for the handicapped; organizations for women; organizations for drug abusers; organizations for men; centers for children; housing agencies; organizations for offenders; organizations for minorities; neighborhood agencies; day-care centers; community centers; animal centers

**Types of Support for Organizations:** Capital support; general operating support; matching grants; program development

**Sample Grants:**
Project for Pride in Living—$1,500
Neighborhood Involvement Program—$750
Mixed Blood Theater—$500

**Financial Data for Year Ending December 31, 1981:**
Assets: $1,138,153
Grants Paid: $1,138,153
Number of Grants: 183
Largest/Smallest: $277,500/$100

**Paid Professional Staff:** Yes

**Contact Made by:** Letter of inquiry or complete proposal

**Available by Request:** Application procedures; annual report

**Board Meetings:** Quarterly, in March, June, September, and December

**Applicants Notified:** Within one to two weeks of decision

**Directors/Trustees:** D. H. Ankeny, Jr., vice-chairman, First Bank System; James L. Hetland, Jr., senior vice-president; Joseph R. Kingman III, vice-chairman of the board

# THE HAROLD AND FLORENCE FISCHBEIN FOUNDATION

5009 Ridge Road
Edina, MN 55424

**Established:** July 1978

**Type:** Private foundation

**Geographic Orientation:** Minnesota

**Sample Grants:**
Minneapolis Federation for Jewish Service—$38,144
Temple Israel—$1,772
University of Minnesota—$510

**Financial Data for Year Ending April 30, 1982:**
Assets: $425,938
Grants Paid: $44,255
Number of Grants: 38
Largest/Smallest: $38,144/$10

**Paid Professional Staff:** No

**Directors/Trustees:** Harold Fischbein, president/treasurer; Florence Fischbein, vice-president; I. George Fischbein, secretary

## S. S. FISHER FOUNDATION

c/o Louis Smerling
5251 West Seventy-third Street
Minneapolis, MN 55435

**Established:** December 1954

**Type:** Private foundation

**Sample Grants:**
Progress Corporation of America—$2,354
Temple Israel—$1,210
Macalester College—$250

**Financial Data for Year Ending November 30, 1981:**
Assets: $104,490
Grants Paid: $6,664
Number of Grants: 10
Largest/Smallest: $2,354/$150

**Paid Professional Staff:** No

**Directors/Trustees:** Louis Smerling, president; Harold Feder, secretary

## THE EDWARD FITERMAN FOUNDATION

910 Plymouth Building
Minneapolis, MN 55402

**Established:** July 1957

**Type:** Private foundation

**Geographic Orientation:** Twin Cities; national

**Sample Grants:**
Minneapolis Federation for Jewish Service—$9,000
Breck School—$5,180
Theater in the Round—$100

**Financial Data for Year Ending December 31, 1981:**
Assets: $12,134
Grants Paid: $46,925
Number of Grants: 57
Largest/Smallest: $9,000/$50

**Paid Professional Staff:** No

**Directors/Trustees:** Edward Fiterman, president; F. A. Stang, vice-president; Matthew Levitt, secretary; Roger Stockmo, treasurer; Patrick Shade (all from 990-AR 1980)

## THE JACK AND BESSIE FITERMAN FOUNDATION

5600 North County Road 18
Minneapolis, MN 55428

**Established:** May 1966

**Type:** Private foundation

**Geographic Orientation:** National

**Sample Grants:**
Minneapolis Federation for Jewish Service—$115,000
United Way—$17,000
Big Brothers—$150

**Financial Data for Year Ending May 31, 1981:**
Assets: $116,499
Grants Paid: $157,900
Number of Grants: 17
Largest/Smallest: $115,000/$50

**Paid Professional Staff:** No

**Directors/Trustees:** Sylvia Sorkin, president; Ben Fiterman, secretary; Michael Fiterman, vice-president

## S. B. FOOT TANNING COMPANY FOUNDATION

Box 73
Red Wing, MN 55066

**Established:** May 1956

**Type:** Corporate foundation

**Geographic Orientation:** Minnesota

**Sample Grants:**
Red Wing YMCA—$70,750
Minnesota Orchestral Association—$3,000
Boy Scouts of America—$850

**Financial Data for Year Ending June 30, 1981:**
Assets: $182,072
Grants Paid: $84,650
Number of Grants: 8
Largest/Smallest: $70,750/$300

**Paid Professional Staff:** No

**Directors/Trustees:** E. H. Foot, Jr., president/treasurer; V. H. Foot, vice-president/secretary

## THE WILLIAM F. FOSS II MEMORIAL FOUNDATION

c/o William F. Foss
Box 325
Milwaukee, WI 53201

**Established:** December 1962

**Type:** Private foundation

**Geographic Orientation:** Minnesota; Wisconsin

**Sample Grants:**
St. Roberts Church, Milwaukee—$2,100
Raymond Plank Chair of Incentive Economics (Carleton College)—$500
American Cancer Society—$25

**Financial Data for Year Ending December 31, 1981:**
Assets: $40,570
Grants Paid: $5,850
Number of Grants: 16
Largest/Smallest: $2,100/$25

Paid Professional Staff: No

Directors/Trustees: William F. Foss, president/treasurer; Anne Marie Foss, vice-president/secretary

## FOUNDATION FOR BROADCASTING ARTS

Box 3726
Minneapolis, MN 55403

Contact Person: T. J. Western, president

Established: 1976

Type: Private foundation

Program's Purpose: To support individuals and organizations producing radio, television, and cablevision; emphasis on those projects that reflect programming neglected by the mass media

Geographic Orientation: National

Fields of Activity: Media/communications

Types of Organizations Funded: Public television/radio; scholarship funds

Type of Support for Organizations: Funding for specific projects

Type of Support for Individuals: Funding for specific projects

Sample Grant:
National Federation of Community Broadcasters' National Conference (scholarships for minority attendance)—$400

Paid Professional Staff: No

Contact Made by: Letter of inquiry

Board Meetings: Annual

Directors/Trustees: T. J. Western, president; Kirk Hokanson, chair and secretary; Brent Johnson, treasurer

## FOUNDATION FOR THE DEVELOPMENT OF PEOPLE

4827 Woodlawn Boulevard
Minneapolis, MN 55417

Established: December 1978

Type: Private foundation

Program's Purpose: To provide "opportunities mainly for the poor and oppressed to develop themselves"

Sample Grant:
Minnesota Council of Churches—$1,500

Financial Data for Year Ending December 31, 1981:
Assets: $14,025
Grants Paid: $1,500
Number of Grants: 1

Directors/Trustees: Gregory G. Brucker, president; Leota K. Brucker, secretary; Nola K. Miller

## THE FRENZEL FOUNDATION

c/o Northwestern National Bank of St. Paul
55 East Fifth Street
St. Paul, MN 55101
(612) 291-2101

Contact Person: Drake J. Lightner, assistant vice-president

Established: December 1959

Type: Private foundation

Geographic Orientation: Generally, Florida

Types of Organizations Funded: Public television/radio; colleges; scholarship funds; hospitals; medical research groups; churches/synagogues; conservation groups; United Way

Types of Support for Organizations: Capital support; continuing support; general operating support

Sample Grants:
United Way, Collier County, Florida—$1,500
Naples Community Hospital—$1,000
Dartmouth College Northwest Regional Scholarships—$500

Financial Data for Year Ending December 31, 1981:
Assets: $213,977
Grants Paid: $15,000
Number of Grants: 15
Largest/Smallest: $2,000/$500

Paid Professional Staff: No

Contact Made by: Letter of inquiry

Available by Request: Annual report

Board Meetings: Annual, in the fall

Applicants Notified: Within one week of decision

Directors/Trustees: Robert P. Frenzel; William E. Frenzel; Peter M. Frenzel; Drake J. Lightner, assistant vice-president, Northwestern National Bank of St. Paul

## FULLER CHARITABLE TRUST

c/o First Bank of Duluth Trust Department
Duluth, MN 55802

Established: December 1963

Type: Private foundation

Geographic Orientation: Minnesota

Sample Grants:
United Way of Duluth—$1,200
Holy Mary Church—$600
Boys' Club of Duluth—$110

**Financial Data for Year Ending December 31, 1981:**
Assets: $21,477
Grants Paid: $2,410
Number of Grants: 5
Largest/Smallest: $1,200/$100

**Paid Professional Staff:** No

**Trustee:** First Bank of Duluth

## • H. B. FULLER COMPANY

2400 Kasota Avenue
St. Paul, MN 55108
(612) 645-3401

**Contact Person:** Karen Muller, community affairs assistant

**Type:** Charitable contributions program

**Program's Limits:** No grants to individuals, to endowments, or for capital campaigns

**Geographic Orientation:** Twin Cities; communities in which H. B. Fuller Company has facilities

**Fields of Activity:** Arts and humanities; education; health; welfare/social services

**Types of Organizations Funded:** Museums/historical societies; theaters/dance groups; music/opera groups; public television/radio; arts councils; education (matching gifts of employees); United Way; legal aid; multiservice centers; organizations for the elderly; organizations for the handicapped; organizations for women; organizations for veterans; organizations for drug abusers; organizations for youth; centers for children; organizations for offenders; organizations for minorities; neighborhood agencies

**Targeted Population Group:** Vietnam veterans

**Employee Matching Gift Programs:** Higher education; elementary/secondary education; vocational education

**Types of Support for Organizations:** General operating support; matching grants; program development; research; federated fund drives

**Type of Support for Individuals:** Scholarship program for children of employees

**Financial Data for Year Ending December 31, 1981:**
Contributions Paid: $582,854
Number of Contributions: 600
Largest/Smallest: $65,000/$25

**Contact Made by:** Telephone inquiry or letter of inquiry

**Available by Request:** Proposal guidelines; annual report on contributions

**Contributions Decisions Made:** Monthly

**Applicants Notified:** Within one week of decision

## FULLERTON FOUNDATION

Suite 1100
608 Second Avenue South
Minneapolis, MN 55402

**Established:** December 1968

**Type:** Private foundation

**Geographic Orientation:** Twin Cities; national

**Sample Grants:**
Courage Center—$6,000
Minneapolis Society of Fine Arts—$1,000
Westminster Presbyterian Church—$250

**Financial Data for Year Ending December 31, 1981:**
Assets: $254,826
Grants Paid: $34,525
Number of Grants: 38
Largest/Smallest: $6,000/$25

**Paid Professional Staff:** No

**Directors/Trustees:** James G. Fullerton III, president; Robert J. Simonsen, treasurer; Thomas A. Gomilak, Jr., secretary

## THE GAINEY FOUNDATION

148 East Broadway
Owatonna, MN 55060

**Type:** Private foundation

**Geographic Orientation:** Twin Cities

**Sample Grant:**
College of Saint Thomas—$498,600

**Financial Data for Year Ending December 31, 1981:**
Assets: $73,832
Grants Paid: $498,600
Number of Grants: 1

**Paid Professional Staff:** No

**Directors/Trustees:** Daniel J. Gainey, president; Catherine H. Gainey, vice-president

## THE GALINSON FOUNDATION

2441 Cedar Lane
Minneapolis, MN 55416

**Established:** May 1960

**Type:** Private foundation

**Geographic Orientation:** National

**Sample Grants:**
Minneapolis Federation for Jewish Service—$10,600
University of California at San Diego Foundation—$1,000
League of Women Voters—$50

**Financial Data for Year Ending May 31, 1981:**
Assets: $277,639
Grants Paid: $29,932
Number of Grants: 35
Largest/Smallest: $10,600/$25

**Paid Professional Staff:** No

**Directors/Trustees:** Murray L. Galinson, president; Kay Galinson, vice-president; Corrine Birnberg, secretary/treasurer

# B. C. GAMBLE AND P. W. SKOGMO FOUNDATION

500 Foshay Tower
Minneapolis, MN 55402
(612) 339-7343

**Contact Person:** Thomas F. Beech, secretary and treasurer

**Established:** April 1982

**Type:** Supporting organization of The Minneapolis Foundation, a community foundation

**Program's Purpose:** Historic emphases of the two family foundations combined to include youth services, health care programs in the field of aging, and educational institutions in the Twin Cities area (the Gamble and Skogmo Foundation, which resulted from the combination of two family foundations [those of Bertin C. Gamble and Philip W. Skogmo], will continue to follow the foundations' giving patterns within the guidelines of The Minneapolis Foundation)

**Geographic Orientation:** Twin Cities

**Fields of Activity:** Vocational education; higher education; medical research; medical care/treatment; medical/health education; religion; religious education; legal education; business/economic education; community affairs; crime/law enforcement; economic development; employment/job training; equal rights/legal aid; family services; recreation; special population groups; welfare

**Types of Organizations Funded:** Public television/radio; secondary schools; vocational schools; colleges; universities; special education; adult education; junior colleges; hospitals; medical schools; medical research groups; counseling services; churches/synagogues; religious service groups; legal aid; multiservice centers; organizations for the elderly; organizations for the handicapped; organizations for youth; centers for children; organizations for minorities; neighborhood agencies; community centers

**Targeted Population Groups:** Aged; children/youth; handicapped; minorities

**Types of Support for Organizations:** Capital support; continuing support; general operating support; matching grants; program development; research; federated fund drives

**Sample Grants:**
Boys' Clubs of Minneapolis—$160,000
Bethel College—$45,000
Minneapolis Society for the Blind—$6,000

**Financial Data Since Founding April 1, 1982:**
Assets: $16,412,614

**Paid Professional Staff:** Yes

**Contact Made by:** Letter of inquiry

**Available by Request:** Proposal guidelines; application procedures; annual report (in 1983)

**Board Meetings:** Semiannual, in May and December

**Applicants Notified:** Within two weeks of decision

**Officers/Trustees:** Henry T. Rutledge, president; Philip B. Harris, vice-president; Thomas F. Beech, secretary and treasurer; Leone Moe, assistant secretary; Bertin C. Gamble; Donald G. Dreblow; Robert H. Engels; Timothy G. Johnson; Raymond O. Mithun

# GANDRUD FOUNDATION

Box 528
Owatonna, MN 55060

**Established:** December 1952

**Type:** Private foundation

**Geographic Orientation:** Minnesota

**Sample Grants:**
Seminary Appeal, American Lutheran Church—$10,000
Owatonna Foundation—$10,000
Salvation Army—$100

**Financial Data for Year Ending December 31, 1981:**
Assets: $195,908
Grants Paid: $22,700
Number of Grants: 10
Largest/Smallest: $10,000/$50

**Paid Professional Staff:** No

**Directors/Trustees:** E. S. Gandrud; E. M. Gandrud

# GASTERLAND CHARITABLE TRUST

c/o Richfield Bank and Trust Company
6625 Lyndale Avenue South
Richfield, MN 55423

**Established:** December 1963

**Type:** Private foundation

**Geographic Orientation:** Twin Cities

**Sample Grants:**
Richfield Lutheran Church—$6,000
Suburban Hennepin Vo-Tech—$3,000
Colonial Church of Edina—$200

**Financial Data for Year Ending December 31, 1981:**
　Assets: $64,689
　Grants Paid: $9,500
　Number of Grants: 4
　Largest/Smallest: $6,000/$200

**Paid Professional Staff:** No

**Directors/Trustees:** Lorin A. Gasterland; Emma E. Gasterland; Richfield Bank and Trust Company (from 990-AR, 1980)

## • THE GELCO FOUNDATION

1 Gelco Drive
Eden Prairie, MN 55344
(612) 828-6214

**Contact Person:** James P. Johnson, director

**Established:** 1973

**Type:** Corporate foundation

**Program's Purpose:** To provide support to nonprofit organizations that work primarily in the metropolitan Twin Cities area; to create a healthy, informed citizenry; to prevent or resolve social problems; to maintain a vital cultural life

**Program's Limits:** No grants to individuals, to political or fraternal organizations, to religious organizations for sectarian purposes, or to fund-raising events; normally, supports United Way agencies through its annual gift to the United Way of the Minneapolis area

**Geographic Orientation:** Twin Cities

**Fields of Activity:** Arts/architecture; music/opera; theater/dance; secondary education; vocational education; higher education; mental health; business/economic education; community affairs; drug-abuse programs; economic development; employment/job training; equal rights/legal aid; family services; recreation

**Types of Organizations Funded:** Museums/historical societies; theaters/dance groups; music/opera groups; public television/radio; cultural centers; secondary schools; vocational schools; colleges; universities; counseling services; conservation groups; United Way; multiservice centers; organizations for the elderly; organizations for the handicapped; organizations for women; organizations for youth; centers for children

**Types of Support for Organizations:** Capital support; continuing support; endowment; general operating support; program development; research; federated fund drives

**Sample Grants:**
　Guthrie Theater—$2,250
　Washburn Child Guidance Center—$500
　Business Economics Education Foundation—$400

**Financial Data for Year Ending June 30, 1982:**
　Assets: $1,385,894
　Grants Paid: $246,948
　Number of Grants: 112
　Largest/Smallest: $39,249/$100

**Paid Professional Staff:** Yes

**Contact Made by:** Request for guidelines

**Available by Request:** Proposal guidelines; annual report

**Proposal Deadlines:** May 1 for consideration for budget year beginning July 1; proposals received any time

**Board Meetings:** Biannual, in October and May

**Applicants Notified:** Within two weeks of decision

**Directors:** N. Bud Grossman, chairman; Stanley Chason; Richard McFerran; Kevin Mitchell; Allan H. Raymond

## • GENERAL MILLS FOUNDATION

Box 1113
Minneapolis, MN 55436
(612) 540-3337

**Contact Person:** James P. Shannon, executive director

**Established:** 1954

**Type:** Corporate foundation

**Program's Limits:** Grants for social service and health, civic affairs, and cultural affairs considered where company has a significant number of employees; no grants to individuals or to organizations for religious purposes

**Geographic Orienta
a significant number of employees**

**Fields of Activity:** Arts/architecture; music/opera; theater/dance; elementary/secondary education; vocational education; higher education; mental health; advocacy; business/economic education; community affairs; crime/law enforcement; drug-abuse programs; economic development; employment/job training; equal rights/legal aid; family services

**Types of Organizations Funded:** Museums/historical societies; theaters/dance groups; music/opera groups; public television/radio; cultural centers; secondary schools; vocational schools; colleges; universities; scholarship funds; clinics; chemical dependency services; United Way; legal aid; multiservice centers; organizations for the elderly; organizations for the handicapped; organizations for women; organizations for drug abusers; organizations for youth; centers for children; housing agencies; organizations for offenders; organizations for minorities; neighborhood agencies; community centers

**Targeted Population Groups:** Children/youth; women/girls; minorities

**Types of Support for Organizations:** General operating support; program development

**Sample Grants:**
Legal Rights Center, Minneapolis—$4,400
Little Brothers of the Poor, Minneapolis—$2,000
Minnesota Youth Symphony—$1,500

**Financial Data for Year Ending May 31, 1982:**
Assets: $9,130,757
Grants Paid: $5,658,633 (includes $406,308 in employee matching gifts to colleges and secondary schools)
Number of Grants: 740
Largest/Smallest: $368,596/$500

**Paid Professional Staff:** Yes

**Contact Made by:** Letter of inquiry; request for guidelines

**Available by Request:** Proposal guidelines; application procedures; annual report

**Applicants Notified:** Within six weeks of decision

**Trustees:** H. B. Atwater, Jr., president; J. P. Shannon, vice-president and executive director; P. L. Parker, vice-president; F. C. Blodgett; D. F. Swanson; M. H. Willes

# GENERAL SERVICE FOUNDATION

c/o John M. Musser
First National Bank Building
St. Paul, MN 55101

**Established:** June 1946

**Type:** Private foundation

**Geographic Orientation:** National

**Sample Grants:**
Minneapolis Public Schools—$175,000
Population Council, New York—$35,000
International Institute for Environment and Development (Antarctic)—$14,000

**Financial Data for Year Ending December 31, 1981:**
Assets: $16,436,930
Grants Paid: $977,526
Number of Grants: 41
Largest/Smallest: $175,000/$1,250

**Paid Professional Staff:** Yes

**Directors/Trustees:** John M. Musser, president/treasurer; Mrs. Marion M. Lloyd, vice-president; Ruth Hezzelwood, secretary

# GEROT FOUNDATION

c/o Paul S. Gerot
735 Cargill Building
Minneapolis, MN 55402

**Established:** 1959

**Type:** Private foundation

**Geographic Orientation:** Minnesota; Florida; Iowa

**Sample Grants:**
United Way of Minneapolis—$600
Iowa Wesleyan College—$500
North American Wildlife Association—$50

**Financial Data for Year Ending December 31, 1981:**
Assets: $47,978
Grants Paid: $2,450
Number of Grants: 10
Largest/Smallest: $600/$25

**Paid Professional Staff:** No

**Directors/Trustees:** Paul S. Gerot, president; Aileen M. Gerot, vice-president/assistant secretary; Helen M. Anderson, secretary/treasurer

# CHARLES D. GILFILLAN MEMORIAL

W-555 First National Bank Building
St. Paul, MN 55101
(612) 291-1215

**Contact Person:** John Bultena, secretary

**Established:** April 1946

**Type:** Private foundation

**Program's Purpose:** To provide medical and surgical care, hospitalization, and care during convalescence for Minnesota residents who are crippled or physically impaired or are women "dependent upon their own exertions" who are unable to pay for the entire cost of their treatment; dental care included in the provisions; preference shown to people from rural areas of the state or those living in towns with populations of fewer than 3,000

**Program's Limits:** Fund assistance not available for terminal illnesses, for uncomplicated hospital confinements, or in situations where long-term care is required for an indefinite period of time and where public assistance is available

**Geographic Orientation:** Minnesota rural communities and towns with populations of fewer than 3,000

**Field of Activity:** Medical care/treatment

**Type of Support for Individuals:** Aid to needy persons

**Financial Data for Year Ending March 31, 1982:**
Assets: $74,266
Grants Paid: $48,891
Number of Grants: 85
Largest/Smallest: $3,740/$12

**Paid Professional Staff:** No

**Contact Made by:** Letter of inquiry

**Available by Request:** Application procedures

**Board Meetings:** Annual, in May

**Directors:** John H. Herrell, president; Odean C. Erickson, vice-president; R. T. Thein, treasurer; John Bultena, secretary; H. L. Danforth, assistant treasurer; Mrs. Charles Hutchinson; Dr. Donald Nelson; Ronald L. Ress

## ARCHIE AND PHEBE MAE GIVENS FOUNDATION

625 East Sixteenth Street
Minneapolis, MN 55404

**Established:** December 1973

**Type:** Private foundation

**Sample Grants:**
United Negro College Fund—$1,000
Saint Mary's Junior College—$300

**Financial Data for Year Ending December 31, 1980:**
Assets:  $6,353
Grants Paid:  $1,300
Number of Grants:  2
Largest/Smallest:  $1,000/$300

**Paid Professional Staff:** No

**Director/Trustee:** Phebe Mae Givens

## THE JACOB E. GOLDENBERG FOUNDATION

7125 Sandburg Road
Minneapolis, MN 55427
(612) 544-3800

**Contact Person:** M. H. Maisel, director

**Established:** December 1943

**Type:** Private foundation

**Geographic Orientation:** Twin Cities

**Fields of Activity:** Research; religious education

**Types of Organizations Funded:** Colleges; hospitals; medical schools; churches/synagogues; religious service groups; religious colleges

**Sample Grant:**
National Jewish Resource Center—$1,000

**Financial Data for Year Ending December 31, 1981:**
Assets:  $5,357
Grants Paid:  $1,000
Number of Grants:  1

**Paid Professional Staff:** No

**Contact Made by:** Letter of inquiry

**Board Meetings:** Annual

**Directors/Trustees:** David L. Goldenberg, chairman; Kalman S. Goldenberg, vice-chairman; M. H. Maisel, director

## ARTHUR AND CONSTANCE GOODMAN FAMILY FOUNDATION

405 Sibley Street
235 Mears Park Place
St. Paul, MN 55101

**Established:** July 1967

**Type:** Private foundation

**Geographic Orientation:** Minnesota

**Sample Grants:**
College of Saint Catherine—$5,000
Sholom Home—$1,100
Children's Cancer Research Fund—$25

**Financial Data for Year Ending December 31, 1981:**
Assets:  $299,950
Grants Paid:  $16,851
Number of Grants:  45
Largest/Smallest:  $5,000/$25

**Paid Professional Staff:** No

**Directors/Trustees:** Constance Goodman, president; Arthur Goodman, vice-president; Mary Ann Reilly, secretary; Stephanie Krey, treasurer

## GOTTSTEIN FAMILY FOUNDATION

2231 Edgewood Avenue South
Minneapolis, MN 55416

**Established:** December 1966

**Type:** Private foundation

**Sample Grants:**
Minneapolis Federation for Jewish Service—$5,400
Beth El Synagogue—$1,300
American Technion Society—$100

**Financial Data for Year Ending June 30, 1981:**
Assets:  $85,697
Grants Paid:  $8,109
Number of Grants:  21
Largest/Smallest:  $5,400/$25

**Paid Professional Staff:** No

**Directors/Trustees:** Leland Gottstein, vice-president/secretary; Nathan Gottstein, president/treasurer

## RANSFORD RAY AND CLARA J. GOULD FOUNDATION

c/o First Trust Company of St. Paul
W-555 First National Bank Building
St. Paul, MN 55101

**Contact Person:** Roland W. Hohman

**Established:** 1959

**Type:** Private foundation

**Program's Purpose:** "Primarily to assist and benefit the youth in and about the donor's home city of Brainerd, Minnesota, and birthplace of Jamestown, New York"

**Program's Limits:** No grants to individuals

**Geographic Orientation:** Brainerd, MN, and Jamestown, NY, areas

**Sample Grants:**
YMCA, Brainerd—$1,400
Paul Bunyan Bronco League—$650
Campfire Girls, Brainerd—$500

**Financial Data for Year Ending December 31, 1981:**
Assets: $160,015
Grants Paid: $8,300
Number of Grants: 14
Largest/Smallest: $1,400/$200

**Paid Professional Staff:** No

**Trustee:** First Trust Company of St. Paul

# GRACO FOUNDATION

60 Eleventh Avenue Northeast
Minneapolis, MN 55413
(612) 623-6222

**Contact Person:** Charles F. Murphy, executive director

**Established:** 1956

**Type:** Corporate foundation

**Program's Limits:** Grants only to 501c-3 organizations; no grants to individuals, to political organizations, or to religious institutions for sectarian purposes; national and international organizations that have broad public support have low priority

**Geographic Orientation:** Twin Cities; Minnesota; cities in which Graco has a significant number of employees

**Fields of Activity:** Arts/architecture; music/opera; arts education; elementary/secondary education; vocational education; higher education; adult/continuing education; medical care/treatment; medical/health education; physical sciences; business/economic education; community affairs; crime/law enforcement; drug-abuse programs; economic development; employment/job training; disaster relief; family services

**Types of Organizations Funded:** Museums/historical societies; music/opera groups; libraries; zoos; public television/radio; elementary schools; secondary schools; vocational schools; colleges; universities; educational councils; scholarship funds; special education; adult education; junior colleges; libraries; hospitals; medical schools; chemical dependency services; family-planning agencies; counseling services; conservation groups; United Way; legal aid; multiservice centers; organizations for the elderly; organizations for the handicapped; organizations for women; organizations for drug abusers; organizations for youth; centers for children; housing agencies; organizations for minorities; neighborhood agencies; day-care centers; community centers

**Targeted Population Groups:** Aged; children/youth; handicapped; minorities

**Types of Support for Organizations:** Capital support; continuing support; general operating support; program development; federated fund drives; program-related investments

**Type of Support for Individuals:** Scholarships

**Sample Grants:**
United Way of Minneapolis Area—$150,000
Junior Achievement of Greater Minneapolis—$4,500
Hospitality House Motor Vehicle Replacement Fund—$1,500

**Financial Data for Year Ending December 31, 1981:**
Assets: $1,427,564
Grants Paid: $437,667
Number of Grants: 145
Largest/Smallest: $120,000/$50

**Paid Professional Staff:** No

**Contact Made by:** Letter of inquiry

**Board Meetings:** Quarterly, in March, June, September, and December

**Applicants Notified:** Within two weeks of decision

**Directors/Trustees:** David A. Koch, president; Russell J. Gray, vice-president; Maynard B. Hasselquist; Charles F. Murphy, executive director, secretary/treasurer

# ● GRAIN TERMINAL FOUNDATION

Box 43594
St. Paul, MN 55164
(612) 646-9433

**Contact Person:** R. A. Pavek, treasurer

**Established:** 1947

**Type:** Corporate foundation

**Geographic Orientation:** Minnesota; national

**Field of Activity:** Higher education (related to agriculture)

**Types of Organizations Funded:** Scholarship funds; United Way

**Sample Grants:**
University of Minnesota Foundation—$75,000
Crop Quality Council—$7,300
Minnesota SPAN Association—$300

**Financial Data for Year Ending May 31, 1981:**
Assets: $2,668,382
Grants Paid: $243,250
Number of Grants: 74
Largest/Smallest: $75,000/$150

**Paid Professional Staff:** No

**Contact Made by:** Letter of inquiry

**Available by Request:** IRS 990AR (available at the office only)

**Board Meetings:** Quarterly

**Applicants notified:** Within two to three weeks of decision

**Directors/Trustees:** Allen D. Hanson, chairman; Gordon H. Matheson, vice-chairman; R. A. Pavek, treasurer

# GRANELDA FOUNDATION

4900 IDS Center
Minneapolis, MN 55402

**Established:** December 1948

**Type:** Private foundation

**Geographic Orientation:** Twin Cities

**Sample Grants:**
Chadwick Foundation—$2,500
Wood-Rill Foundation—$2,500
WM Foundation—$2,500

**Financial Data for Year Ending December 31, 1981:**
Assets: $5
Grants Paid: $12,500
Number of Grants: 5

**Paid Professional Staff:** No

**Directors/Trustees:** Donald C. Dayton, president; Bruce B. Dayton, vice-president/secretary-treasurer; Wallace C. Dayton, vice-president; K. N. Dayton, vice-president; Douglas J. Dayton, vice-president; Ronald N. Gross, vice-president/assistant secretary-treasurer

# GRAYBRIER FOUNDATION

Route 5, Box 85W
Excelsior, MN 55331

**Established:** October 1969

**Type:** Private foundation

**Geographic Orientation:** Twin Cities

**Sample Grants:**
University of Minnesota Foundation—$250
Minnetonka Garden Club—$200
Amicus—$200

**Financial Data for Year Ending December 31, 1981:**
Assets: $37,834
Grants Paid: $3,300
Number of Grants: 20
Largest/Smallest: $250/$50

**Paid Professional Staff:** No

**Directors/Trustees:** John P. Gray, chairman/treasurer; Phillip H. Martin, secretary; Russell J. Gray, vice-chairman

# ALVIN GREENBERG FOUNDATION

2522 Joppa Avenue
St. Louis Park, MN 55416

**Type:** Private foundation

**Sample Grants:**
Minneapolis Federation for Jewish Service—$3,000
Anti-Defamation League—$300
Little City Foundation—$75

**Financial Data for Year Ending November 30, 1981:**
Assets: $30,318
Grants Paid: $3,710
Number of Grants: 7
Largest/Smallest: $3,000/$25

**Paid Professional Staff:** No

**Director/Trustee:** Alvin Greenberg, president

# GREYSTONE FOUNDATION

510 Baker Building
Minneapolis, MN 55402
(612) 332-2454

**Contact Person:** John M. Hollern, trustee

**Established:** December 1948

**Type:** Private foundation

**Geographic Orientation:** National

**Fields of Activity:** Arts/architecture; music/opera; higher education; medical/health education; religion; community affairs; family services

**Types of Organizations Funded:** Museums/historical societies; music/opera groups; public television/radio; universities; scholarship funds; medical research groups; clinics; churches/synagogues; United Way; organizations for women; organizations for youth; organizations for men; animal centers

**Types of Support for Organizations:** Continuing support; general operating support

**Types of Support for Individuals:** Scholarships; research support

**Sample Grants:**
Mayo Foundation, Brooks-Hollern Endowment Fund (to provide scholarships for medical students)—$180,000
Courage Center—$20,000
United Way of Minneapolis Area—$8,500

**Financial Data for Year Ending December 31, 1981:**
Assets: $1,502,950
Grants Paid: $137,910
Number of Grants: 71
Largest/Smallest: $43,500/$35

**Trustees:** John M. Hollern; Michael P. Hollern

## MARY LIVINGSTON GRIGGS AND MARY GRIGGS BURKE FOUNDATION

1400 Northwestern National Bank Building
St. Paul, MN 55101
(612) 227-7683

**Contact Person:** Marvin J. Pertzik, secretary

**Established:** June 1966

**Type:** Private foundation

**Geographic Orientation:** Twin Cities; New York; northern Wisconsin

**Fields of Activity:** Arts/architecture; music/opera; theater/dance; other arts and humanities activities; visual arts education; conservation; United Way

**Types of Organizations Funded:** Museums/historical societies; theaters/dance groups; music/opera groups; zoos; arts councils; other arts and humanities organizations; universities (for specific purposes, not for general grants); family-planning agencies; environmental agencies; conservation groups; United Way

**Sample Grants:**
Metropolitan Opera (three-year operating grant)—$30,000
St. Paul-Ramsey Arts and Science Council (for the United Arts Fund)—$20,000
Cricket Theatre (operating grant)—$2,000

**Financial Data for Year Ending June 30, 1981:**
Assets: $9,142,280
Grants Paid: $518,032
Number of Grants: 67
Largest/Smallest: $46,000/$500

**Paid Professional Staff:** No

**Contact Made by:** Complete proposal

**Available by Request:** IRS 990 during statutory period

**Board Meetings:** Quarterly

**Directors/Trustees:** Mary Griggs Burke, president; Richard A. Moore, vice-president; Orley R. Taylor, treasurer; Marvin J. Pertzik, secretary

## GROSSMAN BROTHERS FOUNDATION

1 Gelco Drive
Eden Prairie, MN 55344

**Type:** Private foundation

**Geographic Orientation:** Twin Cities

**Sample Grants:**
Minneapolis Federation for Jewish Service—$5,000
United Way—$1,500

**Financial Data for Year Ending July 31, 1981:**
Assets: $15,618
Grants Paid: $6,500
Number of Grants: 2
Largest/Smallest: $5,000/$1,500

**Paid Professional Staff:** No

**Directors/Trustees:** Thomas Grossman, president; John Grossman, vice-president; Ronald Link, secretary

## N. BUD AND ALENE GROSSMAN FOUNDATION

1 Gelco Drive
Eden Prairie, MN 55344

**Established:** May 1980

**Type:** Private foundation

**Geographic Orientation:** Twin Cities

**Sample Grants:**
Adath Jeshurun Cemetery Association—$2,700
Guthrie Theater—$500
United Negro College Fund—$100

**Financial Data for Year Ending June 30, 1981:**
Assets: $1,059
Grants Paid: $5,925
Number of Grants: 24
Largest/Smallest: $2,700/$10

**Paid Professional Staff:** No

**Directors/Trustees:** N. Bud Grossman, president; Alene Grossman, vice-president; Sidney Lorber, assistant secretary

## GROTTO FOUNDATION

West 2090 First National Bank Building
St. Paul, MN 55101
(612) 224-9431

**Contact Person:** A. A. Heckman, executive director

**Established:** December 1964

**Type:** Private foundation

**Program's Limits:** No capital fund grants, grants to individuals, grants to foreign organizations; ordinarily grants not made to annual budgets of established organizations

**Geographic Orientation:** Midwest

**Fields of Activity:** History/preservation; language/literature; media/communications; vocational education; adult/continuing education; medical research; medical care/treatment; life sciences; physical sciences; legal education; business/economic education; drug-abuse programs; employment/job training

**Types of Organizations Funded:** Museums/historical societies; public television/radio; secondary schools; colleges; scholarship funds; junior colleges; hospitals; medical research groups; chemical dependency services; organizations for the handicapped

**Targeted Population Groups:** Substance abusers; children/youth; blacks; Hispanics; native Americans; senior citizens

**Types of Support for Organizations:** Matching grants; program development; research

**Types of Support for Individuals:** Scholarships; research support

**Sample Grants:**
Sisters of St. Joseph of Carondolet in Minnesota and adjoining states (support for oral history of the activities)—$18,000 (multiyear grants)
William Mitchell College of Law (scholarships for minority students)—$9,000 (multiyear grants)
Hamline University Law School (counseling and scholarships for American Indian students)—$6,700 (multiyear grants)

**Financial Data for Year Ending April 30, 1982:**
Assets: $1,903,400
Grants Paid: $69,000
Number of Grants: 33
Largest/Smallest: $6,000/$125

**Paid Professional Staff:** Yes

**Contact Made by:** Letter of inquiry

**Available by Request:** Proposal guidelines; application procedures; annual report

**Proposal Deadlines:** Sixty days before quarterly board meetings

**Board Meetings:** Quarterly, in May, August, November, and February

**Applicants Notified:** Within two weeks of decision

**Directors/Trustees:** L. W. Hill, Jr.; Irving Clark; John Diehl; A. A. Heckman; Malcolm McDonald; William Randall

## GROVES FOUNDATION

Box 1267
10,000 Highway 55 West
Minneapolis, MN 55440

**Established:** September 1952

**Type:** Private foundation

**Geographic Orientation:** National

**Sample Grants:**
Minneapolis Society of Fine Arts—$202,062
Groves Learning Center—$188,616
American Cancer Society—$25

**Financial Data for Year Ending September 30, 1981:**
Assets: $9,126,238
Grants Paid: $486,211
Number of Grants: 40 (plus 23 scholarships)
Largest/Smallest: $202,062/$25

**Paid Professional Staff:** No

**Directors/Trustees:** F. N. Groves, president; C. T. Groves, vice-president; O. E. Miller, vice-president; H. A. Beltz, secretary

## THE JEROME HALPER FAMILY FOUNDATION

1780 Pinehurst Avenue
St. Paul, MN 55116

**Established:** November 1960

**Type:** Private foundation

**Geographic Orientation:** Twin Cities; Minnesota

**Sample Grant:**
National Council of Jewish Women—$1,500

**Financial Data for Year Ending December 31, 1981:**
Assets: $47,837
Grants Paid: $1,500
Number of Grants: 1

**Paid Professional Staff:** No

**Directors/Trustees:** Marice Halper, president; Stephen Halper, vice-president; Wendy Rubin, secretary-treasurer

## THE HANSER FAMILY FOUNDATION

1300 First Bank Place West
Minneapolis, MN 55402
(612) 375-9655

**Contact Person:** S. Albert Hanser

**Established:** March 1978

**Type:** Private foundation

**Geographic Orientation:** Minnesota; national

**Fields of Activity:** Medical research; medical care/treatment; business/economic education (which promotes the free enterprise system)

**Types of Organizations Funded:** Elementary schools; secondary schools; colleges; universities; hospitals; medical research groups; medical libraries; United Way; organizations for youth; neighborhood agencies; animal centers

**Types of Support for Organizations:** Capital support; endowment

**Sample Grants:**
Saint Olaf College—$13,578
St. Louis County Day School—$10,078
Intervarsity Christian Fellowship—$100

**Financial Data for Year Ending December 31, 1981:**
Assets: $7,289
Grants Paid: $51,595
Number of Grants: 14
Largest/Smallest: $13,578/$7

**Paid Professional Staff:** No

**Contact Made by:** Letter of inquiry

**Board Meetings:** Biannual, in December and June

**Director:** S. Albert Hanser

## HELEN HARRINGTON CHARITABLE TRUST

c/o First National Bank of Minneapolis
Box A700
Minneapolis, MN 55440

**Established:** March 1962

**Type:** Private foundation

**Program's Limits:** Will stipulates that 50 percent of trust income be paid to predesignated institutions and 50 percent to educational institutions

**Sample Grants:**
Minneapolis Foundation—$29,769
Minneapolis Private College Fund—$28,579
William Hood Dunwoody Institute—$7,442

**Financial Data for Year Ending December 31, 1981:**
Assets: $1,228,628
Grants Paid: $119,078
Number of Grants: 9
Largest/Smallest: $29,769/$1,191

**Paid Professional Staff:** No

**Trustee:** First National Bank of Minneapolis

## HARRIS FOUNDATION

120 South LaSalle Street
Chicago, IL 60603

**Established:** December 1945

**Type:** Private foundation

**Geographic Orientation:** National

**Sample Grants:**
Brown University, Providence, RI—$20,000
Planned Parenthood of Illinois—$10,000
Actors Theatre of St. Paul—$100

**Financial Data for Year Ending December 31, 1981:**
Assets: $7,425,209
Grants Paid: $305,112
Number of Grants: 200
Largest/Smallest: $20,000/$50

**Paid Professional Staff:** No

**Directors/Trustees:** Irving B. Harris, chairman; Benno F. Wolff, secretary; William W. Harris, vice-chairman; Sidney Barrows, assistant vice-chairman

## HARTWELL FOUNDATION

Suite 450
10,000 Highway 55 West
Minneapolis, MN 55441

**Established:** August 1969

**Type:** Private foundation

**Sample Grant:**
Salvation Army—$100

**Financial Data for Year Ending December 31, 1981:**
Assets: $1,023
Grants Paid: $100
Number of Grants: 1

**Paid Professional Staff:** No

**Directors/Trustees:** John M. Hartwell, president; Lucy B. Hartwell, treasurer

## HARTZ FOUNDATION

Thief River Falls, MN 56701

**Type:** Corporate foundation

**Geographic Orientation:** Minnesota

**Sample Grants:**
Bagley Senior Citizens—$10,000
Bemidji Community Hospital—$6,000
Seventh-Day Adventist Charities—$250

**Financial Data for Year Ending July 31, 1981:**
Assets: $3,046,837
Grants Paid: $143,720
Number of Grants: 65
Largest/Smallest: $10,000/$38

**Paid Professional Staff:** No

**Director/Trustee:** Onealee Hartz, secretary

## HARTZELL FOUNDATION

2516 Wabash Avenue
St. Paul, MN 55114

**Established:** August 1969

**Type:** Private foundation

**Geographic Orientation:** Minnesota

**Sample Grants:**
Goodwill Industries—$15,000
Rice Lake Library—$10,000
Oasis Zoo—$2,500

**Financial Data for Year Ending September 30, 1981:**
Assets: $209,298
Grants Paid: $112,109
Number of Grants: 82
Largest/Smallest: $15,000/$15

**Paid Professional Staff:** No

**Directors/Trustees:** James R. Hartzell, president; Robert Hartzell, vice-president

## HARVARD CLUB OF MINNESOTA FOUNDATION

c/o Ralph K. Morris
1500 First National Bank Building
St. Paul, MN 55101

**Established:** December 1967

**Type:** Private foundation

**Geographic Orientation:** Minnesota

**Sample Grant:**
Scholarship to Harvard—$1,100

**Financial Data for Year Ending June 30, 1981:**
Assets: $75,845
Grants Paid: $1,100
Number of Grants: 1

**Paid Professional Staff:** No

## OSCAR AND MADGE HAWKINS FOUNDATION

c/o Carl Flodquist
Route 1
North Branch, MN 55056

**Established:** December 1966

**Type:** Private foundation

**Program's Purpose:** ''To aid research in the areas of social, political, governmental history and development''

**Geographic Orientation:** Minnesota

**Financial Data for Year Ending November 30, 1981:**
Assets: $13,057

**Paid Professional Staff:** No

**Directors/Trustees:** Helvi Savola, president; Carl Flodquist, secretary-treasurer

## HAWTHORNE FOUNDATION

25 Peninsula Road, Dellwood
White Bear Lake, MN 55110

**Established:** December 1953

**Type:** Private foundation

**Sample Grants:**
St. Paul YWCA—$11,000
Minnesota Private College Fund—$6,000
St. Croix Animal Shelter—$1,000

**Financial Data for Year Ending December 31, 1981:**
Assets: $193,003
Grants Paid: $136,800
Number of Grants: 36
Largest/Smallest: $11,000/$100

**Paid Professional Staff:** No

**Directors/Trustees:** Herbert R. Galloway, president/treasurer; Janice T. Galloway, vice-president; Victoria G. Holmen, secretary; Richard B. Galloway

## MENAHEM HEILICHER CHARITABLE FOUNDATION

850 Decatur Avenue North
Minneapolis, MN 55427

**Established:** September 1963

**Type:** Private foundation

**Geographic Orientation:** Twin Cities

**Sample Grants:**
Minneapolis Federation for Jewish Service—$71,348
Community Housing and Service Corporation—$5,000
Guthrie Theater—$100

**Financial Data for Year Ending September 30, 1981:**
Assets: $1,062,379
Grants Paid: $113,418
Number of Grants: 46
Largest/Smallest: $71,348/$10

**Paid Professional Staff:** No

**Directors/Trustees:** Amos Heilicher, president; Daniel Heilicher, vice-president/treasurer/assistant secretary; Marvin Borman, secretary

## THE JACK HEIMANN FAMILY FOUNDATION

1653 Pinehurst Avenue
St. Paul, MN 55116

**Established:** December 1947

**Type:** Private foundation

**Geographic Orientation:** Minnesota

**Sample Grants:**
Indianhead Council, BSA—$500
Harvard University—$500
Toys' N' Things—$50

**Financial Data for Year Ending December 31, 1981:**
Assets: $44,236
Grants Paid: $4,085
Number of Grants: 16
Largest/Smallest: $500/$50

**Paid Professional Staff:** No

**Directors/Trustees:** Jeanne L. Heimann, chairperson; Harold L. Rutchick, vice-chairperson; Jemie J. J. Thorvig, secretary-treasurer

## HENDEL FOUNDATION

1800 Midwest Plaza Building
Minneapolis, MN 55402

**Established:** July 1955

**Type:** Private foundation

**Sample Grants:**
Mount Sinai Hospital Capital Fund—$20,100
United Way of Minneapolis—$690
Walker Art Center—$300

**Financial Data for Year Ending December 31, 1981:**
Assets: $240,090
Grants Paid: $26,349
Number of Grants: 13
Largest/Smallest: $20,100/$13

**Paid Professional Staff:** No

**Directors/Trustees:** Helen Hendel, president; Burt Corwin, vice-president; Marvin Borman, secretary; Jeanne Corwin, treasurer

## THOMAS R. HENNESSY FAMILY CHARITABLE TRUST

Route 2
Lewiston, MN 55952

**Established:** September 1974

**Type:** Private foundation

**Geographic Orientation:** Minnesota

**Sample Grants:**
Lewiston Ecumenical Conference—$500
Williams Fund—$335
Goodfellows—$100

**Financial Data for Year Ending August 31, 1981:**
Assets: $98,190
Grants Paid: $6,020
Number of Grants: 28
Largest/Smallest: $500/$100

**Paid Professional Staff:** No

**Trustee:** Merchants National Bank of Winona

## THE HERMUNDSLIE FOUNDATION

3762 Harrison Road North
Tucson, AZ 85715

**Established:** November 1968

**Type:** Private foundation

**Geographic Orientation:** Minnesota

**Sample Grants:**
American Diabetes Association of Minnesota—$21,000
Minneapolis Medical Research Foundation—$10,500
Minnesota Society for the Prevention of Blindness—$10,500

**Financial Data for Year Ending December 31, 1981:**
Assets: $906,437
Grants Paid: $42,000
Number of Grants: 3
Largest/Smallest: $21,000/$10,500

**Paid Professional Staff:** No

**Directors/Trustees:** Gerold Hermundslie; G. D. Engdahl

## HERSEY FOUNDATION

Room 440
408 St. Peter Street
St. Paul, MN 55102

**Established:** January 1968 (originally Etoile du Nord Foundation)

**Type:** Private foundation

**Geographic Orientation:** Minnesota

**Sample Grants:**
Minneapolis Art Institute—$75,000
Nature Conservancy—$45,000
Abortion Education and Referral Service—$6,800

**Financial Data for Year Ending December 31, 1981:**
Assets: $3,551,664
Grants Paid: $400,940
Number of Grants: 13
Largest/Smallest: $75,000/$140

**Paid Professional Staff:** No

**Director/Trustee:** Edward H. Hamm (from AR-990, 1980)

## MALVIN E. AND JOSEPHINE D. HERZ FOUNDATION

Route 4
Excelsior, MN 55331

**Established:** July 1967

**Type:** Private foundation

**Geographic Orientation:** Minnesota

**Sample Grants:**
Minneapolis Federation for Jewish Service—$10,000
University of Minnesota, Field Biology Program—$1,200
Minnesota Orchestral Association—$300

**Financial Data for Year Ending December 31, 1981:**
Assets: $68,587
Grants Paid: $13,500
Number of Grants: 5
Largest/Smallest: $10,000/$300

**Paid Professional Staff:** No

**Directors/Trustees:** Malvin E. Herz, president/treasurer; Josephine D. Herz, vice-president; Michael J. Herz, vice-president; Benno F. Wolff, secretary

## HOLLY FOUNDATION

215 Elm Avenue
Waseca, MN 56093

**Established:** November 1964

**Type:** Private foundation

**Geographic Orientation:** Minnesota

**Sample Grants:**
Minnesota Opera Company—$200
St. Andrews Episcopal Church—$180
University of Minnesota, Opera Guarantor
Fund—$125

**Financial Data for Year Ending June 30, 1981:**
Assets:  $7,929
Grants Paid:  $505
Number of Grants:  3
Largest/Smallest:  $200/$125

**Paid Professional Staff:** No

**Directors/Trustees:** William C. Hoversten, president;
William B. Patton, secretary-treasurer

# ● HONEYWELL FOUNDATION

Box 524
Minneapolis, MN 55440
(612) 870-6822

**Contact Person:** Pat Hoven, director

**Established:** 1958

**Type:** Corporate foundation

**Program's Interests:** Education (four-year colleges), then
health and welfare, followed by the arts; currently is
decreasing its support to the arts to less than 10
percent of its budget

**Program's Limits:** Average grant between $3,500 and
$5,000; giving restricted to communities in which
Honeywell has major manufacturing operations;
support to education limited to four-year degree-
granting institutions with programs in computer
science, engineering, and business administration

**Geographic Orientation:** Twin Cities; communities in
which Honeywell has major manufacturing operations

**Fields of Activity:** Music/opera; theater/dance; higher
education; computer science; community affairs;
crime/law enforcement; drug-abuse programs;
economic development; employment/job training;
disaster relief; family services; welfare

**Types of Organizations Funded:** Museums/historical
societies; theaters/dance groups; music/opera groups;
libraries; zoos; public television/radio; arts councils;
cultural centers; colleges and universities (four-year
degree-granting institutions with programs in
computer science, engineering, and business
administration); scholarship funds; hospitals; chemical
dependency services; family-planning agencies;
counseling services; United Way; legal aid;
organizations for the elderly; organizations for the
handicapped; organizations for women; organizations
for drug abusers; organizations for youth;
organizations for men; centers for children; housing
agencies; organizations for offenders; organizations for
minorities; neighborhood agencies; day-care centers;
community centers

**Matching Gift Programs:** Public television and public
radio (matched one to one); public educational
institutions (matched one to one); private and
independent institutions of higher education (matched
two to one)

**Targeted Population Groups:** Aged; children/youth;
criminal offenders/exoffenders; handicapped;
men/boys; women/girls; refugees; Asian Americans;
blacks; Hispanics; native Americans

**Types of Support for Organizations:** Capital support;
endowment; general operating support; matching
grants (of employees); program development;
federated fund drives

**Types of Support for Individuals:** Scholarships and
fellowships (made payable to school, with school
naming the recipient); scholarship program for
children of employees through the National Merit
Scholarship Fund

**Sample Grants:**
University of Minnesota, Institute of
Technology—$500,000
American Indian OIC, Minneapolis—$20,000
Minnesota Dance Theatre and School,
Minneapolis—$5,000

**Financial Data for Year Ending December 31, 1981:**
Contributions Paid:  $4,500,581
Number of Contributions:  576 (excluding matching
gifts)
Largest/Smallest:  $500,000/$500

**Contact Made by:** Complete proposal

**Available by Request:** Annual report on contributions

**Contributions Decisions Made:** Quarterly

**Applicants Notified:** Within three weeks of decision

# W. R. HOTCHKISS FOUNDATION

1080 West County Road F
St. Paul, MN 55112

**Established:** November 1958

**Type:** Corporate foundation

**Geographic Orientation:** Minnesota

**Sample Grants:**
Minnesota Private College Fund—$20,000
Lutheran Social Service of Minnesota—$9,960
Minnesota Literacy Council—$3,000

**Financial Data for Year Ending June 30, 1981:**
Assets:  $4,325,069
Grants Paid:  $263,628
Number of Grants:  93 (includes 65 scholarships)
Largest/Smallest:  $20,000/$334

**Paid Professional Staff:** No

**Directors/Trustees:** M. J. Welch, president; R. L.
Swanson, vice-president; S. L. Peterson, secretary;
F. H. Cloutier, treasurer

## THE HUBBARD FOUNDATION

3415 University Avenue
St. Paul, MN 55114

**Established:** August 1958

**Type:** Private foundation

**Geographic Orientation:** Minnesota; national

**Sample Grants:**
St. Croix Valley Youth Center—$35,000
Hazelden Foundation—$8,000
National Right to Work Foundation—$500

**Financial Data for Year Ending November 30, 1981:**
Assets: $4,213,269
Grants Paid: $446,647
Number of Grants: 197
Largest/Smallest: $35,000/$60

**Paid Professional Staff:** No

**Directors/Trustees:** Stanley E. Hubbard, president;
Stanley S. Hubbard, vice-president/treasurer; Karen H.
Hubbard, vice-president; Gerald D. Deeney, secretary

## LAURA AND WALTER HUDSON FOUNDATION

Northwestern National Bank of Minneapolis Trust
    Department
Minneapolis, MN 55479

**Established:** April 1961

**Type:** Private foundation

**Program's Purpose:** To give preference "to Minnesota
institutions in the fields of education, health, and
conservation"

**Program's Limits:** No scholarships or grants to
individuals

**Geographic Orientation:** Twin Cities

**Sample Grants:**
Blake School—$5,000
Film in the Cities—$1,000
U.S. Ski Team Fund—$100

**Financial Data for Year Ending December 31, 1981:**
Assets: $451,471
Grants Paid: $29,980
Number of Grants: 39
Largest/Smallest: $5,000/$25

**Paid Professional Staff:** No

**Directors/Trustees:** Sewall D. Andrews, Jr., president;
Craig A. Nalen, vice-president/secretary; John Crosby,
vice-president/assistant secretary; Lilla A. Patterson,
treasurer

## NEVIN N. HUESTED FOUNDATION FOR HANDICAPPED CHILDREN

208 Commerce Building
St. Paul, MN 55101

**Established:** June 1961

**Type:** Private foundation

**Program's Purpose:** "To promote the general welfare of
the handicapped children...in the state of
Minnesota"

**Geographic Orientation:** Minnesota

**Sample Grants:**
University of Minnesota—$3,600
Segum Center—$2,920
Bay Totem Town—$800

**Financial Data for Year Ending December 31, 1981:**
Assets: $433,197
Grants Paid: $28,121
Number of Grants: 20
Largest/Smallest: $3,600/$350

**Paid Professional Staff:** No

**Directors/Trustees:** Ellsworth Stenswick, president;
James J. Geary, secretary-treasurer; Vernon Schultz;
Betty Bassett; August Gehrke

## MARY ANDERSEN HULINGS FOUNDATION

Bayport, MN 55003

**Established:** March 1962

**Type:** Private foundation

**Geographic Orientation:** Minnesota; national

**Sample Grants:**
Washington County Association for Senior
Citizens—$68,960
National Ataxia Foundation—$1,500
Congregational Foundation for Theological
Studies—$500

**Financial Data for Year Ending February 28, 1982:**
Assets: $2,371,365
Grants Paid: $178,660
Number of Grants: 54
Largest/Smallest: $68,960/$100

**Paid Professional Staff:** No

**Directors/Trustees:** Mary A. Hulings, president; Albert
D. Hulings, vice-president; Mark B. Christian,
secretary-treasurer

# HUBERT H. HUMPHREY FOUNDATION

1404 TCF Tower
121 South Eighth Street
Minneapolis, MN 55402

**Established:** November 1967

**Type:** Private foundation

**Geographic Orientation:** Twin Cities

**Financial Data for Year Ending December 31, 1981:**
  Assets:   $74,601
  Grants Paid:   $0

**Paid Professional Staff:** No

**Directors/Trustees:** Muriel F. Humphrey, chairman of
  the board; Hubert H. Humphrey III, president;
  Nancy H. Solomonson, secretary-treasurer; C. Bruce
  Solomonson, vice-president; Robert Humphrey

# INGRAM FOUNDATION

c/o First Trust Company of St. Paul
W-555 First National Bank Building
St. Paul, MN 55101

**Established:** October 1955

**Type:** Private foundation

**Geographic Orientation:** National

**Sample Grants:**
  Nashville Symphony Association—$15,000
  Princeton University—$2,000
  U.S. Olympic Committee—$100

**Financial Data for Year Ending October 31, 1981:**
  Assets:   $646,055
  Grants Paid:   $45,335
  Number of Grants:   40
  Largest/Smallest:   $15,000/$35

**Paid Professional Staff:** No

**Directors/Trustees:** E. Bronson Ingram, chairman;
  Frederic B. Ingram, vice-chairman; Martha R. Ingram,
  secretary

# • INTERNATIONAL MULTIFOODS CHARITABLE FOUNDATION

Multifoods Tower
Box 2942
Minneapolis, MN 55402
(612) 340-3302

**Contact Person:** Fran Kolb, manager, Corporate Support
  Programs

**Established:** 1970

**Type:** Corporate foundation

**Program's Purpose:** To focus on education, with
  emphasis on economic education, culture and arts,
  health and welfare, civic programs

**Geographic Orientation:** Twin Cities; Minnesota;
  locations where International Multifoods operates
  facilities

**Fields of Activity:** Arts/architecture; history/preservation;
  music/opera; theater/dance; elementary/secondary
  education; vocational education; higher education;
  research; other educational activities; medical research;
  medical care/treatment; medical/health education;
  mental health; physical sciences; social sciences; legal
  education; business/economic education; community
  affairs; crime/law enforcement; drug-abuse programs;
  economic development; employment/job training;
  environment/energy; equal rights/legal aid; family
  services; recreation; safety; special population groups;
  welfare; consumer interests

**Types of Organizations Funded:** Museums/historical
  societies; theaters/dance groups; music/opera groups;
  libraries; zoos; public television/radio; historic
  preservation; cultural centers; elementary schools;
  secondary schools; colleges; universities; educational
  councils; scholarship funds; special education; junior
  colleges; libraries; hospitals; medical research groups;
  clinics; chemical dependency services; counseling
  services; religious colleges; research/study institutes;
  environmental agencies; conservation groups; United
  Way; legal aid; multiservice centers; organizations for
  the handicapped; organizations for drug abusers;
  organizations for youth; organizations for minorities;
  neighborhood agencies

**Types of Support for Organizations:** Capital support;
  continuing support; endowment; general operating
  support; matching grants; program development;
  research; federated fund drives; program-related
  investments

**Sample Grants:**
  United Way of Minneapolis Area—$70,000
  Junior Achievement of Greater Minneapolis—$5,500
  Learning Center for Economics, Minneapolis Public
  Schools—$2,675

**Financial Data for Year Ending February 28, 1982:**
  Assets:   $640,225
  Grants Paid:   $364,580
  Number of Grants:   29 (plus matching educational
  gifts)
  Largest/Smallest:   $75,000/$25

**Contact Made by:** Letter of inquiry

**Available by Request:** IRS 990PF

**Board Meetings:** Quarterly, additional meetings as
  required

**Applicants Notified:** Within two weeks of decision

**Directors:** William G. Phillips, president; Richard H.
  King, vice-president and treasurer; Atherton Bean

## • INTER-REGIONAL FINANCIAL GROUP FOUNDATION

100 Dain Tower
Box 1160
Minneapolis, MN 55440
(612) 371-2809

**Contact Person:** Elizabeth Hermanson, executive director

**Established:** 1962

**Type:** Corporate foundation

**Program's Purpose:** To serve the social and cultural needs of the communities in which the corporation operates; has a strong commitment to education, particularly to business and economic education

**Program's Limits:** First priority given to projects located in geographic areas in which corporation has branch offices and to organizations in which employees are involved

**Geographic Orientation:** National, areas in which corporation has branch offices

**Fields of Activity:** Media/communications; music/opera; theater/dance; arts education; vocational education; higher education; medical research; medical care/treatment; business/economic education; community affairs; drug-abuse programs; economic development

**Types of Organizations Funded:** Museums/historical societies; theaters/dance groups; music/opera groups; libraries; public television/radio; vocational schools; colleges; universities; educational councils; hospitals; chemical dependency services; family-planning agencies; counseling services; United Way; legal aid; organizations for the elderly; organizations for women; organizations for drug abusers; organizations for youth; housing agencies; neighborhood agencies

**Targeted Population Groups:** Substance abusers; children/youth

**Types of Support for Organizations:** Capital support; continuing support; general operating support; matching grants; federated fund drives

**Sample Grants:**
Minnesota Private College Fund—$5,000
Junior Achievement—$3,000
Johnson Institute—$2,000

**Financial Data for Year Ending December 31, 1981:**
Assets: $100,408
Grants Paid: $191,700
Number of Grants: 454
Largest/Smallest: $8,333/$25

**Paid Professional Staff:** No

**Contact Made by:** Letter of inquiry

**Available by Request:** Proposal guidelines; application procedures

**Proposal Deadline:** December 15

**Board Meetings:** Quarterly

**Applicants Notified:** Within two weeks of decision

**Directors/Trustees:** Thomas E. Holloran, president; Douglas R. Coleman; Joseph J. Gallick; Robert W. Goodfellow; Dale Pugh; Noel Rahn

## • INVESTORS DIVERSIFIED SERVICES (IDS)

3300 IDS Tower, Unit 61
Minneapolis, MN 55402
(612) 372-3695

**Contact Person:** Alice S. Reimann, manager, community relations

**Type:** Charitable contributions program

**Program's Interests:** Economic education

**Program's Limits:** Most grants in the area of economic education and matching employee gifts to schools and community service organizations

**Geographic Orientation:** Twin Cities; Minnesota; national

**Fields of Activity:** Media/communications; music/opera; theater/dance; arts education; elementary/secondary education; higher education; medical research; life sciences; business/economic education; employment/job training; family services

**Types of Organizations Funded:** Museums/historical societies; theaters/dance groups; music/opera groups; zoos; public television/radio; cultural centers; arts councils; elementary schools; secondary schools; vocational schools; colleges; universities; educational councils; scholarship funds; special education; junior colleges; hospitals; medical research groups; chemical dependency services; conservation groups; United Way; multiservice centers; organizations for the handicapped; organizations for women; organizations for minorities; day-care centers; community centers

**Employee Matching Gift Programs:** Higher education; elementary/secondary education; many nonprofit organizations

**Targeted Population Groups:** Handicapped; women/girls; minorities

**Types of Support for Organizations:** General operating support; matching grants; program development (in economic education)

**Sample Grants:**
Sojourner Shelter—$2,500
Urban Coalition—$2,000
St. Paul Council of Arts—$1,000

**Financial Data for Year Ending December 31, 1982:**
Contributions Budgeted: $750,000
Number of Contributions: 315 (from January 1 through August 24, 1982)
Largest/Smallest: $100,000/$500

**Contact Made by:** Letter of inquiry

**Available by Request:** Proposal guidelines; application procedures

**Proposal Deadlines:** January, August

**Contribution Decisions Made:** Monthly

**Applicants Notified:** Within six weeks of decision

# THE JACKLEY FOUNDATION

4301 Highway 7
Minneapolis, MN 55416

**Established:** September 1967 (as Winter Tree Foundation)

**Type:** Private foundation

**Program's Purpose:** To make "general purpose contributions to well established...organizations which are publicly supported"

**Geographic Orientation:** Minnesota

**Sample Grants:**
Minnesota Dance Theatre—$1,169
Children's Museum—$500
Leader Dogs for the Blind—$88

**Financial Data for Year Ending December 31, 1981:**
Assets: $64
Grants Paid: $8,900
Number of Grants: 36
Largest/Smallest: $1,169/$25

**Paid Professional Staff:** No

**Director/Trustee:** C. A. Jackley

# THE JEFFERSON FOUNDATION

219 Main Street Southeast
Minneapolis, MN 55414
(612) 379-1316

**Contact Person:** June Jensen, secretary

**Type:** Corporate foundation

**Program's Interests:** Arts; education

**Geographic Orientation:** Twin Cities; national

**Fields of Activity:** Arts/architecture; history/preservation; music/opera; theater/dance; vocational education; higher education; advocacy; family services; safety

**Types of Organizations Funded:** Museums/historical societies; theaters/dance groups; music/opera groups; libraries; public television/radio; historic preservation; colleges; universities; scholarship funds; special education; libraries; conservation groups; United Way; organizations for youth; centers for children; neighborhood agencies; community centers

**Employee Matching Gift Programs:** No

**Types of Support for Organizations:** Capital support; continuing support; endowment; general operating support; research

**Financial Data for Year Ending December 31, 1981:**
Grants Paid: $27,200
Number of Grants: 14
Largest/Smallest: $7,500/$250

**Paid Professional Staff:** No

**Contact Made by:** Letter of inquiry

**Contributions Decisions Made:** Annually, in March

**Directors:** Louis N. Zelle, president; James J. Viera, treasurer; June H. Jensen, secretary; Daniel F. Prins

# • JEROME FOUNDATION

W-2090 First National Bank Building
St. Paul, MN 55101
(612) 224-9431

**Contact Person:** Cynthia A. Gehrig, executive director

**Established:** May 1965

**Type:** Private foundation

**Program's Purpose:** To support programs in the arts and humanities; focus on emerging artists of promise in each of the arts disciplines and in certain areas of the humanities

**Geographic Orientation:** Minnesota; Iowa; Wisconsin; North Dakota; South Dakota; New York City

**Fields of Activity:** Creative writing; dance; film-video; music; theater; visual arts; humanities

**Types of Organizations Funded:** Museums/historical societies; theaters/dance groups; music/opera groups; libraries; public television/radio; arts councils; cultural centers; other arts and humanities organizations; universities

**Targeted Population Group:** Emerging artists

**Types of Support for Organizations:** Continuing support; general operating support; matching grants; program development; research; project support

**Type of Support for Individuals:** Fellowships (in selected disciplines)

**Sample Grants:**
Minnesota Composers Forum (composers' commissioning program)—$56,000
Playwrights' Center (playwrights' stipends and developmental pool)—$25,630
Center for the Study and Exhibition of Drawings (exhibitions of works by emerging artists, New York City)—$16,000

**Financial Data for Year Ending April 30, 1982:**
Assets: $20,091,125
Grants Paid: $1,094,002
Number of Grants: 85
Largest/Smallest: $56,000/$200

**Paid Professional Staff:** Yes

**Contact Made by:** Letter of inquiry; request for guidelines

**Available by Request:** Proposal guidelines; application procedures; annual report

**Board Meetings:** Bimonthly

**Applicants Notified:** Within one week of decision

**Directors/Trustees:** A. A. Heckman, president and treasurer; Irving Clark, vice-president and assistant secretary; Patricia Bratnober Anderson; Gaylord Glarner; Thelma Hunter; Archibald Leyasmeyer

# D. W. JIMMERSON FOUNDATION

505 South Willow Drive
Long Lake, MN 55356

**Established:** 1969

**Type:** Private foundation

**Geographic Orientation:** Twin Cities

**Financial Data for Year Ending December 31, 1981:**
Assets: $25,028
Grants Paid: $0

**Paid Professional Staff:** No

**Directors/Trustees:** D. W. Jimmerson; Josephine Jimmerson; John B. Fischer

# JNM 1966 GIFT TRUST

c/o First National Bank of Duluth Trust Department
Duluth, MN 55801

**Established:** March 1966

**Type:** Private foundation

**Geographic Orientation:** National

**Sample Grants:**
Duluth YMCA—$10,000
College of Saint Scholastica—$8,000
American Friends Service Committee—$50

**Financial Data for Year Ending December 31, 1981:**
Assets: $1,130,438
Grants Paid: $74,950
Number of Grants: 22
Largest/Smallest: $10,000/$50

**Paid Professional Staff:** No

**Directors/Trustees:** Newell Marshall; Caroline Marshall

# LEWIS H. JOHNSON FAMILY FOUNDATION

1000 TCF Tower
Minneapolis, MN 55402

**Established:** September 1964

**Type:** Private foundation

**Geographic Orientation:** Twin Cities

**Sample Grants:**
St. Paul United Jewish Fund—$14,000
Temple of Aaron—$1,818
Zion Orphanage of Jerusalem—$50

**Financial Data for Year Ending December 31, 1981:**
Assets: $288,398
Grants Paid: $17,994
Number of Grants: 8
Largest/Smallest: $14,000/$50

**Paid Professional Staff:** No

**Directors/Trustees:** Lewis H. Johnson, president/treasurer; Rivian Johnson, vice-president; Marie Heckel, secretary

# LLOYD K. AND MARION JOHNSON FOUNDATION

517 Torrey Building
Duluth, MN 55802

**Established:** September 1975

**Type:** Private foundation

**Geographic Orientation:** Duluth area

**Sample Grants:**
United Way of Duluth—$2,000
Cook County Historical Society—$500
Boys' Club of Duluth—$500

**Financial Data for Year Ending December 31, 1981:**
Assets: $78,648
Grants Paid: $5,050
Number of Grants: 8
Largest/Smallest: $2,000/$50

**Paid Professional Staff:** No

**Directors/Trustees:** Lloyd K. Johnson; Darryl E. Coons; J. Thomas Johnson

# THE HARRY V. JOHNSTON FOUNDATION

Box 6
Circle Pines, MN 55014

**Contact Person:** Madrienne J. Larson

**Established:** September 1964

**Type:** Private foundation

**Geographic Orientation:** Minnesota; South Dakota

**Sample Grants:**
Episcopal Community Services, Minneapolis—$8,000
Huron College, South Dakota—$5,000
Native American Indian Clubs of Northern State College—$500

**Financial Data for Year Ending December 31, 1981:**
Assets: $79,470
Grants Paid: $20,826
Number of Grants: 6
Largest/Smallest: $8,000/$326

**Paid Professional Staff:** No

**Contact Made by:** Letter of inquiry

**Directors/Trustees:** Madrienne J. Larson; Ira N. Burhans; Robert S. C. Peterson

## JOSEPH FOUNDATION

777 Grain Exchange
Minneapolis, MN 55415

**Established:** August 1944

**Type:** Private foundation

**Geographic Orientation:** National

**Sample Grants:**
Hebrew Union College—$50,000
Hubert H. Humphrey Institute—$20,000
Workers Defense League—$700

**Financial Data for Year Ending July 31, 1981:**
Assets: $7
Grants Paid: $437,680
Number of Grants: 63
Largest/Smallest: $50,000/$100

**Paid Professional Staff:** No

**Director/Trustee:** Burton M. Joseph, president

## JOSHUA FOUNDATION

1350 First Bank Place West
Minneapolis, MN 55402

**Established:** December 1957

**Type:** Private foundation

**Geographic Orientation:** National

**Sample Grants:**
National Council—Young Israel—$55,000
Kenesseth Israel Congregation—$10,060
Big Brothers—$200

**Financial Data for Year Ending December 31, 1981:**
Assets: $230,934
Grants Paid: $116,077
Number of Grants: 40
Largest/Smallest: $55,000/$13

**Paid Professional Staff:** No

**Directors/Trustees:** Herbert Joshua; Rose Joshua (from 990-AR, 1980)

## JOSTENS

5501 Norman Center Drive
Bloomington, MN 55437
(612) 830-8429

**Contact Person:** Ellis F. Bullock, Jr., director of public affairs

**Type:** Charitable contributions program

**Program's Interests:** Programs and events not covered by the Jostens Foundation (see separate entry); emphasis on youth programs

**Geographic Orientation:** Twin Cities; Minnesota; national

**Fields of Activity:** Arts/architecture; history/preservation; language/literature; media/communications; music/opera; theater/dance; arts education; elementary/secondary education; vocational education; higher education; medical research; medical care/treatment; medical/health education; public health; mental health; advocacy; business/economic education; community affairs; crime/law enforcement; drug-abuse programs; economic development; employment/job training; environment/energy; equal rights/legal aid; disaster relief; family services; recreation; safety; special population groups; welfare

**Types of Organizations Funded:** Museums/historical societies; theaters/dance groups; music/opera groups; libraries; zoos; public television/radio; arts councils; historic preservation; cultural centers; universities; educational councils; scholarship funds; hospitals; chemical dependency services; family-planning agencies; counseling services; environmental agencies; conservation groups; United Way; legal aid; multiservice centers; organizations for the elderly; organizations for the handicapped; organizations for women; organizations for veterans; organizations for drug abusers; organizations for youth; organizations for men; centers for children; housing agencies; organizations for offenders; organizations for minorities; neighborhood agencies; day-care centers; community centers

**Targeted Population Group:** Children/youth

**Employee Matching Gift Programs:** Higher education; elementary/secondary education; any nonprofit organization (matching gift programs through Jostens Foundation)

**Types of Support for Organizations:** Capital support; continuing support; endowment; general operating support; matching grants; program development; federated fund drives

**Types of Support for Individuals:** Scholarships; scholarship program for children of employees (through National Merit Scholarship program)

**Sample Grants:**
   U.S. Chamber of Commerce—$3,500
   Minnesota Coalition for Health Care Costs—$1,000
   Freshwater Biological Research Foundation—$250

**Financial Data for Year Ending June 30, 1982:**
   Contributions Paid: $322,900 (in addition, plants have their own contributions budget and during 1982 gave more than $54,000 to their communities)
   Largest/Smallest: $250,000 (special one-time-only grant)/$100

**Contact Made by:** Letter of inquiry

**Available by Request:** Proposal guidelines; application procedures; annual report on contributions


## • THE JOSTENS FOUNDATION

Box 20367
Bloomington, MN 55420
(612) 830-8461

**Contact:** Ellis F. Bullock, Jr., director

**Established:** 1976

**Type:** Corporate foundation

**Program's Purpose:** To help young people between the ages of twelve and twenty-four

**Program's Limits:** Grants normally not made to independent educational institutions, school districts, churches, or political organizations

**Geographic Orientation:** Twin Cities; locations where there are Jostens plants

**Fields of Activity:** Music/opera; theater/dance; arts education; elementary/secondary education; vocational education; higher education; medical/health education; business/economic education; drug-abuse programs; employment/job training; recreation; special population groups

**Types of Organizations Funded:** Museums/historical societies; theaters/dance groups; music/opera groups; public television/radio; cultural centers; educational institutions (elementary, secondary, and vocational schools, colleges and universities) through employee matching gift programs; educational councils; chemical dependency services; family-planning agencies; counseling services; United Way; legal aid; multiservice centers; organizations for the handicapped; organizations for women; organizations for drug abusers; organizations for youth; organizations for minorities; neighborhood agencies; community centers

**Targeted Population Group:** Children/youth (ages twelve to twenty-four)

**Types of Support for Organizations:** Capital support; general operating support; matching grants (in-house matching programs); program development; federated fund drives

**Type of Support for Individuals:** Scholarships (through specific program)

**Sample Grants:**
   KIDS (scholarships)—$1,500
   Camp Sunrise (program support)—$1,500
   Omegon (educational programing)— $1,000

**Financial Data for Year Ending June 30, 1981:**
   Grants Paid: $377,000
   Number of Grants: 340
   Largest/Smallest: $10,000/$200

**Paid Professional Staff:** Yes

**Contact Made by:** Request for guidelines

**Available by Request:** Proposal guidelines; application procedures; annual report

**Proposal Deadlines:** Last days of August, October, December, February, April, and June

**Board Meetings:** Third Thursdays of September, November, January, March, May, and July

**Directors/Trustees:** H. William Lurton, chairman of the board/chief executive officer; Robert W. Leslie, president/chief operating officer; Don C. Lein, executive vice-president/chief financial officer


## JUDSON FUND

4308 IDS Center
Minneapolis, MN 55402

**Established:** December 1937 (as Joel Foundation)

**Type:** Private foundation

**Geographic Orientation:** Twin Cities

**Sample Grant:**
   Macalester College—$5,000

**Financial Data for Year Ending December 31, 1981:**
   Assets: $37,758
   Grants Paid: $5,000
   Number of Grants: 1

**Paid Professional Staff:** No

**Directors/Trustees:** David J. Winton; Katherine D. Winton; Margaret W. Anderson; David M. Winton; Katherine W. Evans (from 990-AR, 1980)


## • THE KAHLER FOUNDATION

20 Second Avenue Southwest
Rochester, MN 55901
(507) 282-2581

**Contact Person:** Jerry Harrington, chairman

**Established:** October 1962

**Type:** Corporate foundation

**Program's Limits:** Grants confined to communities where corporation is involved in business operations

**Geographic Orientation:** Minnesota

**Fields of Activity:** Arts/architecture; history/preservation; media/communications; music/opera; theater/dance; vocational education; higher education; medical research; medical care/treatment; mental health; family services; recreation

**Types of Organizations Funded:** Museums/historical societies; theaters; music; public television/radio; arts councils; vocational schools; colleges; scholarship funds; hospitals; medical research groups; counseling services; United Way; organizations for the elderly; organizations for the handicapped; organizations for youth; day-care centers

**Types of Support for Organizations:** Capital support; program development; research

**Type of Support for Individuals:** Scholarships (Rochester area only)

**Sample Grants:**
United Ways (five)—$19,588 (Rochester Area United Way—$17,563 of that amount)
Minnesota Private College Fund—$2,200
Rochester Art Center—$1,100

**Financial Data for Year Ending June 30, 1982:**
Assets: $30,814
Grants Paid: $43,659
Number of Grants: 44
Largest/Smallest: $17,500/$55

**Paid Professional Staff:** No

**Contact Made by:** Request for guidelines

**Available by Request:** Proposal guidelines

**Proposal Deadline:** Thirty days prior to meetings of board

**Board Meetings:** Fourth Monday in February, May, August, and October

**Applicants Notified:** Within one week of decision

**Trustees:** Gerald L. Harrington, chairman; Ray L. Roberts, vice-chairman; Jean H. Freeman, secretary-treasurer; Dr. Francis A. Tyce, assistant secretary; Charles Withers; Harvey L. Hollenback; Howard T. Stewart; Dr. Harry Vakos

# GEORGE KAPLAN MEMORIAL FOUNDATION

c/o Sol Minsberg
Box 4412
St. Paul, MN 55104
(612) 647-0111

**Contact Persons:** Sol Minsberg, president; Allan Baumgarten, treasurer

**Established:** 1948

**Type:** Private foundation

**Program's Purpose:** To foster Jewish education and the Jewish religion; to promote religion, charity, and education of members of the Jewish faith; to aid and assist institutions of learning for persons of the Jewish faith

**Program's Limits:** No grants to individuals

**Geographic Orientation:** Twin Cities

**Fields of Activity:** Arts education; elementary/secondary education; higher education; religion; religious education; family services; recreation

**Types of Organizations Funded:** Cultural centers; elementary schools; universities; synagogues; religious schools; religious colleges; community centers

**Targeted Population Groups:** Children/youth; Jews

**Types of Support for Organizations:** Capital support; continuing support; general operating support; program development; federated fund drives

**Sample Grants:**
United Jewish Fund and Council, St. Paul—$15,000
Jewish Community Center, St. Paul—$1,000
Talmud Torah of St. Paul—$500

**Financial Data for Year Ending December 31, 1981:**
Assets: $438,000
Grants Paid: $35,500
Number of Grants: 9
Largest/Smallest: $15,000/$100

**Paid Professional Staff:** No

**Contact Made by:** Letter of inquiry

**Board Meetings:** Quarterly

**Trustees:** Sol Minsberg, president; Solly Robins, vice-president; Allan Baumgarten, treasurer/recording secretary; Rabbi Louis Milgrom; A. J. Geller; David Touchin

# HYMAN S. KAPLAN FAMILY FOUNDATION

345 Shepard Road
St. Paul, MN 55102

**Established:** December 1974

**Type:** Private foundation

**Geographic Orientation:** Twin Cities

**Sample Grants:**
United Jewish Fund and Council, St. Paul—$36,000
Sholom Home—$10,000

**Financial Data for Year Ending October 31, 1981:**
Assets: $117,628
Grants Paid: $46,000
Number of Grants: 2

**Paid Professional Staff:** No

**Director/Trustee:** Reuben Kaplan, president

# FATHER KASAL CHARITABLE TRUST

c/o Minnesota Trust Company
Box 463
107 West Oakland Avenue
Austin, MN 55912
(507) 437-3231

**Contact Person:** The Right Reverend Monsignor B. P. Mangan

**Established:** September 1963

**Type:** Private foundation

**Program's Purpose:** To support Catholic charities and education of young men and women for religious life

**Program's Limits:** No gifts for maintenance or construction of buildings; no gifts to individuals

**Geographic Orientation:** National

**Fields of Activity:** Higher education; adult/continuing education; religious education; Catholic charities

**Types of Organizations Funded:** Colleges; universities; scholarship funds; adult education; chemical dependency services; religious service groups; religious schools; religious colleges

**Types of Support for Organizations:** Matching grants; program development; scholarships to institutions

**Sample Grants:**
Naeve Hospital Foundation Trust—$11,000
Saint Teresa College—$10,000
Diocese of Winona—$2,000

**Financial Data for Year Ending September 30, 1981:**
Assets: $1,277,154
Grants Paid: $78,250
Number of Grants: 18
Largest/Smallest: $11,000/$1,000

**Paid Professional Staff:** No

**Contact Made by:** Request for guidelines

**Available by Request:** Proposal guidelines; application procedures; annual report

**Board Meetings:** Quarterly, in January, April, July, and October

**Applicants Notified:** Within six months of decision

**Directors/Trustees:** Warren F. Plunkett, president; Mary Matuska, secretary; the Right Reverend Monsignor B. P. Mangan, treasurer

# KEF FOUNDATION

312 East Superior Street
Duluth, MN 55802

**Established:** December 1952

**Type:** Private foundation

**Geographic Orientation:** Minnesota

**Sample Grants:**
Duluth YMCA—$1,160
United Way of Duluth—$663

**Financial Data for Year Ending December 31, 1981:**
Assets: $14,863
Grants Paid: $3,248
Number of Grants: 4

**Paid Professional Staff:** No

**Directors/Trustees:** C. G. Evans; R. B. Evans; J. E. Koenig (from 990-AR, 1980)

# KELM FOUNDATION

15 West Snapper Point Drive
Key Largo, FL 33037

**Established:** December 1962

**Type:** Private foundation

**Geographic Orientation:** Twin Cities

**Sample Grants:**
United Way of Minneapolis—$6,400
KTCA—$1,000
Pick-a-Pet Welfare—$100

**Financial Data for Year Ending December 31, 1981:**
Assets: $241,084
Grants Paid: $28,650
Number of Grants: 27
Largest/Smallest: $6,400/$100

**Paid Professional Staff:** No

**Directors/Trustees:** Erwin E. Kelm, president; David E. Kelm, vice-president (from 990-AR, 1980)

# M. J. KENNEDY FOUNDATION

c/o Green, Merrigan, Johnson & Quayle
Suite 800
400 Second Avenue South
Minneapolis, MN 55401

**Established:** May 1975

**Type:** Private foundation

**Geographic Orientation:** Twin Cities

**Sample Grant:**
Elderfriends—$15,000

**Financial Data for Year Ending December 31, 1981:**
Assets: $191,110
Grants Paid: $15,000
Number of Grants: 1

**Paid Professional Staff:** No

**Directors/Trustees:** Maribeth Jennings; John E. Jennings; Lee N. Johnson

## KLASEN

306 Physicians and Surgeons Building
St. Cloud, MN 56301

**Established:** April 1960

**Type:** Private foundation

**Geographic Orientation:** St. Cloud area

**Sample Grants:**
Holy Angels Church—$600
Saint John's University—$500
United Way of St. Cloud—$100

**Financial Data for Year Ending September 30, 1981:**
Assets: $15,520
Grants Paid: $1,529
Number of Grants: 4
Largest/Smallest: $600/$100

**Paid Professional Staff:** No

**Director/Trustee:** M. A. Klasen, president

## JULIUS AND SOPHIE KLEIN FAMILY FOUNDATION

535 South Lexington Parkway
St. Paul, MN 55116

**Established:** December 1958

**Type:** Private foundation

**Geographic Orientation:** Twin Cities

**Sample Grants:**
United Jewish Fund and Council—$2,650
Temple Solel—$500
Hadassah—$48

**Financial Data for Year Ending December 31, 1981:**
Assets: $31,391
Grants Paid: $3,731
Number of Grants: 9
Largest/Smallest: $2,650/$36

**Paid Professional Staff:** No

**Directors/Trustees:** Julius Klein; Harvey Klein; E. Gary Klein

## KLEVEN FOUNDATION

6201 Ryan Avenue South
Minneapolis, MN 55424

**Established:** December 1959

**Geographic Orientation:** Minnesota

**Sample Grants:**
Normandale Lutheran Church—$3,700
Saint Olaf College—$2,000
Gustavus Adolphus College—$100

**Financial Data for Year Ending December 31, 1980:**
Assets: $50,632
Grants Paid: $6,150
Number of Grants: 5
Largest/Smallest: $3,700/$100

**Paid Professional Staff:** No

**Director/Trustee:** E. Milton Kleven

## HESS KLINE FOUNDATION

35W North and County Road C
Roseville, MN 55113

**Established:** December 1956

**Type:** Private foundation

**Geographic Orientation:** National

**Sample Grants:**
Multiple Sclerosis Society—$3,800
Jewish National Fund—$1,000
Jewish Community Center—$100

**Financial Data for Year Ending December 31, 1981:**
Assets: $123,393
Grants Paid: $6,200
Number of Grants: 8
Largest/Smallest: $3,800/$100

**Paid Professional Staff:** No

**Directors/Trustees:** Hess Kline, president/treasurer; Renee Kline, vice-president; Judith Lund, second vice-president; Arnold A. Karlins, secretary

## JAESON H. KLINE FOUNDATION

1221 West Lake Street
Minneapolis, MN 55408

**Established:** December 1947

**Type:** Private foundation

**Geographic Orientation:** Twin Cities

**Sample Grants:**
Minneapolis Federation for Jewish Service—$28,873
Multiple Sclerosis Society—$1,000
Sister Kenny Institute—$25

**Financial Data for Year Ending December 31, 1981:**
Assets: $164,740
Grants Paid: $58,848
Number of Grants: 28
Largest/Smallest: $28,873/$25

**Paid Professional Staff:** No

**Directors/Trustees:** J. H. Kline, president-treasurer; A. A. Karling, secretary

# • LAND O'LAKES

4001 Lexington Avenue North
Arden Hills, MN 55112
(612) 481-2222

**Contact Person:** Debra Boyles, community relations
manager

**Established:** 1975

**Type:** Charitable contributions program

**Program's Interests:** Agriculture-related activities; social
services; youth programs; arts; civic affairs

**Geographic Orientation:** Twin Cities

**Fields of Activity:** Arts/architecture; history/preservation;
music/opera; theater/dance; cooperative and business
education programs; mental health; business/economic
education; community affairs; crime/law enforcement;
drug-abuse programs; economic development;
employment/job training; family services; safety

**Types of Organizations Funded:** Museums/historical
societies; theaters/dance groups; music/opera groups;
public television/radio; arts councils; historic
preservation; chemical dependency services; family-
planning agencies; counseling services; conservation
groups; United Way; legal aid; multiservice centers;
organizations for the elderly; organizations for the
handicapped; organizations for women; organizations
for drug abusers; organizations for youth; centers for
children; organizations for offenders; organizations for
minorities; neighborhood agencies; day-care centers;
community centers

**Employee Matching Gift Programs:** No

**Types of Support for Organizations:** Capital support;
general operating support; program development;
program-related investments

**Sample Grants:**
Future Farmers of America—$2,000
Hospitality House—$2,000
Children's Theatre—$1,000

**Financial Data for Year Ending December 31, 1981:**
Contributions Paid:  $162,000
Number of Contributions:  400
Largest/Smallest:  $6,000/$75

**Contact Made by:** Letter of inquiry

**Available by Request:** Proposal guidelines; application
procedures

**Contributions Decisions Made:** Every other month
(February through December)

**Applicants Notified:** Within one week of decision

# HELEN LANG CHARITABLE TRUST

c/o First Trust Company of St. Paul
W-555 First National Bank Building
St. Paul, MN 55101

**Established:** February 1972

**Type:** Private foundation

**Geographic Orientation:** Twin Cities

**Sample Grant:**
St. Paul Academy/Summit School—$50,000

**Financial Data for Year Ending August 31, 1981:**
Assets:  $1,067,132
Grants Paid:  $50,000
Number of Grants:  1

**Paid Professional Staff:** No

**Trustee:** First Trust Company of St. Paul

# JOSEPH N. LARSON FOUNDATION

c/o Northwestern National Bank of Minneapolis Trust
Tax Division
Seventh and Marquette
Minneapolis, MN 55479

**Established:** October 1971

**Type:** Private foundation

**Financial Data for Year Ending March 31, 1981:**
Assets:  $249,576
Grants Paid:  $0

**Paid Professional Staff:** No

**Trustee:** Northwestern National Bank of Minneapolis

# THE LEAVITT FOUNDATION

512 Sibley Street
St. Paul, MN 55101

**Established:** August 1953 (as Jerome Hirsh Foundation)

**Type:** Private foundation

**Geographic Orientation:** Minnesota

**Sample Grants:**
United Jewish Fund and Council, St. Paul—$16,000
University of Minnesota Foundation—$1,100
Viking Council, BSA—$150

**Financial Data for Year Ending March 31, 1982:**
Assets:  $82,417
Grants Paid:  $33,425
Number of Grants:  30
Largest/Smallest:  $16,000/$25

**Paid Professional Staff:** No

**Directors/Trustees:** Charles L. Leavitt, Jr.; Ella Hirsh;
Helen H. Leavitt

# LEIFMAN MEMORIAL FOUNDATION

1500 American National Bank Building
St. Paul, MN 55101

**Established:** November 1952

**Type:** Private foundation

**Geographic Orientation:** Twin Cities

**Sample Grant:**
  Sholom Home—$3,000

**Financial Data for Year Ending December 31, 1981:**
  Assets: $13,088
  Grants Paid: $3,000
  Number of Grants: 1

**Paid Professional Staff:** No

**Director/Trustee:** Herbert L. Leifman, manager


# LEISURE DYNAMICS FOUNDATION

4400 West Seventy-eighth Street
Minneapolis, MN 55435

**Established:** October 1976

**Type:** Corporate foundation

**Geographic Orientation:** National

**Sample Grants:**
  Harvard University Business School—$5,000
  Phoenix House—$2,000
  Walker Art Center—$250

**Financial Data for Year Ending December 31, 1981:**
  Assets: $495,727
  Grants Paid: $30,050
  Number of Grants: 20
  Largest/Smallest: $5,000/$100

**Paid Professional Staff:** No

**Directors/Trustees:** Louis F. Polk, Jr., president; Louis F. Polk, Sr., vice-president; Dyanne R. Holmes, treasurer; Richard N. Flint, secretary


# LERNER FOUNDATION

241 First Avenue North
Minneapolis, MN 55401

**Established:** September 1968

**Type:** Private foundation

**Geographic Orientation:** Twin Cities; national

**Sample Grants:**
  American Jewish Committee—$3,498
  American Cancer Society—$1,100
  Minnesota March of Dimes—$25

**Financial Data for Year Ending August 31, 1981:**
  Assets: $25,509
  Grants Paid: $15,043
  Number of Grants: 53
  Largest/Smallest: $3,498/$10

**Paid Professional Staff:** No
**Director/Trustee:** Harry J. Lerner


# GEORGE AND MARION LEVINE FOUNDATION

5005 Cedar Lake Road
Minneapolis, MN 55416

**Established:** June 1964

**Type:** Private foundation

**Financial Data for Year Ending December 31, 1981:**
  Assets: $16,942
  Grants Paid: $0

**Paid Professional Staff:** No

**Directors/Trustees:** M. Levine, president; R. Simon, vice-president (from 990-AR, 1980)


# LIEBERMAN-OKINOW FOUNDATION

9549 Penn Avenue South
Minneapolis, MN 55431

**Established:** August 1959

**Type:** Private foundation

**Geographic Orientation:** Twin Cities; national

**Sample Grants:**
  Minneapolis Federation for Jewish Service—$100,000
  United Way of Minneapolis Area—$25,000
  Opportunity Workshop—$400

**Financial Data for Year Ending September 30, 1981:**
  Assets: $3,900
  Grants Paid: $236,402
  Number of Grants: 42
  Largest/Smallest: $100,000/$10

**Paid Professional Staff:** No

**Directors/Trustees:** Adele Lieberman, president; David Lieberman, vice-president; Stephen Lieberman, secretary; Harold Okinow, treasurer


# RICHARD COYLE LILLY FOUNDATION

c/o First Trust Company of St. Paul
W-555 First National Bank Building
St. Paul, MN 55101
(612) 291-5061

**Contact Person:** Thomas H. Patterson

**Type:** Private foundation

**Program's Limits:** No grants to individuals or to organizations that require expenditure responsibility

**Geographic Orientation:** National

**Sample Grants:**
  Carleton College—$65,000
  Catholic Services for the Elderly—$25,000
  Walker Art Center—$5,000

**Financial Data for Year Ending December 31, 1981:**
  Assets:   $2,147,185
  Grants Paid:   $218,600
  Number of Grants:   40
  Largest/Smallest:   $65,000/$500

**Paid Professional Staff:** No

**Contact Made by:** Complete proposal

**Directors/Trustees:** David M. Lilly, president; Elizabeth Lilly, vice-president; Andrew Scott, secretary

## THE HANNAH LIPS FOUNDATION

12 Northeast Second Avenue
Faribault, MN 55021

**Established:** October 1978

**Type:** Private foundation

**Program's Purpose:** "To make grants and gifts to health care service associations, hospitals, medical research programs or organizations"

**Geographic Orientation:** Minnesota

**Sample Grants:**
  St. Lucas Hospital—$15,473
  Rice County District #1 Hospital—$8,000
  Faribault Area Vocational School—$5,000

**Financial Data for Year Ending October 31, 1981:**
  Assets:   $304,633
  Grants Paid:   $34,923
  Number of Grants:   4
  Largest/Smallest:   $15,473/$5,000

**Paid Professional Staff:** No

**Directors/Trustees:** Ruth McCormick; Richard Carlander; Clarence Berg; Gerald Heyer

## LOTUS LAKE FOUNDATION

Box 398
Chanhassen, MN 55317

**Established:** December 1979

**Type:** Private foundation

**Geographic Orientation:** Twin Cities

**Sample Grants:**
  Hopkins Project—$1,000
  Minnesota Association for Children with Learning Disabilities—$200

**Financial Data for Year Ending December 31, 1981:**
  Assets:   $152,743
  Grants Paid:   $1,200
  Number of Grants:   2
  Largest/Smallest:   $1,000/$200

**Paid Professional Staff:** No

**Contact Made by:** Letter of inquiry

**Directors/Trustees:** Robert R. Conklin, president-treasurer; Nadine Conklin, vice-president; Leonard M. Addington, secretary

## RUSSELL T. LUND CHARITABLE TRUST

c/o First National Bank of Minneapolis
120 South Sixth Street
Minneapolis, MN 55402

**Established:** December 1950

**Type:** Private foundation

**Geographic Orientation:** Minnesota

**Sample Grants:**
  Sister Kenny Institute—$10,000
  Tuskegee Institute—$5,000
  WAMSO—$1,000

**Financial Data for Year Ending December 31, 1981:**
  Assets:   $532,924
  Grants Paid:   $56,976
  Number of Grants:   20
  Largest/Smallest:   $10,000/$100

**Paid Professional Staff:** No

**Trustee:** First National Bank of Minneapolis

## THE CARGILL MACMILLAN FAMILY FOUNDATION

c/o D. E. Billbe
Department 28, Box 9300
Minneapolis, MN 55440

**Established:** November 1961

**Type:** Private foundation

**Geographic Orientation:** Minnesota; national

**Sample Grants:**
  Stearns County Historical Society—$1,600
  National Audubon Society—$200
  Lupus Foundation—$50

**Financial Data for Year Ending December 31, 1981:**
  Assets:   $122,896
  Grants Paid:   $10,610
  Number of Grants:   40
  Largest/Smallest:   $1,600/$25

**Paid Professional Staff:** No

## GEORGE A. MACPHERSON FUND

c/o First Trust Company of St. Paul
W-555 First National Bank Building
St. Paul, MN 55101
(612) 291-5128

**Contact Person:** John L. Jerry

**Established:** November 1954

**Type:** Private foundation

**Program's Limits:** No grants to individuals

**Geographic Orientation:** St. Paul area

**Sample Grants:**
  Macalester College—$15,098
  Minnesota Historical Society—$15,098
  Saint John's University—$15,098

**Financial Data for Year Ending December 31, 1981:**
  Assets: $627,818
  Grants Paid: $45,296
  Number of Grants: 3

**Paid Professional Staff:** No

**Contact Made by:** Complete proposal

**Directors/Trustees:** Oliver W. Hedeen; Pierce Butler; Dr. John B. Davis

## MALAKOFF FOUNDATION

Suite 1350
100 Washington Square
Minneapolis, MN 55401

**Established:** December 1964

**Type:** Private foundation

**Geographic Orientation:** Minnesota; Iowa

**Sample Grants:**
  Micah Corporation—$21,735
  Amnesty International—$1,000
  Minneapolis Public Library—$250

**Financial Data for Year Ending December 31, 1981:**
  Assets: $195,832
  Grants Paid: $78,580
  Number of Grants: 10
  Largest/Smallest: $21,735/$50

**Paid Professional Staff:** No

**Directors/Trustees:** Bernard Mercer, president; Chad L. Hensley, vice-president; Sheldon Karlins, secretary-treasurer

## MALESKA ROTHFORK FAMILY FOUNDATION

Box 176
224 First Street South
Melrose, MN 56352

**Established:** October 1978

**Type:** Private foundation

**Financial Data for Year Ending August 31, 1981:**
  Assets: $197,193
  Grants Paid: $0

**Paid Professional Staff:** No

**Director/Trustee:** Frank Maleska

## MANITOU FUND

444 Lafayette Road
St. Paul, MN 55101

**Established:** January 1966

**Type:** Private foundation

**Geographic Orientation:** Minnesota; California

**Sample Grants:**
  Community Hospital of Monterey Peninsula—$5,000
  Guthrie Theater—$1,000
  Mzuri Safari Foundation—$200

**Financial Data for Year Ending December 31, 1981:**
  Assets: $807,103
  Grants Paid: $21,125
  Number of Grants: 51
  Largest/Smallest: $5,000/$25

**Paid Professional Staff:** No

**Directors/Trustees:** Donald C. McNeely; Marjorie R. McNeely

## MANKATO CITIZENS TELEPHONE COMPANY FOUNDATION

Box 3248
221 East Hickory Street
Mankato, MN 56002

**Established:** December 1962

**Type:** Corporate foundation

**Geographic Orientation:** Southern Minnesota

**Sample Grants:**
  University Associates, Mankato State University—$7,200
  Twin Valley Council, BSA—$3,000
  Fellowship of Christian Athletes—$100

**Financial Data for Year Ending February 28, 1982:**
  Assets: $369,101
  Grants Paid: $37,046
  Number of Grants: 26
  Largest/Smallest: $7,200/$50

**Paid Professional Staff:** No

**Directors/Trustees:** Paul L. Stevens, president; Thomas R. Borchert, vice-president; David R. Lindenberg, secretary-treasurer

## • MARBROOK FOUNDATION

510 Baker Building
Minneapolis, MN 55403
(612) 332-2454

**Contact Person:** Conley Brooks, executive director

**Established:** November 1948

**Type:** Private foundation

**Program's Purpose:** To promote broad philanthropic objectives through grants and investments in the areas of health and medicine, education, social welfare, visual and performing arts, conservation, and recreation

**Geographic Orientation:** Twin Cities; Minnesota

**Fields of Activity:** Arts/architecture; history/preservation; media/communications; music/opera; theater/dance; arts education; elementary/secondary education; vocational education; higher education; medical research; medical care/treatment; medical/health education; mental health; business/economic education; community affairs; crime/law enforcement; economic development; employment/job training; environment/energy; family services; recreation

**Types of Organizations Funded:** Museums/historical societies; theaters/dance groups; music/opera groups; public television/radio; arts councils; historic preservation; elementary schools; secondary schools; vocational schools; colleges; universities; educational councils; special education; hospitals; medical schools; clinics; family-planning agencies; counseling services; conservation groups; United Way; multiservice centers; organizations for the handicapped; organizations for women; organizations for drug abusers; organizations for youth; centers for children; organizations for offenders

**Types of Support for Organizations:** Capital support; continuing support; general operating support; matching grants; program development; federated fund drives; program-related investments

**Sample Grants:**
Breck School Business/Economics Project—$7,500
Business Economic Education Foundation—$2,000
The Neighborhood Center—$1,000

**Financial Data for Year Ending December 31, 1981:**
Assets:   $3,150,259
Grants Paid:   $250,550
Number of Grants:   59
Largest/Smallest:   $22,000/$250

**Paid Professional Staff:** No

**Contact Made by:** Letter of inquiry

**Available by Request:** Annual report

**Proposal Deadlines:** April 15 and October 15

**Board Meetings:** Biannual, in May and November

**Applicants Notified:** Within three weeks of decision

**Directors/Trustees:** Conley Brooks, executive director; John E. Andrus III; Conley Brooks, Jr.; William R. Humphrey, Jr.

## • MARDAG FOUNDATION

1120 Northwestern National Bank Building
St. Paul, MN 55101
(612) 224-5463

**Contact Person:** Paul A. Verret, secretary

**Established:** 1969

**Type:** Private foundation

**Program's Limits:** Giving limited to Minnesota; no grants to individuals; generally no grants to endowment funds or sectarian religious programs

**Geographic Orientation:** Minnesota

**Fields of Activity:** Arts/architecture; history/preservation; music/opera; theater/dance; arts education; other arts and humanities; elementary/secondary education; vocational education; higher education; adult/continuing education; other education; public health; life sciences; physical sciences; social sciences; community affairs; crime/law enforcement; drug-abuse programs; economic development; employment/job training; environment/energy; family services; welfare; other welfare/social services

**Types of Organizations Funded:** Museums/historical societies; theaters/dance groups; music/opera groups; libraries; zoos; public television/radio; arts councils; historic preservation; cultural centers; other arts and humanities organizations; elementary schools; secondary schools; vocational schools; colleges; universities; special education; adult education; libraries; other educational organizations; hospitals; medical schools; chemical dependency services; counseling services; environmental agencies; energy agencies; conservation groups; other science/social science organizations; United Way; multiservice centers; organizations for the elderly; organizations for the handicapped; organizations for women; organizations for drug abusers; organizations for youth; centers for children; housing agencies; organizations for offenders; organizations for minorities; neighborhood agencies; day-care centers; community centers; other welfare/social service organizations

**Targeted Population Group:** Aged

**Types of Support for Organizations:** Capital support; matching grants; program development; federated fund drives; program-related investments

**Sample Grants:**
University of Minnesota Raptor Research and Rehabilitation—$15,000
City of Bagley Senior Center—$10,000
Mainstay (employment counselor)—$7,424

**Financial Data for Year Ending December 31, 1981:**
Assets: $10,905,768
Grants Paid: $634,822
Number of Grants: 53
Largest/Smallest: $100,000/$900

**Paid Professional Staff:** Yes

**Contact Made by:** Request for guidelines

**Available by Request:** Proposal guidelines; application procedures; annual report

**Proposal Deadlines:** Two months prior to board meetings

**Board Meetings:** Quarterly

**Applicants Notified:** Within two weeks of decision

**Directors/Trustees:** Thomas G. Mairs, principal officer; Stephen S. Ober, financial officer; James E. Davidson; Virginia D. Iverson; Edgar B. Ober, Jr.

# MARTIN HOMES FOUNDATION

6901 West Old Shakopee Road
Bloomington, MN 55438

**Established:** December 1976

**Type:** Corporate foundation

**Geographic Orientation:** Twin Cities

**Sample Grants:**
Camp Ramah—$500
Neighborhood House—$200
National Association to Ban Handguns—$25

**Financial Data for Year Ending December 31, 1981:**
Assets: $134
Grants Paid: $975
Number of Grants: 6
Largest/Smallest: $500/$25

**Paid Professional Staff:** No

**Directors/Trustees:** Martin Capp; Robert S. Bein; Joel S. Bernick

# MASLON FOUNDATION

1800 Midwest Plaza Building
Minneapolis, MN 55442

**Established:** December 1955

**Type:** Private foundation

**Geographic Orientation:** National; international

**Sample Grants:**
Minnesota Orchestral Association—$11,250
Palm Springs Desert Museum—$3,900
Mount Sinai Hospital Association—$1,000

**Financial Data for Year Ending December 31, 1981:**
Assets: $403,375
Grants Paid: $66,499
Number of Grants: 81
Largest/Smallest: $11,250/$12

**Paid Professional Staff:** No

**Directors/Trustees:** Samuel H. Maslon, president; Luella R. Maslon, treasurer; James I. Maslon, vice-president; Enid M. Starr, vice-president; F. S. Sigal, secretary

# MCFARLAND FOUNDATION

Suite 450
10,000 Highway 55 West
Minneapolis, MN 55441

**Established:** September 1969

**Type:** Private foundation

**Geographic Orientation:** Twin Cities

**Sample Grants:**
St. Martins by the Lake Episcopal Church—$700
Amos Tuck School—$400
Boys' Clubs of Minneapolis—$200

**Financial Data for Year Ending December 31, 1981:**
Assets: $17,719
Grants Paid: $1,300
Number of Grants: 3
Largest/Smallest: $700/$200

**Paid Professional Staff:** No

**Directors/Trustees:** James P. McFarland, president; Shirley F. McFarland, secretary; Ruth A. Meyer, assistant treasurer; T. R. Anderson, treasurer

# • THE MCKNIGHT FOUNDATION

410 Peavey Building
730-Second Avenue South
Minneapolis, MN 55402
(612) 333-4220

**Contact Person:** Russell V. Ewald, executive vice-president

**Established:** August 1953

**Type:** Private foundation

**Program's Purpose:** To concentrate on making general grants in the area of human service programming

**Program's Limits:** No grants to individuals, religious organizations for religious purposes, fund raisers, or conferences

**Geographic Orientation:** Seven-county Twin Cities metropolitan area (primary focus); outstate Minnesota

**Fields of Activity\*:** Arts Funding Plan (contact the foundation directly for information); public elementary/secondary education; vocational education; higher private education (contact the foundation for specific guidelines); medical care/treatment; public health; mental health; life sciences; advocacy; community affairs; crime/law enforcement; economic development; employment/job training; equal rights/legal aid; family services; Comprehensive Program in Developmental Disabilities (contact the foundation directly for information); special population groups

**Types of Organizations Funded\*:** Public television/radio; public elementary schools; public secondary schools; colleges; universities; special education; community clinics; family-planning agencies; counseling services; conservation groups; United Way; legal aid; multiservice centers; organizations for the elderly; organizations for the handicapped; organizations for women; organizations for youth; centers for children; housing agencies; organizations for offenders; organizations for minorities; neighborhood agencies; community centers

**Targeted Population Groups\*:** Aged; children/youth; criminal offenders/exoffenders; developmentally disabled; mentally ill; women/girls (battered, sexually abused women); refugees; Asian Americans; blacks; Hispanics; native Americans

**Types of Support for Organizations:** Capital support; endowment; general operating support; matching grants; program development; research; federated fund drives

**Financial Data for Year Ending December 31, 1981:**
Assets: $338,143,248
Grants Paid: $24,796,148
Largest/Smallest: $5,000,000/$591

**Paid Professional Staff:** Yes

**Contact Made by:** Telephone inquiry or letter of inquiry

**Available by Request:** Proposal guidelines; annual report

**Proposal Deadlines:** Two and a half months before board meetings

**Board Meetings:** Quarterly, in February, May, August, and November

**Applicants Notified:** Within one week of decision

**Directors:** Virginia M. Binger, president; James H. Binger, treasurer; Russell V. Ewald, executive vice-president; Judith Binger; James M. Binger; Cynthia Boynton

\*The McKnight Foundation has a number of comprehensive programs; contact the foundation for specific information about current programs and guidelines.

# • THE SUMNER T. MCKNIGHT FOUNDATION

c/o Northwestern National Bank of Minneapolis
Seventh and Marquette
Minneapolis, MN 55479

**Contact Persons:** Malcolm G. Pfunder, secretary (phone: 612-332-6080); Iva Kroeger, executive secretary (phone: 612-448-3035)

**Established:** December 1956

**Type:** Private foundation

**Program's Purpose:** To support organizations with primary interests in education, culture, health and education, environment, and aid to the disadvantaged

**Program's Limits:** No grants to individuals, to organizations for political purposes, to endowments or to capital campaigns, for trips or tours, or for religious purposes

**Geographic Orientation:** Minneapolis; Baltimore, MD; areas where directors are located

**Fields of Activity:** Arts/architecture; vocational education; medical care/treatment; public health; mental health

**Types of Organizations Funded:** Museums/historical societies; zoos; vocational schools; chemical dependency services; other health organizations; environmental agencies; United Way; organizations for veterans; organizations for drug abusers; neighborhood agencies

**Types of Support for Organizations:** Continuing support; general operating support; matching grants

**Type of Support for Individuals:** Aid to needy persons

**Financial Data for Year Ending December 31, 1981:**
Assets: $2,772,434
Grants Paid: $166,850 ($51,583—inner-city programs; $50,833—educational programs; $50,000—environmental programs; $14,434—health programs)
Number of Grants: 27
Largest/Smallest: $50,000/$600

**Paid Professional Staff:** No

**Contact Made by:** Complete proposal

**Available by Request:** Annual report

**Proposal Deadlines:** At least six weeks prior to meetings held in January, April, and October

**Applicants Notified:** Within two weeks of decision

**Directors:** H. Turney McKnight, president; Peter A. Heegaard, vice-president; Sumner T. McKnight II, vice-president; Eugene F. Trumble, vice-president; Malcolm G. Pfunder, secretary-treasurer; Duane E. Joseph, counsel; Christina McKnight Kippen; Russell B. Jones, Jr.; John T. Westrom; Wheelock Whitney

# THE MCNEELY FOUNDATION

444 Lafayette Road
St. Paul, MN 55101

**Established:** December 1980

**Type:** Private foundation

**Geographic Orientation:** Minnesota

**Sample Grants:**
College of Saint Thomas—$40,000
United Way of St. Paul—$12,333
Homeward Bound—$50

**Financial Data for Year Ending December 31, 1981:**
    Assets: $2,627,316
    Grants Paid: $99,841
    Number of Grants: 162
    Largest/Smallest: $40,000/$50

**Paid Professional Staff:** No

**Directors/Trustees:** Harry G. McNeely; Gregory McNeely; Frank A. Koscielak; Adelaide F. McNeely

## MCQUAY-PERFEX FOUNDATION OF MINNESOTA

5401 Gamble Drive
Box 9316
Minneapolis, MN 55440

**Established:** October 1976

**Type:** Corporate foundation

**Geographic Orientation:** National

**Sample Grants:**
    United Way of the Minneapolis Area—$32,500
    Dunwoody Industrial Institute—$8,500
    Camp New Hope—$1,000

**Financial Data for Year Ending December 31, 1981:**
    Assets: $27,727
    Grants Paid: $168,621
    Number of Grants: 78 (includes matching grants)
    Largest/Smallest: $32,500/$25

**Paid Professional Staff:** No

**Directors/Trustees:** Daniel K. Sewell, president; Earl T. Lyons, vice-president; Carl O. Steinnagel, vice-president; Walter H. Robilliard, treasurer; Jay R. Resch, secretary

## MEDICLINICS EDUCATIONAL FUND

2000 Midwest Plaza Building
Minneapolis, MN 55402

**Established:** May 1971

**Type:** Corporate foundation

**Program's Purpose:** To work toward "supporting education by contributions to existing educational institutions, endowing a professional chair, contributing to an educational institution to enable it to carry on research, awarding scholarships and making loans"

**Geographic Orientation:** International

**Sample Grants:**
    University of Minnesota—$35,000
    British Orthopaedic Association—$2,000
    Peer Education—$1,000

**Financial Data for Year Ending April 30, 1981:**
    Assets: $296,804
    Grants Paid: $39,500
    Number of Grants: 4
    Largest/Smallest: $35,000/$1,000

**Paid Professional Staff:** No

**Directors/Trustees:** Karl F. Diessner, president; Dr. Harold F. Buchstein, secretary-treasurer; Dr. Donald R. Lanin, vice-president

## • THE MEDTRONIC FOUNDATION

Box 1453
Minneapolis, MN 55440
(612) 574-3024

**Contact Person:** Jan Schwarz, manager

**Established:** 1977

**Type:** Corporate foundation

**Program's Purpose:** To make contributions concentrated on programs that improve the quality of life for the elderly, provide education in fields related to Medtronic businesses, promote cardiovascular and neuromuscular health

**Program's Limits:** Capital requests, special events, fund raisers, and advertising generally not considered; only youth programs related to areas of interest

**Geographic Orientation:** Communities where Medtronic operations are located

**Fields of Activity:** Arts/architecture; language/literature; music/opera; theater/dance; educational activities; medical/health education; health activities; life sciences; physical sciences; business/economic education; employment/job training; equal rights/legal aid; special population groups

**Types of Organizations Funded:** Museums/historical societies; theaters/dance groups; music/opera groups; public television/radio; cultural centers; educational organizations; clinics; health organizations; religious service groups; United Way; legal aid; organizations for the elderly; organizations for the handicapped; organizations for minorities

**Targeted Population Groups:** Aged; handicapped

**Types of Support for Organizations:** General operating support; matching grants; program development

**Sample Grants:**
    Metro Community Health Consortium, Minneapolis—$10,000
    National Medical Fellowships, New York (scholarships for minority medical students)—$5,000
    Coffeehouse Extempore, Minneapolis (series of concerts for senior citizens)—$2,000

**Financial Data for Year Ending April 30, 1982:**
Assets: $1,683,224
Grants Paid: $756,337
Number of Grants: 135
Largest/Smallest: $50,000 (other than United Way)/$500

**Paid Professional Staff:** Yes

**Contact Made by:** Telephone inquiry

**Available by Request:** Application procedures

**Directors/Trustees:** Lowell P. Jacobsen, chairman; Raymond Dittrich, vice-chairman; B. Kristine Johnson, treasurer; Donald Stone, secretary; Peter Mulier; David L. Duclos; Lawrence W. Shearon; Kent VanKampen; John A. Meslow

## MELAMED FOUNDATION

820 Midwest Plaza Building
Minneapolis, MN 55402

**Established:** December 1947

**Type:** Private foundation

**Geographic Orientation:** National

**Sample Grants:**
Minneapolis Federation for Jewish Service—$45,000
Yale University—$15,000
Music of the Baroque—$500

**Financial Data for Year Ending December 31, 1981:**
Assets: $632,153
Grants Paid: $97,475
Number of Grants: 65
Largest/Smallest: $45,000/$5

**Paid Professional Staff:** No

**Directors/Trustees:** Arthur C. Melamed, president-treasurer; Ruth Melamed, vice-president/secretary; Arthur D. Melamed, vice-president; Robert L. Melamed, vice-president; Irene Petersen, assistant secretary

## ROY E. AND MERLE MEYER FOUNDATION

Suite M-101
408 Main Street
Red Wing, MN 55066

**Established:** November 1967

**Type:** Private foundation

**Program's Limits:** No grants to building funds

**Geographic Orientation:** Red Wing area

**Sample Grants:**
Northwestern Lutheran Theological Seminary, St. Paul (scholarship)—$750
Citizens Action Council—$750
A.R.C. Retreat Community, Stanchfield, MN—$500

**Financial Data for Year Ending December 31, 1981:**
Assets: $72,843
Grants Paid: $6,250
Number of Grants: 10
Largest/Smallest: $750/$500

**Paid Professional Staff:** No

**Directors/Trustees:** Roy E. Meyer, president; Merle Meyer, secretary; Carolyn Mahn; Judith Penniman

## BENJAMIN A. MILLER FAMILY FOUNDATION

500 Pillsbury Center
Minneapolis, MN 55402

**Established:** December 1953 (as The Miller Foundation of Winona)

**Type:** Private foundation

**Geographic Orientation:** Minnesota

**Sample Grants:**
St. Paul Foundation—$1,000,000
YMCA—$14,000
Minnesota Private College Fund—$1,200

**Financial Data for Year Ending November 30, 1981:**
Assets: $15,360
Grants Paid: $1,029,000
Number of Grants: 5
Largest/Smallest: $1,000,000/$1,200

**Paid Professional Staff:** No

**Directors/Trustees:** B. A. Miller; R. W. Miller, M. A. Goldberg

## THE GLADYS AND RUDOLPH MILLER FOUNDATION

5007 Hyatt Regency Mart
Minneapolis, MN 55403

**Established:** December 1980

**Type:** Private foundation

**Geographic Orientation:** National

**Sample Grants:**
Mount Sinai Hospital—$27,879
Sloan Kettering Cancer Center—$25,000
Minnesota Dance Theatre—$200

**Financial Data for Year Ending November 30, 1981:**
Assets: $1,022,032
Grants Paid: $111,929
Number of Grants: 11
Largest/Smallest: $27,879/$200

**Paid Professional Staff:** No

**Director/Trustee:** Rudolph W. Miller, president

# SAM MILLER FOUNDATION

861 East Hennepin Avenue
Minneapolis, MN 55403

**Established:** July 1964

**Type:** Private foundation

**Geographic Orientation:** Twin Cities

**Sample Grants:**
Mount Sinai Hospital—$50,200
United Way—$1,400
United Arts Fund—$25

**Financial Data for Year Ending December 31, 1981:**
Assets: $657,589
Grants Paid: $118,689
Number of Grants: 41
Largest/Smallest: $50,200/$5

**Paid Professional Staff:** No

**Directors/Trustees:** Martin Miller, manager; Ben Miller; Beryl Miller

# • THE MINNEAPOLIS FOUNDATION

500 Foshay Tower
Minneapolis, MN 55402
(612) 339-7343

**Contact Person:** Thomas F. Beech, executive director

**Established:** 1915

**Type:** Community foundation

**Program's Purpose:** To administer funds entrusted to the foundation to assist the needy, to improve living conditions, to further education, and to support other beneficial activities in the community; highest priority to support projects that deal with the underlying causes of community needs; lower priority to support projects that deal with symptoms of such needs

**Program's Limits:** Grants restricted to the seven-county metropolitan area; foundation tends to concentrate on one-time, one-year grants for projects or programs that address emerging community needs; as a general rule, undesignated funds are not used for grants to general operating budgets, for basic research, or for capital or construction purposes

**Geographic Orientation:** Seven-county metropolitan area

**Fields of Activity:** Arts/architecture; media/communications; music/opera; theater/dance; arts education; elementary/secondary education; vocational education; higher education; adult/continuing education; medical care/treatment; medical/health education; mental health; advocacy; community affairs; crime/law enforcement; drug-abuse programs; economic development; employment/job training; equal rights/legal aid; family services; special population groups; welfare

**Types of Organizations Funded:** Theaters/dance groups; music/opera groups; public television/radio; cultural centers; elementary schools; secondary schools; vocational schools; colleges; universities; special education; adult education; junior colleges; clinics; chemical dependency services; family-planning agencies; counseling services; religious service groups; United Way; legal aid; multiservice centers; organizations for the elderly; organizations for the handicapped; organizations for women; organizations for drug abusers; organizations for youth; organizations for men; centers for children; housing agencies; organizations for offenders; organizations for minorities; neighborhood agencies; day-care centers; community centers

**Type of Support for Organizations:** Program development

**Type of Support for Individuals:** Aid to needy persons upon referral from a nonprofit agency

**Sample Grants:**
Beltrami Health Center (to establish a volunteer program)—$10,000
Project for Pride in Living (for start-up funding for a business that will employ low-income people)—$5,400
Minnesota Literacy Council (to improve and expand volunteer tutoring services to non-English-speaking adults)—$5,000

**Financial Data for Year Ending March 31, 1982:**
Assets: $23,417,664
Grants Paid: $2,417,664 ($424,956 from undesignated funds)
Number of Grants: 52 (from undesignated funds)
Largest/Smallest: $20,000/$2,500 (from undesignated funds)

**Paid Professional Staff:** Yes

**Contact Made by:** Telephone inquiry; letter of inquiry

**Available by Request:** Proposal guidelines; application procedures; annual report

**Board Meetings:** Quarterly, in June, September, December, and March

**Applicants Notified:** Within one week of decision

**Directors/Trustees:** Conley Brooks, president; Marvin Borman, vice-president; Edward C. Lund, vice-president; Frances Naftalin, vice-president; Clinton Morrison, treasurer; Thomas F. Beech, assistant treasurer; Richard A. Nordbye, secretary; Thomas M. Crosby, assistant secretary

## • MINNEAPOLIS KIWANIS FOUNDATION

Leamington Hotel
Minneapolis, MN 55404

**Established:** 1941

**Type of Foundation:** Private foundation

**Geographic Orientation:** Twin Cities

**Sample Grants:**
Minneapolis Society for the Blind—$5,000
Hospitality House—$2,000
Chemical Abuse Center—$500

**Financial Data for Year Ending September 30, 1981:**
Assets: $210,264
Grants Paid: $24,898
Number of Grants: 24
Largest/Smallest: $5,000/$500

**Paid Professional Staff:** No

**Directors/Trustees:** Vincent Abramson, president; John Jerrard, vice-president; John P. Montgomery, secretary; Lloyd O. Swanson, treasurer

## • MINNEAPOLIS STAR AND TRIBUNE FOUNDATION

Sixth Floor, IDS Tower
Minneapolis, MN 55402

**Contact Person:** Hazel H. Reinhardt

**Established:** May 1945

**Type:** Corporate foundation

**Geographic Orientation:** Minnesota

**Sample Grants:**
Augsburg College—$70,000
Minneapolis Society of Fine Arts—$40,000
Reporters Committee for the Freedom of the Press, Washington, D.C.—$4,000

**Financial Data for Year Ending February 27, 1982:**
Assets: $898,827
Grants Paid: $421,500
Number of Grants: 18
Largest/Smallest: $70,000/$2,500

**Paid Professional Staff:** No

**Directors/Trustees:** Otto A. Silha, chairman of the board; John Cowles, Jr., president; Michael F. Koch, treasurer; Norton L. Armour, secretary

## MINNESOTA FOUNDATION

1120 Northwestern National Bank Building
St. Paul, MN 55101
(612) 224-5463

**Contact Person:** Paul A. Verret, vice-president

**Established:** 1949

**Type:** Private foundation

**Program's Limits:** Grantees designated by restricted funds; no discretionary grants made

**Geographic Orientation:** Twin Cities; national

**Types of Organizations Funded:** Designated recipients selected by donors

**Type of Support for Organizations:** General operating

**Sample Grants:**
Amherst H. Wilder Foundation for the Eisenmenger Learning Center—$120,000
Friends of the St. Paul Public Library, continuing education—$5,000
Communications Center, Radio Talking Book Program—$50

**Financial Data for Year Ending June 30, 1981:**
Assets: $2,880,374
Grants Paid: $157,879
Number of Grants: 23
Largest/Smallest: $93,000/$19

**Paid Professional Staff:** Yes

**Directors/Trustees:** Frank Hammond, chairman; G. Richard Slade, first vice-chairman; James C. Otis, second vice-chairman; H. James Seesel, Jr., treasurer; Leonard H. Wilkening, president/secretary; Elisabeth W. Doermann; Elizabeth M. Kiernat; David M. Lilly; Malcolm W. McDonald; Mary Bigelow McMillan

## MINNESOTA MASONIC FOUNDATION

200 East Plato Boulevard
St. Paul, MN 55107

**Established:** December 1971

**Type:** Independent foundation

**Geographic Orientation:** Twin Cities

**Sample Grants:**
St. Louis Park Medical Center Research Foundation—$3,000
Le Sueur JC Women's LaFond Fund—$1,000
Scholarship (for individual)—$500

**Financial Data for Year Ending February 28, 1982:**
Assets: $89,862
Grants Paid: $5,500
Number of Grants: 5
Largest/Smallest: $3,000/$500

**Paid Professional Staff:** No

**Contact Made by:** Letter of inquiry

**Applicants Notified:** Within twelve weeks

**Directors/Trustees:** Lyman M. Moore, president; Robert S. Johnsen, secretary; Frederick B. Vihovde, treasurer

# • MINNESOTA MUTUAL LIFE CHARITABLE TRUST

400 North Robert Street
St. Paul, MN 55116
(612) 298-3501

**Contact Person:** William J. Smith

**Established:** July 1979

**Type:** Corporate trust

**Program's Limits:** Generally, no contributions to endowment funds; most gifts to Minnesota organizations, with Twin Cities emphasis; in field of education, private colleges preferred except where program can only be provided through a tax-supported facility; organizations preferably supported through federated campaigns, but grants to new organizations or to organizations whose purposes are not embraced by a federated program considered

**Geographic Orientation:** Twin Cities; Minnesota; national (in a limited way)

**Fields of Activity:** History/preservation; media/communications; music/opera; theater; higher education; medical research; medical/health education; life sciences; advocacy; business/economic education; community affairs; crime/law enforcement; drug-abuse programs; economic development; employment/job training; equal·rights/legal aid; family services; safety; special population groups; welfare

**Types of Organizations Funded:** Museums/historical societies; theaters; music/opera groups; zoos; public television/radio; arts councils; historic preservation; colleges; universities; medical schools; medical research groups; clinics; chemical dependency services; health referral organizations; research/study institutes—science/social science; United Way; organizations for the elderly; organizations for the handicapped; organizations for drug abusers; organizations for youth; centers for children; housing agencies; organizations for offenders; organizations for minorities

**Types of Support for Organizations:** Capital support; continuing support; general operating support; program development; research; federated fund drives

**Sample Grants:**
United Way—$76,000
Minnesota Orchestra—$10,000
Science Museum of Minnesota—$5,000

**Financial Data for Year Ending December 31, 1981:**
Assets: $3,500,000
Grants Paid: $297,927
Number of Grants: 90
Largest/Smallest: $76,000/$250

**Paid Professional Staff:** Yes

**Contact Made by:** Telephone inquiry; complete proposal

**Available by Request:** Proposal guidelines

**Board Meetings:** Quarterly, in March, June, September, and December

**Applicants Notified:** Within one week of decision

**Trustees:** Coleman Bloomfield, president; Joe Bird, vice-president; Keith Campbell, vice-president

**Contributions Committee:** Keith Campbell, chairman; Dr. Warren Kleinsasser; Milt Hildebrandt

## MINNESOTA NATURAL FOUNDATION

c/o E. H. Swetman, Jr.
Minnesota Gas Company
733 Marquette Avenue
Minneapolis, MN 55402

**Established:** May 1971

**Type:** Corporate foundation

**Geographic Orientation:** Minnesota

**Sample Grants:**
Greater Mankato United Way—$3,500
Senior Citizens Center, Mankato—$2,500
Minnesota Historical Society—$200

**Financial Data for Year Ending June 30, 1981:**
Assets: $63,464
Grants Paid: $20,415
Number of Grants: 23
Largest/Smallest: $3,500/$120

**Paid Professional Staff:** No

**Directors/Trustees:** E. H. Swetman, president; L. W. Albrecht, vice-president; R. A. Ellingson, vice-president; A. L. Gessner, secretary- treasurer

## THE MINNESOTA RUBBER FOUNDATION

3630 Wooddale Avenue
Minneapolis, MN 55416

**Established:** February 1979

**Type:** Corporate foundation

**Geographic Orientation:** National

**Sample Grants:**
United Way of Minneapolis—$11,996
Methodist Hospital Foundation—$5,000
Climb—$200

**Financial Data for Year Ending December 31, 1981:**
Assets: $240,452
Grants Paid: $41,723
Number of Grants: 71
Largest/Smallest: $11,996/$25

**Paid Professional Staff:** No

**Directors/Trustees:** Robert Carlson, president; Floyd Vincent, administrative assistant; David Koenig, vice president-secretary; Robert Dye, treasurer

# MINNESOTA STATE BAR FOUNDATION

Minnesota Bar Center
Suite 403
430 Marquette Avenue
Minneapolis, MN 55401
(612) 333-1183

**Contact Person:** George King, president

**Established:** December 1932

**Program's Purpose:** To make grants to programs and causes that attract the special interest and support of Minnesota's lawyers, including programs of law-related education, legal assistance to the poor and disadvantaged groups, programs designed to improve the administration of justice, and programs supporting or promoting public interest legal work

**Geographic Orientation:** Minnesota

**Fields of Activity:** Law-related education or legal education at all levels; drug-abuse programs (Lawyers Concerned for Lawyers); equal rights/legal aid; legal assistance; administration of justice

**Types of Organizations Funded:** Libraries; scholarship funds; chemical dependency services (Lawyers Concerned for Lawyers); legal aid; organizations with programs relating to legal rights of specific groups (e.g., Hmongs' tenants' rights handbook)

**Types of Support for Organizations:** Continuing support; general operating support; matching grants; program development; program-related investments

**Type of Support for Individuals:** Scholarships

**Sample Grants:**
Tel-Law Program—$7,597
Child Abuse Workshops, Young Lawyers Section, Minnesota State Bar Association—$5,000
Minnesota State Law Library—$4,500

**Financial Data for Year Ending December 31, 1981:**
Assets: $355,976
Grants Paid: $38,597
Number of Grants: 9
Largest/Smallest: $7,597/$1,000

**Paid Professional Staff:** No

**Contact Made by:** Complete proposal

**Available by Request:** Annual report; financial statement; mission statement; articles and bylaws

**Proposal Deadlines:** Ten days before meetings so proposal can be circulated

**Board Meetings:** Quarterly, in March, June, September, and December

**Directors/Trustees:** George C. King, president; Christie B. Eller, vice-president/treasurer; James H. Martin, secretary; C. Blaine Harstad; Robert F. Eaton, Jr.; Sheldon Larson; Elton A. Kuderer; Cara Lee Neville; Robert J. Sheran; Richard L. Pemberton

# MINNESOTA TITLE FOUNDATION

400 Second Avenue South
Minneapolis, MN 55401
(612) 371-1199

**Contact Person:** Pat Kubal, administrative secretary

**Established:** January 1978

**Type:** Corporate foundation

**Program's Purpose:** To contribute to projects and programs benefiting the company, employees, customers, and the market in which the company operates; such programs include those involving the environment, minority needs, special education, community health services, youth programs, and art and cultural activity

**Geographic Orientation:** Within the communities in which the company operates

**Fields of Activity:** Arts/architecture; media/communications; music/opera; theater/dance; higher education; medical research; medical care/treatment; business/economic education; community affairs; crime/law enforcement; employment/job training; family services; recreation; special population groups; welfare

**Types of Organizations Funded:** Museums/historical societies; theaters/dance groups; music/opera groups; libraries; public television/radio; colleges; universities; scholarship funds; hospitals; medical research groups; United Way; multiservice centers; organizations for the handicapped; organizations for drug abusers; organizations for youth; housing agencies

**Sample Grants:**
United Way of the Minneapolis Area—$20,000
William Mitchell College of Law—$2,000
Central Texas Girls Choir—$50

**Financial Data for Year Ending December 31, 1981:**
Assets: $24,137
Grants Paid: $47,259
Number of Grants: 104
Largest/Smallest: $20,000/$25

**Paid Professional Staff:** No

**Contact Made by:** Letter of inquiry

**Board Meetings:** Annual, in February

**Trustees:** C. J. McConville, president; Robert G. Rove, vice-president/secretary; Douglas D. Donovan, executive secretary; John B. Cleaveland, treasurer; Charles G. Gregory, controller; Patsy J. Kubal, administrative secretary; Henry S. Kingman, Jr., chairman; D. H. Ankeny; R. A. Cecchettini

## WILDEY H. MITCHELL FAMILY FOUNDATION

702 Alworth Building
Duluth, MN 55802

**Established:** December 1979

**Type:** Private foundation

**Geographic Orientation:** National

**Sample Grants:**
St. Luke's Hospital, Duluth—$700
Yale Alumni Fund—$400
Culver Military Academy, Indiana—$200

**Financial Data for Year Ending December 31, 1981:**
Assets: $63,043
Grants Paid: $2,900
Number of Grants: 6
Largest/Smallest: $700/$200

**Paid Professional Staff:** No

**Directors/Trustees:** Wildey H. Mitchell, president; Bruce W. Potter, vice-president; James F. French, secretary-treasurer

## MSI FOUNDATION

2 Pine Tree Drive
Arden Hills, MN 55112
(612) 631-7320

**Contact Person:** Jerry M. Friedmann, vice-president, personnel and corporate relations

**Established:** 1980

**Type:** Corporate foundation

**Geographic Orientation:** Twin Cities

**Fields of Activity:** Arts/architecture; music/opera; higher education; research; medical research; community affairs; safety

**Types of Organizations Funded:** Public television/radio; colleges; universities; medical research groups; United Way; organizations for youth; neighborhood agencies

**Types of Support for Organizations:** Capital support; matching grants; federated fund drives

**Sample Grants:**
United Way of the St. Paul Area (capital campaign)—$5,000
University of Minnesota (chair in agriculture)—$5,000
Minnesota Private College Fund—$1,850

**Financial Data for Year Ending December 31, 1981:**
Assets: $612,098
Grants Paid: $35,285
Number of Grants: 21
Largest/Smallest: $23,270/$25

**Paid Professional Staff:** No

**Contact Made by:** Complete proposal

**Available by Request:** Proposal guidelines; application procedures

**Proposal Deadlines:** Proposals usually submitted during last quarter of the year for the next grant year

**Applicants Notified:** Within two weeks of decision

**Directors/Trustees:** Roman N. Eller, president; Jerry M. Friedmann, vice-president; Chester A. Zinn, Jr., secretary; Richard G. Rosel, treasurer

## MTS SYSTEMS CORPORATION

Box 24012
Minneapolis, MN 55424
(612) 937-4000

**Contact Person:** G. N. Butzow, chairman

**Type:** Charitable contributions program

**Program's Interests:** Technical education; business education

**Geographic Orientation:** National

**Fields of Activity:** Research; physical sciences; business/economic education; drug-abuse programs; economic development

**Types of Organizations Funded:** Public television/radio; vocational schools; colleges; universities; scholarship funds; chemical dependency services; United Way; organizations for drug abusers

**Targeted Population Group:** Blacks (one scholarship)

**Employee Matching Gift Programs:** Higher education; United Way; public radio and television; Camp Courage

**Types of Support for Organizations:** Capital support; continuing support; matching grants; program development

**Types of Support for Individuals:** Scholarships; fellowships

**Financial Data for Year Ending December 31, 1982:**
Contributions Paid: $50,000 to $99,000 range

**Contact Made by:** Letter of inquiry

**Contributions Decisions Made:** Primarily in the period October through December

## THE INA AND HARRY MURPHY FOUNDATION

6105 Eden Prairie Road
Edina, MN 55436

**Established:** September 1969

**Type:** Private foundation

**Geographic Orientation:** National

**Sample Grants:**
Massachusetts General Hospital—$2,000
Emory University—$1,000
Freedom Foundation—$75

**Financial Data for Year Ending December 31, 1981:**
  Assets: $59,462
  Grants Paid: $4,985
  Number of Grants: 14
  Largest/Smallest: $2,000/$10

**Paid Professional Staff:** No

**Directors/Trustees:** Ina Reed, secretary-treasurer; Douglas Murphy, vice-chairman; Susan Murphy

## • MWVE FUND

807 Lonsdale Building
Duluth, MN 55802
(612) 722-4757

**Contact Person:** K. E. Maine

**Established:** 1968

**Type:** Private foundation

**Program's Purpose:** To make grants for charitable, religious, and educational purposes

**Geographic Orientation:** Duluth; northeastern Minnesota

**Types of Support for Organizations:** Capital support; continuing support; endowment; general operating support; matching grants; federated fund drives; other

**Type of Support for Individuals:** Scholarships

**Sample Grants:**
  Institute for World Order, New York—$7,000
  Duluth Summer Festival of the Arts—$2,050
  American Indian Fund, AAIA—$50

**Financial Data for Year Ending December 31, 1981:**
  Assets: $31,627
  Grants Paid: $51,273
  Number of Grants: 91
  Largest/Smallest: $7,000/$10

**Paid Professional Staff:** No

**Contact Made by:** Letter of inquiry

**Available by Request:** IRS 990 available in the MWVE Fund's office

**Directors/Trustees:** Mary C. Van Evera; William P. Van Evera

## MYERS FOUNDATION

1200 Town Square
445 Minnesota Street
St. Paul, MN 55101

**Established:** December 1952

**Type:** Private foundation

**Geographic Orientation:** Minnesota

**Sample Grants:**
  St. Paul Chamber Orchestra—$20,000
  Episcopal Church Foundation, New York—$1,000
  Planned Parenthood—$500

**Financial Data for Year Ending December 31, 1981:**
  Assets: $633,307
  Grants Paid: $61,950
  Number of Grants: 33
  Largest/Smallest: $20,000/$100

**Paid Professional Staff:** No

**Directors/Trustees:** John H. Myers, president; Elizabeth B. Myers, vice-president

## • PAUL N. MYERS, JR., FOUNDATION

c/o Taylor, McCaskill & Company
1200 Town Square
445 Minnesota Street
St. Paul, MN 55101
(612) 457-1381

**Contact Person:** Mrs. Paul N. Myers, Jr.

**Established:** December 1966

**Type:** Private foundation

**Geographic Orientation:** Twin Cities

**Fields of Activity:** History/preservation; music/opera; arts education; elementary/secondary education; vocational education; higher education; medical care/treatment; mental health; religious activities; life sciences; physical sciences; social sciences; business/economic education; crime/law enforcement; drug-abuse programs; employment/job training; family services

**Types of Organizations Funded:** Museums/historical societies; music/opera groups; public television/radio; arts councils; historic preservation; cultural centers; elementary schools; secondary schools; colleges; scholarship funds; special education; adult education; hospitals; chemical dependency services; counseling services; religious service groups; religious schools; religious colleges; research/study institutes; environmental agencies; conservation groups; United Way; organizations for drug abusers

**Types of Support for Organizations:** Capital support; continuing support; endowment; general operating support; matching grants; program development; research

**Sample Grants:**
  Minnesota Orchestra Guaranty Fund—$1,700
  Science Museum of Minnesota—$1,500
  New Connections Programs—$1,000

**Financial Data for Year Ending December 31, 1981:**
  Assets: $820,200
  Grants Paid: $60,903
  Number of Grants: 24
  Largest/Smallest: $10,000/$600

**Paid Professional Staff:** No

**Contact Made by:** Complete proposal

**Board Meetings:** Quarterly, in February, May, August, and November

**Applicants Notified:** Within two weeks of decision, following quarterly meeting

**Directors/Trustees:** Genevieve P. Myers, president; Catherine M. Busher, secretary; Caroline M. Baillon, treasurer

# NADLER FOUNDATION

5401 Gamble Drive, #204
Minneapolis, MN 55416

**Established:** August 1977

**Type:** Private foundation

**Geographic Orientation:** National

**Sample Grants:**
Jewish Federation of Youngstown—$10,000
Walter F. George School of Law—$5,054
Children's Theatre—$200

**Financial Data for Year Ending December 31, 1981:**
Assets: $967
Grants Paid: $33,750
Number of Grants: 21
Largest/Smallest: $10,000/$51

**Paid Professional Staff:** No

**Directors/Trustees:** G. E. Nadler, president; Myron J. Nadler; Charles E. Nadler

# • THE NASH FOUNDATION

Northwestern National Bank Trust Tax Division
Seventh and Marquette
Minneapolis, MN 55480
(612) 372-5820

**Contact Person:** Barry Kelner, secretary

**Established:** April 1922

**Type:** Private foundation

**Program's Limits:** Rarely accepts proposals from new organizations

**Geographic Orientation:** Minnesota; Upper Midwest

**Fields of Activity:** Arts/architecture; media/communications; music/opera; theater/dance; arts education; medical care/treatment; mental health; drug-abuse programs; environment/energy; family services

**Types of Organizations Funded:** Museums/historical societies; theaters/dance groups; music/opera groups; zoos; public television/radio; arts councils; chemical dependency services; family-planning agencies; counseling services; conservation groups; United Way; organizations for youth

**Types of Support for Organizations:** Capital support; continuing support

**Sample Grants:**
Courage Center—$500
Citizens League—$500
Minnesota Orchestra—$500

**Financial Data for Year Ending December 31, 1981:**
Assets: $829,000
Grants Paid: $65,000
Number of Grants: 43
Largest/Smallest: $5,000/$400

**Paid Professional Staff:** No

**Contact Made by:** Letter of inquiry

**Available by Request:** Proposal guidelines; application procedures

**Proposal Deadlines:** Proposals preferably received before September 1 for the following year

**Board Meetings:** Biannual, in November and May

**Directors/Trustees:** John M. Nash, president; Nicholas D. Nash, vice-president; Barry Kelner, secretary; Charles H. Nash, treasurer

# • NATIONAL CITY BANK FOUNDATION

Box E1919
Minneapolis, MN 55480
(612) 340-3122

**Contact Person:** Elaine Hartmann, secretary-treasurer

**Established:** February 1971

**Type:** Corporate foundation

**Program's Interests:** Social service; education; community affairs; arts

**Program's Limits:** No contributions to national health organizations or to national organizations that do not have a substantial local relationship

**Geographic Orientation:** Twin Cities

**Fields of Activity:** Arts/architecture; media/communications; music/opera; theater/dance; elementary/secondary education; vocational education; higher education; medical research; medical care/treatment; public health; business/economic education; community affairs; crime/law enforcement; drug-abuse programs; economic development

**Types of Organizations Funded:** Theaters/dance groups; music/opera groups; libraries; public television/radio; elementary schools; secondary schools; vocational schools; colleges; universities; educational councils; hospitals; medical research groups; chemical dependency services; United Way; organizations for the elderly; organizations for the handicapped; housing agencies; organizations for minorities; neighborhood agencies

**Employee Matching Gift Programs:** No

**Types of Support for Organizations:** Capital support; continuing support; general operating support; program development

**Sample Grants:**
United Way of Minneapolis—$25,000
Metropolitan Economic Development Association—$1,200
Minnesota Independent School Fund—$600

**Financial Data for Year Ending December 31, 1981:**
Grants Made: $46,280
Number of Grants: 63
Largest/Smallest: $25,000/$50

**Contact Made by:** Complete proposal

**Applicants Notified:** Within two weeks of decision

**Directors/Trustees:** C. Bernard Jacobs, president; James H. Hearon III, vice-president; Elaine E. Hartmann, secretary-treasurer

## NAVANOD FOUNDATION

1080 Montreal Avenue
St. Paul, MN 55116

**Established:** December 1969

**Type:** Private foundation

**Geographic Orientation:** Twin Cities

**Financial Data for Year Ending November 30, 1981:**
Assets: $2,990
Grants Paid: $0

**Paid Professional Staff:** No

**Directors/Trustees:** John F. Donovan, president-treasurer; Eleanor M. Donovan, vice-president/secretary; Gerald J. Donovan

## ● GEORGE W. NEILSON FOUNDATION

c/o Northwestern National Bank of Minneapolis Trust Department
Seventh and Marquette
Minneapolis, MN 55479
(612) 372-6717

**Contact Person:** Henry Doerr, treasurer

**Established:** 1962

**Type:** Private foundation

**Program's Purpose:** To promote matching funds for community needs, including environmental, recreational, and educational facilities and support, in the Bemidji area

**Geographic Orientation:** Minnesota

**Fields of Activity:** Education; community affairs and development; environment; health

**Sample Grants:**
The Nature Conservancy—$20,000
Twin City Institute of Talented Youth—$5,000
Bemidji Community Arts Council—$4,500

**Financial Data for Year Ending December 31, 1981:**
Assets: $1,084,603
Grants Paid: $66,500
Number of Grants: 14
Largest/Smallest: $20,000/$400

**Board Meetings:** Annual, on August 1 or shortly thereafter

**Directors/Trustees:** E. M. Arundel; Katharine N. Cram; Henry Doerr

## J. S. AND ROSE NEMER FOUNDATION

535 Lexington Parkway, #504
St. Paul, MN 55116

**Established:** December 1961

**Type:** Private foundation

**Geographic Orientation:** Twin Cities

**Sample Grants:**
United Jewish Fund and Council—$2,000
Mount Zion Temple—$1,100
Sholom Home—$500

**Financial Data for Year Ending November 30, 1981:**
Assets: $17,039
Grants Paid: $3,800
Number of Grants: 4
Largest/Smallest: $2,000/$200

**Paid Professional Staff:** No

**Director/Trustee:** Rose B. Nemer

## AXEL NEWMAN FAMILY FOUNDATION

1608 Como Avenue
St. Paul, MN 55108

**Established:** September 1967

**Type:** Private foundation

**Geographic Orientation:** Minnesota

**Sample Grants:**
United Way—$6,500
Eastern Minnesota Speed Skating Association—$4,200
Girl Scouts of the St. Croix Valley—$200

**Financial Data for Year Ending December 31, 1981:**
Assets: $108,870
Grants Paid: $30,064
Number of Grants: 26
Largest/Smallest: $6,500/$39

**Paid Professional Staff:** No

**Directors/Trustees:** Lucille Newman, president/treasurer; Richard O'Connell, vice-president; Richard Newman, secretary

# NORLING BROTHERS FOUNDATION

c/o American National Bank and Trust Company
370 Minnesota Street
St. Paul, MN 55101
(612) 298-6276

**Contact Person:** Robert E. Jenkins

**Established:** July 1963

**Type:** Private foundation

**Program's Purpose:** To make grants to organizations "generally of a religious character and usually limited to the Willmar area"

**Geographic Orientation:** Willmar

**Sample Grants:**
Salvation Army of Willmar—$1,500
Gustavus Adolphus College—$1,000
Gideons of Willmar—$200

**Financial Data for Year Ending December 31, 1981:**
Assets:  $208,652
Grants Paid:  $15,600
Number of Grants:  21
Largest/Smallest:  $1,500/$200

**Paid Professional Staff:** No

**Contact Made by:** Letter of inquiry

**Trustee:** American National Bank and Trust Company

# JANE AND WILLIAM C. NORRIS FOUNDATION

W-1781 First National Bank Building
St. Paul, MN 55101

**Established:** December 1969

**Type:** Private foundation

**Geographic Orientation:** Twin Cities

**Sample Grant:**
Our Lady of Good Counsel Free Cancer Home—$209

**Financial Data for Year Ending December 31, 1981:**
Assets:  $4,264
Grants Paid:  $209
Number of Grants:  1

**Paid Professional Staff:** No

**Directors/Trustees:** Jane Norris; William C. Norris; Harry L. Holtz; Richard G. Lareau

# NORTH STAR RESEARCH FOUNDATION

500 Foshay Tower
Minneapolis, MN 55402
(612) 339-7343

**Contact Person:** Henry Doerr, consultant

**Established:** 1982

**Type:** Private foundation

**Program's Purpose:** To make grants for the support of scientific research leading to new technology or new businesses to produce or retain high-quality jobs to strengthen this region; emphasis on seed grants, on grants where matching funds can be attracted, and on grants to research-oriented tax-exempt organizations that can provide technical support to appropriate businesses or individuals; loans to businesses or individuals in the form of program-related investments considered

**Program's Limits:** No grants for buildings or new construction; usually, grants not to exceed $50,000 to any single applicant

**Geographic Orientation:** Minnesota and surrounding region

**Fields of Activity:** Medical and electronic research; life sciences; physical sciences

**Types of Organizations Funded:** Nonprofit educational or research organizations providing advanced support to businesses and individuals; loans to businesses or individuals in the form of program-related investments

**Financial Data for Year Ending October 31, 1981:**
Assets:  $1,200,000

**Contact Made by:** Requesting loan or grant application form

**Board Meetings:** Quarterly

**Directors:** John N. Dempsey, president; Lester A. Malkerson, vice-president; John E. Haaland, secretary; Philip B. Harris, treasurer

# NORTHERN STAR FOUNDATION

440 Hamm Building
St. Paul, MN 55102

**Established:** November 1960 (originally William and Edward Hamm Foundation)

**Type:** Private foundation

**Geographic Orientation:** National

**Sample Grants:**
Yale Alumni Fund—$37,500
San Francisco Opera—$5,500
Outward Bound—$200

**Financial Data for Year Ending October 31, 1981:**
Assets:  $2,092,859
Grants Paid:  $197,380
Number of Grants:  62
Largest/Smallest:  $37,500/$25

**Paid Professional Staff:** No

**Directors/Trustees:** William H. Hamm, president; Edward H. Hamm, vice-president/treasurer; Candace S. Hamm, vice-president; Joseph A. Maun, secretary

## ● NORTHERN STATES POWER COMPANY

414 Nicollet Mall
Minneapolis, MN 55401
(612) 330-6395

**Contact Person:** Merrill Blaskey, general manager, consumer affairs

**Type:** Charitable contributions program

**Program's Interests:** Human service; education

**Program's Limits:** No grants to individuals

**Geographic Orientation:** Service territory

**Fields of Activity:** Arts and humanities; education; health; welfare/social services

**Types of Organizations Funded:** Theaters/dance groups; music/opera groups; libraries; zoos; public television/radio; cultural centers; vocational schools; colleges; universities; scholarship funds; adult education; clinics; chemical dependency services; family-planning agencies; counseling services; United Way; legal aid; multiservice centers; organizations for the elderly; organizations for the handicapped; organizations for women; organizations for drug abusers; organizations for youth; organizations for men; centers for children; housing agencies; organizations for offenders; organizations for minorities; neighborhood agencies; day-care centers; community centers

**Employee Matching Gift Programs:** Higher education

**Types of Support for Organizations:** Capital support; general operating support; federated fund drives

**Financial Data for Year Ending December 31, 1981:**
Contributions Paid: $1,400,000
Number of Contributions: 350
Largest/Smallest: $196,000/$25 (matching gift)

**Contact Made by:** Letter of inquiry

**Available by Request:** Proposal guidelines; application procedures

**Contributions Decisions Made:** Monthly

**Applicants Notified:** Within six weeks of decision

## ● NORTHWEST AREA FOUNDATION

W-975 First National Bank Building
St. Paul, MN 55101
(612) 224-9635

**Contact Person:** John D. Taylor, president

**Established:** December 1934

**Type:** Private foundation

**Program's Purpose:** To promote public welfare through funding programs in the arts; youth education; higher education; medical sciences and health, environmental and physical sciences; human services; and social sciences

**Program's Limits:** No grants to programs or services that have already proven effective elsewhere; campaigns for physical plants, equipment, or endowments; operating budgets or annual fund drives; scholarships, fellowships, travel, lobbying activities, propaganda, religious concerns, publications, films, or other audiovisual materials (except as selected examples grow out of, report on, or support research and experiments underwritten by the foundation)

**Geographic Orientation:** Minnesota; Iowa; North Dakota; South Dakota; Montana; Idaho; Oregon; Washington

**Fields of Activity:** Arts (contact Foundation to determine current program focus); elementary, secondary, and higher education (contact Foundation to determine current program focus); medical care and treatment, and medical health education, physical sciences, environment/energy (contact Foundation to determine current program focus); social science, economic development, employment/job training, family services, special population groups

**Types of Organizations Funded:** Theaters/dance groups; music/opera groups; public television/radio; arts councils; elementary schools; secondary schools; colleges; universities; clinics; family-planning agencies; counseling services; environmental agencies; legal aid; organizations for the elderly; organizations for the handicapped; organizations for women; organizations for youth; centers for children; housing agencies; organizations for offenders; organizations for minorities; neighborhood agencies

**Targeted Population Groups:** Aged; children/youth; handicapped; women; refugees; Asian Americans; blacks; Hispanics; native Americans

**Types of Support for Organizations:** Program development; program-related investments

**Sample Grants:**
Minnesota Diversified Industries—$50,000
Pike Market Senior Center, Seattle—$42,715
Minnesota Independent School Fund—$38,000

**Financial Data for Year Ending February 28, 1982:**
Assets: $118,180,033
Grants Paid: $5,870,135
Number of Grants: 160
Largest/Smallest: $200,000/$350

**Paid Professional Staff:** Yes

**Contact Made by:** Telephone inquiry; request for guidelines

**Available by Request:** Proposal guidelines; annual report; Program Focus RFP

**Board Meetings:** Bimonthly on the first Friday of the month

**Applicants Notified:** Within one week of decision

Directors: W. John Driscoll, chairman of the board/treasurer; Irving Clark, vice-chairman; Dr. Shirley M. Clark; Dr. Joseph T. Ling; Carlos Luis; Norman Lorentzsen; Dr. Francis B. Tiffany; Jean M. West; Stanley E. Williams

# • NORTHWEST BANCORPORATION FOUNDATION

1200 Northwestern Bank Building
Seventh and Marquette
Minneapolis, MN 55480
(612) 372-8393

Contact Person: Peter R. Spokes, president and treasurer

Established: November 1979

Type: Corporate foundation

Program's Purpose: To coordinate contributions to national, regional, and statewide organizations in the Banco seven-state area

Program's Limits: Contributions normally limited to organizations that have at least a statewide impact; national organizations must have an impact on the Banco seven-state region; no grants to individuals

Geographic Orientation: Minnesota; Iowa; South Dakota; North Dakota; Montana; Nebraska; Wisconsin

Fields of Activity: History/preservation; media/communications; theater/dance; vocational education; higher education; physical sciences; business/economic education; community affairs

Types of Organizations Funded: Museums/historical societies; theaters/dance groups; music/opera groups; zoos; historic preservation; vocational schools; colleges; universities; educational councils; scholarship funds; junior colleges; research/study institutes; United Way

Types of Support for Organizations: Capital support; continuing support; general operating support; research; federated fund drives; program-related investments

Financial Data for Year Ending December 31, 1981:
Assets:   $103,005
Grants Paid:   $300,043
Number of Grants:   55
Largest/Smallest:   $20,000/$100

Paid Professional Staff: No

Contact Made by: Letter of inquiry

Proposal Deadlines: December 31

Board Meetings: Annual

Directors/Trustees: Peter R. Spokes, president/treasurer; Roger D. Bryan, vice-president/secretary

# • NORTHWESTERN BELL TELEPHONE COMPANY

200 South Fifth Street
Minneapolis, MN 55402
(612) 344-4349

Contact Person: Sandra Erickson, customer relations

Type: Charitable contributions program

Program's Limits: Company policy restricts giving to tax-supported agencies, religious organizations, controversial projects, or United Way-funded organizations

Geographic Orientation: Minnesota

Fields of Activity: Music/opera; arts education; vocational education; higher education; research; medical research; business/economic education; crime/law enforcement; economic development

Types of Organizations Funded: Music/opera groups; public television/radio; cultural centers; vocational schools; colleges; universities; scholarship funds; chemical dependency services; environmental agencies; United Way; legal aid; multiservice centers; organizations for the elderly; organizations for youth; organizations for minorities; neighborhood agencies

Employee Matching Gift Programs: Higher education; cultural and educational organizations

Types of Support for Organizations: Capital support; general operating support

Sample Grants:
United Way
Hospitality House
Reach-out

Financial Data for Year Ending December 31, 1982:
Contributions Paid:   More than $1 million

Contact Made by: Complete proposal

Available by Request: Proposal guidelines; application procedures

Applicants Notified: Within two weeks of decision

# • NORTHWESTERN NATIONAL BANK OF MINNEAPOLIS

Seventh and Marquette
Minneapolis, MN 55480
(612) 372-6743

Contact Persons: John Doyle, assistant director, social policy; Janet Dudrow, social policy officer

Type: Charitable contributions program

Program's Interests: Education; arts; social action and community development; health and welfare

Program's Limits: No contributions to individuals or to religious, political, fraternal, or veterans' organizations except for those programs that directly relate to the community rather than provide direct benefit to the organization itself (account relationship with the bank has no bearing on contributions considerations)

**Geographic Orientation:** Seven-county metropolitan area

**Fields of Activity:** Arts/architecture; history/preservation; language/literature; media/communications; music/opera; theater/dance; arts education; elementary/secondary education; vocational education; higher education; adult/continuing education; medical care/treatment; medical/health education; public health; mental health; social sciences; legal education; advocacy; business/economic education; community affairs; crime/law enforcement; drug-abuse programs; economic development; employment/job training; environment/energy; equal rights/legal aid; family services; recreation; special population groups; consumer interests

**Types of Organizations Funded:** Museums/historical societies; theaters/dance groups; music/opera groups; libraries; zoos; public television/radio; arts councils; historic preservation; cultural centers; elementary schools; secondary schools; vocational schools; colleges; universities; scholarship funds; adult education; hospitals; clinics; chemical dependency services; family-planning agencies; counseling services; research/study institutes; environmental agencies; conservation groups; United Way; legal aid; multiservice centers; organizations for the elderly; organizations for the handicapped; organizations for women; organizations for veterans; organizations for drug abusers; organizations for youth; centers for children; housing agencies; organizations for offenders; organizations for minorities; neighborhood agencies; day-care centers; community centers

**Targeted Population Groups:** Aged; handicapped; women/girls; minorities

**Employee Matching Gift Programs:** Higher education; elementary/secondary education

**Types of Support for Organizations:** Capital support; continuing support; endowment; general operating support; matching grants (education only); program development; federated fund drives

**Type of Support for Individuals:** Scholarship program for children of employees, through Banco (holding company)

**Sample Grants:**
Greater Minneapolis Metropolitan Housing Corporation (for administration of low- and moderate-income housing program)—$25,000
The Network, coalition of small arts organizations (for feasibility study on joint box-office and shared marketing services for small performing companies)—$1,000
Center for Community Action (for summer youth-employment program)—$500

**Financial Data for Year Ending December 31, 1981:**
Contributions Paid: $1,087,000
Number of Contributions: Approximately 200
Largest/Smallest: $38,000/$25

**Contact Made by:** Letter of inquiry

**Available by Request:** Proposal guidelines; application procedures; report on contributions

**Contributions Decisions Made:** Monthly for requests under $3,000; quarterly for larger requests

**Applicants Notified:** Within one week of decision

## • NORTHWESTERN NATIONAL LIFE INSURANCE COMPANY

20 Washington Avenue South
Minneapolis, MN 55440
(612) 372-5580

**Contact Person:** David K. Cummings, second vice-president, corporate relations

**Established:** 1980

**Type:** Charitable contributions program

**Program's Limits:** No grants to individuals or for religious or political purposes

**Geographic Orientation:** Twin Cities; Minnesota; national

**Fields of Activity:** Arts and humanities; education; health; welfare/social services

**Types of Organizations Funded:** Museums/historical societies; public television/radio; colleges; universities; United Way

**Employee Matching Gift Programs:** Higher education

**Types of Support for Organizations:** Capital support; general operating support; research; federated fund drives

**Types of Support for Individuals:** Scholarships; scholarship program for children of employees

**Sample Grants:**
Metro Community Health Consortium (operating grant)—$1,250
Minnesota Public Radio (program support)—$1,000
Neighborhood Involvement Program (operating grant)—$600

**Financial Data for Year Ending December 31, 1981:**
Contributions Paid: $462,072
Number of Contributions: 154
Smallest: $25

**Contact Made by:** Request for guidelines; complete proposal

**Available by Request:** Proposal guidelines; application procedures; annual report on contributions

**Contributions Decisions Made:** Quarterly

**Applicants Notified:** Within three weeks of decision

## NUMERO-STEINFELDT FOUNDATION

c/o Laventhol and Horwath
100 Washington Square
Minneapolis, MN 55401

**Established:** December 1944 (originally Numero
Foundation)

**Type:** Private foundation

**Geographic Orientation:** Twin Cities

**Sample Grants:**
Minneapolis Federation for Jewish Service—$23,938
Torah Institute in Jerusalem—$10,000
Williams Fund—$375

**Financial Data for Year Ending December 31, 1981:**
Assets:  $257,585
Grants Paid:  $51,213
Number of Grants:  36
Largest/Smallest:  $23,938/$45

**Paid Professional Staff:** No

**Director/Trustee:** J. A. Numero, president


## OAKLEAF FOUNDATION

4900 IDS Center
Minneapolis, MN 55402

**Established:** November 1967

**Type:** Private foundation

**Program's Purpose:** "Particularly....to encourage and
promote the development of and the public
understanding, appreciation and enjoyment of music"

**Geographic Orientation:** Minnesota

**Financial Data for Year Ending December 31, 1981:**
Assets:  $177,540
Grants Paid:  $0

**Paid Professional Staff:** No

**Directors/Trustees:** K. N. Dayton, president-treasurer;
Julia W. Dayton, vice-president/secretary; Judson M.
Dayton; Duncan N. Dayton


## ERNEST C. OBERHOLTZER FOUNDATION

3100 Prudential Plaza
Chicago, IL 60601

**Established:** July 1962

**Type:** Private foundation

**Program's Purpose:** In part, to make "awards to
individuals whether Indian or White in recognition of
significant contributions to the advancement...of
American Indians and/or to a better understanding of
the gifts and culture of Indians on the part of White
people"

**Sample Grants:**
Powwow (unspecified)—$125
North American Indian Fellowship Center of
International Falls—$75

**Financial Data for Year Ending July 31, 1981:**
Assets:  $16,985
Grants Paid:  $200
Number of Grants:  2
Largest/Smallest:  $125/$75

**Paid Professional Staff:** No

**Directors/Trustees:** C. A. Kelly, president; T. A.
Tarbox, secretary-treasurer


## ALICE M. O'BRIEN FOUNDATION

324 Forest
Mahtomedi, MN 55115

**Established:** December 1951

**Type:** Private foundation

**Geographic Orientation:** Minnesota

**Sample Grants:**
Minnesota Historical Society—$25,000
Hazelden Foundation—$15,000
Bach Society of Minnesota—$500

**Financial Data for Year Ending December 31, 1981:**
Assets:  $1,573,981
Grants Paid:  $126,878
Number of Grants:  29
Largest/Smallest:  $25,000/$100

**Paid Professional Staff:** No

**Directors/Trustees:** Julia O. Wilcox, president; Terance
G. O'Brien; Thomond O'Brien; William J. O'Brien


## THE OLSON FOUNDATION

124 Ardmore Drive
Minneapolis, MN 55422

**Established:** December 1971

**Type:** Private foundation

**Geographic Orientation:** Minnesota

**Sample Grants:**
Mount Olivet Lutheran Church—$1,520
Big Brothers—$425
National Right to Work Legal Defense
Foundation—$25

**Financial Data for Year Ending December 31, 1981:**
Assets:  $73,886
Grants Paid:  $4,250
Number of Grants:  20
Largest/Smallest:  $1,520/$25

**Paid Professional Staff:** No

**Directors/Trustees:** Robert C. Olson, president; Bruce R.
Olson, vice-president; William C. Olson, secretary

# ONAN CORPORATION

1400 Seventy-third Avenue Northeast
Minneapolis, MN 55432
(612) 574-5641

**Contact Person:** Charlotte Wilkinson, community relations coordinator

**Type:** Charitable contributions program

**Program's Interests:** Education; health; community services; community welfare

**Program's Limits:** Contributions made at the local level only; contributions not made to individuals or to groups based outside of the United States; company does not make multiyear contribution commitments or serve as sole contributor to any group; no grants to fraternal groups, social groups, or veterans' groups, to religious organizations, to capital fund campaigns, to contests, to book or magazine publication, or to production of films

**Geographic Orientation:** Twin Cities

**Fields of Activity:** Higher education; health; business/economic education; community affairs; economic development; equal rights/legal aid; family services

**Types of Organizations Funded:** Arts councils; scholarship funds; clinics; chemical dependency services; counseling services; United Way; organizations for the handicapped; organizations for women; organizations for youth; organizations for minorities; neighborhood agencies

**Employee Matching Gift Programs:** No

**Targeted Population Groups:** Handicapped; women/girls; Asian Americans; blacks; Hispanics; native Americans

**Type of Support for Organizations:** General operating support

**Types of Support for Individuals:** Aid to needy persons; scholarships; scholarship program for children of employees

**Sample Grants:**
Chrysalis, A Center for Women—$2,000
Urban Coalition of Minneapolis—$500
Multiple Sclerosis Society—$150

**Financial Data for Year Ending December 31, 1981:**
Contributions Paid:  $50,000 to $99,999
Number of Contributions:  40
Largest/Smallest:  $67,000/$50

**Contact Made by:** Telephone inquiry; letter of inquiry; request for guidelines; complete proposal

**Available by Request:** Proposal guidelines; application procedures

**Contributions Decisions Made:** Annually, by August 1

**Applicants Notified:** Within six weeks of decision

# • ONAN FAMILY FOUNDATION

475 Shelard Plaza North
300 South County Road 18
Minneapolis, MN 55426
(612) 544-4702

**Contact Person:** Susan J. Smith, executive director

**Established:** 1942

**Type:** Private foundation

**Program's Purpose:** To provide support to programs in the areas of education, social welfare, cultural and civic affairs, and religion

**Program's Limits:** No grants to individuals; for political purposes; to endowments or capital funds; or for trips and tours

**Geographic Orientation:** Twin Cities

**Sample Grants:**
Twin Cities Public Television—$46,950
Children's Home Society—$17,100
Hennepin Avenue Methodist Church—$1,850

**Types of Support for Organizations:** Grants; loans

**Financial Data for Year Ending December 31, 1981:**
Assets:  $2,476,323
Grants Paid:  $265,615
Number of Grants:  33
Largest/Smallest:  $46,950/$1,000

**Paid Professional Staff:** Yes

**Contact Made by:** Letter of inquiry

**Available by Request:** Application procedures; annual report

**Board Meetings:** Biannual, in November and May

**Trustees:** David W. Onan II, president/treasurer; Bruce R. Smith, secretary; C. W. Onan; Lois Onan

# ALBERT T. O'NEIL FOUNDATION

American National Bank and Trust Company
St. Paul, MN 55101

**Established:** February 1965

**Type:** Private foundation

**Geographic Orientation:** National

**Sample Grants:**
Holy Rosary Red Cloud Indian School—$15,000
Catholic Diocese of Northern Alaska—$10,000
Humane Society of Winona—$500

**Financial Data for Year Ending June 30, 1981:**
Assets:  $1,521,578
Grants Paid:  $86,900
Number of Grants:  23
Largest/Smallest:  $15,000/$500

**Paid Professional Staff:** No

**Directors/Trustees:** Albert T. O'Neil; Brother I. Patrick F.S.C., secretary/treasurer; David C. McKenzie

# THE OR FOUNDATION

200 West Old Shakopee Road
Bloomington, MN 55420

**Established:** December 1976

**Type:** Private foundation

**Geographic Orientation:** Minnesota

**Sample Grants:**
Wooddale Baptist Church—$10,562
Open Bible Church—$9,854
Ironwood Springs Christian Church—$5,000

**Financial Data for Year Ending November 30, 1981:**
Assets: $312,995
Grants Paid: $25,416
Number of Grants: 3
Largest/Smallest: $10,562/$5,000

**Paid Professional Staff:** No

**Directors/Trustees:** William F. Reimer, president;
Richard L. Ozment, vice-president/secretary

## • ORDEAN FOUNDATION

501 Ordean Building
Duluth, MN 55802
(218) 722-3373

**Contact Person:** Ernest S. Petersen, executive director

**Established:** December 1933

**Type:** Private foundation

**Program's Purpose:** To make grants to organizations
that provide services or facilities for treatment, care,
and rehabilitation of persons chronically or
temporarily mentally ill or physically impaired by
injury, illness, birth defects, age, alcoholism, or other
causes; to support youth guidance programs designed
to prevent delinquency

**Program's Limits:** Grants made to organizations located
in Duluth or providing services to its residents

**Geographic Orientation:** Duluth

**Fields of Activity:** Nursing scholarships; public health;
drug-abuse programs; equal rights/legal aid; family
services; welfare

**Types of Organizations Funded:** Scholarship funds for
nurses' training; clinics; United Way; legal aid;
organizations for the elderly; organizations for the
handicapped; organizations for women; organizations
for drug abusers; organizations for youth; centers for
children

**Types of Support for Organizations:** Capital support;
general operating support; matching grants; program-
related investments

**Types of Support for Individuals:** Aid to needy
persons; scholarships

**Sample Grants:**
Goodwill Industries, Duluth—$100,000
Women's Coalition, Duluth—$18,000
Duluth Indian Action Council—$2,407

**Financial Data for Year Ending December 31, 1981:**
Assets: $10,500,000
Grants Paid: $401,416
Number of Grants: 23
Largest/Smallest: $250,000/$1,229

**Paid Professional Staff:** Yes

**Contact Made by:** Request for guidelines

**Available by Request:** Proposal guidelines

**Proposal Deadlines:** Fifteenth of month prior to board
meeting

**Board Meetings:** Bimonthly

**Applicants Notified:** Within two weeks of decision

**Directors:** Dennis W. Dunne, president; Arthur C.
Josephs, vice-president; Ernest S. Petersen, secretary-
treasurer; Roger M. Bowman; Howard P. Clarke;
Donald G. Wirtanen; Willis D. Wyard

## • I. A. O'SHAUGHNESSY FOUNDATION

W-555 First National Bank Building
St. Paul, MN 55101

**Contact Person:** Paul J. Kelly, secretary-treasurer

**Established:** December 1941

**Type:** Private foundation

**Geographic Orientation:** Minnesota; Kansas; Texas;
Illinois

**Sample Grants:**
Lyric Opera of Chicago—$150,000
Kansas Newman College—$50,000
United Arts Fund, St. Paul—$2,500

**Financial Data for Year Ending December 31, 1981:**
Assets: $16,562,652
Grants Paid: $1,371,100
Number of Grants: 55
Largest/Smallest: $150,000/$1,000

**Paid Professional Staff:** No

**Contact Made by:** Complete proposal

**Directors/Trustees:** Lawrence O'Shaughnessy, president;
John F. O'Shaughnessy, vice-president; Paul Kelly,
secretary-treasurer

## PAUL M. OTTESON FOUNDATION

213 South Lincoln
Owatonna, MN 55060

**Established:** October 1968

**Type:** Private foundation

**Geographic Orientation:** National

**Sample Grants:**
Trinity Lutheran Church, Owatonna—$2,815
American Lutheran Church, Big Timber, MT—$105
Christmas Seals—$10

**Financial Data for Year Ending December 31, 1981:**
Assets: $74,054
Grants Paid: $3,755
Number of Grants: 22
Largest/Smallest: $2,815/$10

**Paid Professional Staff:** No

**Director/Trustee:** Paul M. Otteson, president

# OUELLETTE FOUNDATION

W-2062 First National Bank Building
St. Paul, MN 55101
(612) 222-8478

**Contact Person:** George C. Power, Jr., treasurer

**Established:** December 1959

**Type:** Private foundation

**Program's Limits:** Most grants to family's personal charities

**Geographic Orientation:** Minnesota

**Fields of Activity:** Elementary/secondary education; higher education; family services

**Types of Organizations Funded:** Colleges; hospitals; churches/synagogues; religious service groups; day-care centers

**Sample Grants:**
Dorothy Day Center, Catholic Charities—$1,000
Cretin High School—$1,000
Children's Hospital—$1,000

**Financial Data for Year Ending December 31, 1981:**
Assets: $72,809
Grants Paid: $6,100
Number of Grants: 8
Largest/Smallest: $1,000/$100

**Paid Professional Staff:** No

**Board Meetings:** Annual

**Directors/Trustees:** Genevieve S. Ouellette, president; Mary O. Weinberger, secretary; George C. Power, Jr., treasurer

# THE BEN AND JEANNE OVERMAN CHARITABLE TRUST

230 West Superior Street
Duluth, MN 55802

**Established:** September 1980

**Type:** Private foundation

**Geographic Orientation:** Minnesota

**Sample Grants:**
Temple Israel—$5,000
Van Gordon Foundation—$2,000
College of Saint Scholastica—$500

**Financial Data for Year Ending December 31, 1981:**
Assets: $84,025
Grants Paid: $7,500
Number of Grants: 3
Largest/Smallest: $5,000/$500

**Paid Professional Staff:** No

**Directors/Trustees:** Ben Overman; Jeanne Overman; William Overman; Manley Goldfine; Beverly Goldfine

# GRACE OVERTON FOUNDATION

207 Kellogg Square Building
St. Paul, MN 55101

**Established:** April 1980

**Type:** Private foundation

**Geographic Orientation:** Minnesota

**Sample Grants:**
University of Minnesota Medical School—$17,750
American Cancer Society—$1,000
Franciscan Sisters—$500

**Financial Data for Year Ending May 31, 1981:**
Assets: $26,018
Grants Paid: $37,298
Number of Grants: 5
Largest/Smallest: $17,750/$500

**Paid Professional Staff:** No

**Directors/Trustees:** Grace Overton, president; Dr. George T. Tani, secretary-treasurer; Yutaka Semba; Joseph L. Nordquist

# OWEN FAMILY FUND

2200 First Bank Place East
Minneapolis, MN 55402

**Established:** December 1958

**Type:** Private foundation

**Financial Data for Year Ending December 31, 1981:**
Assets: $177,875
Grants Paid: $0

**Paid Professional Staff:** No

**Directors/Trustees:** David L. Owen, president/treasurer; Elizabeth B. Owen, vice-president; William B. Owen, secretary; Carol Dittel, assistant secretary

## P & B FOUNDATION

1702 Midwest Plaza Building
Minneapolis, MN 55402

**Established:** September 1970

**Type:** Private foundation

**Sample Grant:**
Bible Baptist College, North Carolina—$12,000

**Financial Data for Year Ending August 31, 1981:**
Assets: $1,350,492
Grants Paid: $12,000
Number of Grants: 1

**Paid Professional Staff:** No

**Directors/Trustees:** C. Wilbur Peters, manager; Duane G. Hanson, secretary-treasurer


## THE PACIFIC FOUNDATION

2521 First Avenue
Hibbing, MN 55746

**Established:** March 1957

**Type:** Private foundation

**Geographic Orientation:** Northern Minnesota; national

**Sample Grants:**
YMCA—$2,500
Opportunity Workshop—$1,500
Hibbing Little League—$150

**Financial Data for Year Ending March 31, 1982:**
Assets: $62,799
Grants Paid: $29,464
Number of Grants: 35
Largest/Smallest: $2,500/$34

**Paid Professional Staff:** No

**Directors/Trustees:** Donald V. Larson, president; Bruce R. Toivola, secretary; Conrad A. Mertely, treasurer


## THE CLAYTON PACKARD FOUNDATION

Route 4, Box 87
Excelsior, MN 55331

**Established:** October 1969

**Type:** Private foundation

**Geographic Orientation:** National

**Sample Grants:**
The Cenacle—$800
Faith Broadcasting Network—$500
Amnesty International—$100

**Financial Data for Year Ending December 31, 1980:**
Assets: $167
Grants Paid: $8,600
Number of Grants: 41
Largest/Smallest: $800/$30

**Paid Professional Staff:** No

**Directors/Trustees:** James J. Emmer, president; Mary P. Emmer; Marcy Graham


## ● PAKO CORPORATION

6300 Olson Highway
Minneapolis, MN 55440
(612) 540-6339

**Contact Person:** John Ziegenhagen, director of community relations

**Established:** 1972

**Type:** Charitable contributions program (note: Pako established a corporate foundation in 1982)

**Program's Interests:** Broad range of community needs

**Program's Limits:** No grants to political or lobbying organizations, for "good-will" advertising, to fund-raising events, or for direct support to individuals

**Geographic Orientation:** Minneapolis; Twin Cities; Minnesota; national

**Types of Organizations Supported:** Public television/radio; colleges; universities; United Way; multiservice centers; organizations for minorities

**Employee Matching Gift Programs:** No

**Type of Support for Organizations:** General operating support

**Financial Data for Year Ending October 31, 1981:**
Contributions Paid: $50,000 to $99,999 range
Number of Contributions: 40
Largest/Smallest: $1,500/$250

**Contact Made by:** Letter of inquiry

**Available by Request:** Proposal guidelines; application procedures

**Contributions Decisions Made:** Quarterly

**Applicants Notified:** Within two weeks of decision


## GEORGE M. PALMER FOUNDATION

Box 544
Mankato, MN 56001

**Established:** April 1959

**Type:** Private foundation

**Geographic Orientation:** Minnesota; South Dakota

**Sample Grants:**
United Fund, Mankato Area—$5,300
Minnesota Private College Fund—$2,900
Blue Earth County Historical Society—$400

**Financial Data for Year Ending April 30, 1982:**
Assets: $149,224
Grants Paid: $38,130
Number of Grants: 44
Largest/Smallest: $5,300/$50

**Paid Professional Staff:** No

**Directors/Trustees:** Ogden W. Confer, president; Mary C. Koehler, vice-president; Richard P. Confer, secretary

## JOSEPH PAPER FOUNDATION

Box 3186
St. Paul, MN 55165

**Contact Person:** Mrs. Joseph Paper, president

**Established:** January 1948

**Type:** Private foundation

**Program's Limits:** No contributions involving expense responsibility; giving confined to the Twin Cities area (primarily St. Paul)

**Geographic Orientation:** Twin Cities

**Types of Support for Organizations:** Capital support; continuing support; endowment; general operating support; federated fund drives

**Sample Grants:**
  Jewish Vocational Service—$13,200
  United Hospitals, St. Paul—$1,000
  Amicus—$150

**Financial Data for Year Ending December 31, 1981:**
  Assets: $841,478
  Grants Paid: $44,865
  Number of Grants: 32
  Largest/Smallest: $13,200/$110

**Paid Professional Staff:** No

**Contact Made by:** Request for guidelines; complete proposal

**Available by Request:** Annual report

**Board Meetings:** Annual

**Trustees:** Mrs. Joseph Paper, president; Mrs. Willis Forman, secretary; Lewis Paper, treasurer

## • LEWIS AND ANNIE F. PAPER FOUNDATION

Box 3186
St. Paul, MN 55165
(612) 631-1111

**Contact Person:** Lewis Paper, president

**Established:** December 1947

**Program's Limits:** Few contributions involving expense responsibility; few grants far from this region and only grants to organizations outside the area when they have significant local impact

**Geographic Orientation:** Ninth Federal Reserve District

**Types of Support for Organizations:** Capital support; continuing support; endowment; general operating support; federated fund drives

**Sample Grants:**
  United Jewish Fund and Council, St. Paul—$101,300
  Goodwill Industries Vocational Enterprises, Duluth—$2,500
  Minnesota Press Council—$275

**Financial Data for Year Ending December 31, 1981:**
  Assets: $2,496,870
  Grants Paid: $259,985
  Number of Grants: 46
  Largest/Smallest: $101,300/$100

**Paid Professional Staff:** No

**Contact Made by:** Request for guidelines; complete proposal

**Available by Request:** Annual report

**Board Meetings:** Annual

**Trustees:** Lewis Paper, president; Lewis R. Harris, vice-president; Mrs. Willis Forman, secretary-treasurer; Mrs. Joseph Paper

## PAULUCCI FAMILY FOUNDATION

525 Lake Avenue South
Duluth, MN 55802

**Established:** November 1966

**Type:** Private foundation

**Geographic Orientation:** National

**Sample Grants:**
  National Italian American Foundation—$27,400
  Duluth Clinic Education and Research Foundation—$10,000
  American Indian OIC—$2,500

**Financial Data for Year Ending December 31, 1981:**
  Assets: $1,342,450
  Grants Paid: $70,143
  Number of Grants: 23
  Largest/Smallest: $27,400/$100

**Paid Professional Staff:** No

**Directors/Trustees:** Jeno F. Paulucci, president; Lois M. Paulucci, vice-president; Michael J. Paulucci, vice-president; Robert E. Heller, secretary; Robert L. Cotton, treasurer

## PEERLESS CHAIN FOUNDATION

Winona, MN 55987

**Established:** December 1967

**Type:** Corporate foundation

**Geographic Orientation:** Minnesota

**Sample Grants:**
  United Way, Greater Winona Area—$9,200
  Saint Mary's College—$5,000
  Women's Resource Center—$1,000

**Financial Data for Year Ending March 31, 1982:**
Assets: $175,368
Grants Paid: $52,000
Number of Grants: 16
Largest/Smallest: $9,200/$300

**Paid Professional Staff:** No

**Directors/Trustees:** A. J. Bambenek, president; J. J. Jeresek, vice-president/treasurer; R. D. Bambenek, secretary

# • PERKINS FOUNDATION

1485 Fox Street
Wayzata, MN 55391
(612) 473-6308

**Contact Person:** Richard W. Perkins, president

**Established:** February 1969

**Type:** Private foundation

**Program's Purpose:** To provide financial assistance to youth-oriented and other tax-exempt organizations

**Program's Limits:** Assistance primarily limited to programs serving young people

**Geographic Orientation:** Primarily Minnesota

**Fields of Activity:** Drug-abuse programs; family services; recreation; religion

**Types of Organizations Funded:** Organizations for drug abusers; organizations for youth; centers for children; churches/synagogues; religious service groups; United Way

**Targeted Population Group:** Children/youth

**Types of Support for Organizations:** Continuing support; program development

**Type of Support for Individuals:** Scholarships

**Sample Grants:**
YMCA, Camp Olson—$4,000
Minneapolis Boys' Club—$200
Viking Council, Boy Scouts of America—$50

**Financial Data for Year Ending December 31, 1981:**
Assets: $162,818
Grants Paid: $6,097
Number of Grants: 20
Largest/Smallest: $4,000/$25

**Paid Professional Staff:** No

**Contact Made by:** Complete proposal

**Available by Request:** Annual report

**Board Meetings:** Annual, in December

**Applicants Notified:** Within two weeks of decision

**Directors/Trustees:** Richard W. Perkins, president; Pamela L. Blumberg, vice-president; Richard C. Perkins, treasurer; Daniel S. Perkins, secretary

# NORMAN PERL FOUNDATION

20670 Linwood Road
Excelsior, MN 55331

**Established:** November 1967

**Type:** Private foundation

**Geographic Orientation:** Twin Cities

**Sample Grants:**
Lubavitch—$1,000
Hadassah—$525
American Heart Association—$10

**Financial Data for Year Ending December 31, 1981:**
Assets: $38,772
Grants Paid: $3,461
Number of Grants: 36
Largest/Smallest: $1,000/$5

**Paid Professional Staff:** No

**Director/Trustee:** Norman Perl, president

# PERRY FOUNDATION

Suite 450
10,000 Highway 55W
Minneapolis, MN 55441

**Established:** October 1969

**Type:** Private foundation

**Geographic Orientation:** National

**Sample Grants:**
Scripps Memorial Hospital Foundation—$2,000
Friends of Scicon—$500
Reader's Digest Fund for the Blind—$50

**Financial Data for Year Ending December 31, 1981:**
Assets: $19,830
Grants Paid: $3,150
Number of Grants: 10
Largest/Smallest: $2,000/$50

**Paid Professional Staff:** No

**Directors/Trustees:** Herbert O. Perry, president; James Perry, vice-president; Ruth A. Meyer, assistant secretary; L. L. Arnevik, assistant treasurer

# MARVIN J. PERTZIK FOUNDATION

1400 Northwestern National Bank Building
St. Paul, MN 55101

**Established:** October 1979

**Type:** Private foundation

**Geographic Orientation:** National

**Sample Grants:**
American Jewish Historical Society—$200
Schubert Club, St. Paul—$100
Lawyers Concerned for Lawyers—$50

**Financial Data for Year Ending December 31, 1981:**
Assets: $12,502
Grants Paid: $600
Number of Grants: 6
Largest/Smallest: $200/$50

**Paid Professional Staff:** No

**Directors/Trustees:** Marvin J. Pertzik, president/treasurer; William F. Orme, secretary; Rene Fishman, vice-president

# PETOMBOB FOUNDATION

212 Colfax Avenue North
Minneapolis, MN 55403

**Type:** Private foundation

**Geographic Orientation:** Twin Cities

**Sample Grant:**
United Way—$450

**Financial Data for Year Ending December 31, 1981:**
Assets: $219
Grants Paid: $650
Number of Grants: 2

**Paid Professional Staff:** No

**Director/Trustee:** E. R. Wood (from AR-990, 1980)

# P.G.N. FOUNDATION

68 Woodland Circle
Minneapolis, MN 55424

**Established:** September 1961

**Type:** Private foundation

**Geographic Orientation:** Twin Cities; national

**Sample Grants:**
United Way of the Minneapolis Area—$2,000
Harvard College Fund—$1,000
Whale Protection Fund, Hawaii—$300

**Financial Data for Year Ending August 31, 1981:**
Assets: $290,343
Grants Paid: $21,800
Number of Grants: 49
Largest/Smallest: $2,000/$100

**Paid Professional Staff:** No

**Directors/Trustees:** Paula C. Kinross-Wright, president; John D. Curtin, vice-president; John S. Curtin, treasurer; Andrea N. Curtin, secretary

# PHELAN FOUNDATION

6566 France Avenue South, #703
Edina, MN 55435

**Established:** July 1967

**Type:** Private foundation

**Program's Purpose:** "To conduct and carry on medical research"

**Financial Data for Year Ending December 31, 1981:**
Assets: $1,461
Grants Paid: $600

**Paid Professional Staff:** No

**Directors/Trustees:** Loraine A. Phelan; James A. Polzak

# • THE PHILLIPS FOUNDATION

2345 Kennedy Northeast
Minneapolis, MN 55413
(612) 331-6230

**Contact Person:** Thomas P. Cook, executive director and trustee

**Established:** 1942

**Type:** Private foundation

**Program's Purpose:** To support education, health, research, and unmet human and social needs

**Program's Limits:** No support for testimonial dinners for fund-raising purposes; prefer to restrict grants to Midwest, except for family and foundation commitments to projects in Israel and Italy

**Geographic Orientation:** Twin Cities; Minnesota; national; international

**Fields of Activity:** Arts/architecture; media/communications; music/opera; theater/dance; vocational education; higher education; research; medical research; medical/health education; mental health; religious education; business/economic education; community affairs; crime/law enforcement; drug-abuse programs; economic development; employment/job training; equal rights/legal aid; welfare

**Sample Grants:**
Harvard University, Henry Levin Chair in Literature—$600,000
Mayo Foundation—$100,000
National Council on Alcoholism—$1,000

**Financial Data for Year Ending December 31, 1981:**
Assets: $34,606,694
Grants Paid: $2,740,363
Number of Grants: 227
Largest/Smallest: $600,000/$15

**Paid Professional Staff:** Yes

**Trustees:** Jay Phillips, president; Rose Phillips, vice-president; Samuel H. Maslon, secretary; Thomas P. Cook, executive director; Morton B. Phillips; Helen Phillips Levin; Jack Levin; Paula Phillips Bernstein

## • THE PILLSBURY COMPANY FOUNDATION

M.S. 3290 Pillsbury Center
Minneapolis, MN 55402
(612) 330-4184

**Contact Person:** Robert W. Bonine, secretary

**Established:** 1957

**Type:** Corporate foundation (in addition to its foundation, the Pillsbury Company has a direct corporate giving program; most of these contributions are made directly by subsidiaries and plants; the same guidelines and application procedures apply; in fiscal 1982, the company paid $480,000 in corporate contributions)

**Program's Purpose:** To help meet the needs of communities where there are Pillsbury employees and facilities; focuses on community service, food and nutrition, higher education, and arts and culture

**Program's Limits:** Generally, no contributions to individuals; projects operating outside of the United States; general support for higher education institutions; intermediary funding agencies serving solely as conduits for channeling monies from donor to donee organizations; appeals for product donations; religious projects; lobbying efforts; fund-raising events; academic or scientific research activities; travel support, or subsidization of books, magazines, or articles in professional journals

**Geographic Orientation:** Twin Cities; Minnesota; communities where the company has a significant number of employees

**Fields of Activity:** Donated food programs; higher education; arts and culture; human service

**Types of Organizations Funded:** Museums/historical societies; theaters/dance groups; music/opera groups; public television/radio; vocational schools; colleges; universities; scholarship funds; junior colleges; hospitals; chemical dependency services; family-plannning agencies; United Way; organizations for the elderly; organizations for the handicapped; organizations for women; organizations for youth; organizations for minorities

**Employee Matching Gift Programs:** United Way campaigns; higher education

**Targeted Population Groups:** Aged; handicapped; women/girls; minorities

**Types of Support for Organizations:** General operating support; matching grants; program development

**Sample Grants:**
Citizens' Crime Commission of Greater Miami (challenge grant)—$25,000
Lake Country Food Bank (for costs related to distribution of government surplus cheese to needy in Minnesota)—$10,000
City of Glencoe, Glencoe Volunteer Fire Department (for purchase of life-saving equipment)—$1,135

**Financial Data for Year Ending May 31, 1982:**
Assets: $5,505,062
Grants Paid: $2,613,370
Number of Grants: 500
Largest/Smallest: $175,000/$25 (matching gift)

**Paid Professional Staff:** Yes

**Contact Made by:** Letter of inquiry

**Available by Request:** Proposal guidelines; application procedures; annual report

**Board Meetings:** Quarterly

**Applicants Notified:** Within two weeks of decision

**Directors/Trustees:** William H. Spoor, president; Edward C. Stringer, vice-president; Frances I. Gamble, treasurer; Robert W. Bonine, secretary

## • PIPER, JAFFRAY AND HOPWOOD

800 Multifoods Building
Minneapolis, MN 55402
(612) 371-6063

**Contact Person:** Walter E. Pratt

**Type:** Charitable contributions program

**Fields of Activity:** Arts and humanities; education; health; religious activities; science; welfare/social services

**Types of Organizations Funded:** Museums/historical societies; theaters/dance groups; music/opera groups; libraries; zoos; public television/radio; arts councils; historic preservation; colleges; universities; educational councils; scholarship funds; junior colleges; hospitals; medical research groups; chemical dependency services; family-planning agencies; counseling services; other health organizations; religious service groups; religious colleges; research/study institutes; conservation groups; United Way; legal aid; multiservice centers; organizations for the elderly; organizations for the handicapped; organizations for women; organizations for veterans; organizations for drug abusers; organizations for youth; organizations for men; centers for children; housing agencies; organizations for offenders; organizations for minorities; neighborhood agencies; day-care centers; community centers

**Employee Matching Gift Programs:** Higher education

**Types of Support for Organizations:** Capital support; endowment; general operating support; matching grants; program development; research; federated fund drives

**Financial Data for Year Ending September 24, 1982:**
Contributions Paid: $100,000 to $499,999 range
Number of Contributions: 150
Largest/Smallest: $25,000/$100

**Contact Made by:** Letter of inquiry

**Available by Request:** Annual report on contributions

**Proposal Deadlines:** Before end of the company's fiscal year (September)

**Contributions Decisions Made:** Quarterly

# PRUDENTIAL INSURANCE COMPANY

North Central Home Office
3701 Wayzata Boulevard
Minneapolis, MN 55416
(612) 349-1210

**Contact Person:** Robert E. Borgstrom, CLU, director, public relations

**Established:** 1977

**Type:** Charitable contributions program

**Program's Interests:** Urban affairs; minority assistance; health; education

**Program's Limits:** Grants of $1,000 or more funded through the Prudential Foundation; grants of less than $1,000 funded through the company's direct giving program

**Geographic Orientation:** Twin Cities; nine-state north-central area

**Fields of Activity:** Arts/architecture; history/preservation; media/communications; music/opera; theater/dance; arts education; vocational education; higher education; research; other educational activities; medical research; medical care/treatment; medical/health education; mental health; other health activities; legal education; business/economic education; community affairs; crime/law enforcement; drug-abuse programs; economic development; employment/job training; equal rights/legal aid; family services; recreation; safety; special population groups; consumer interests

**Types of Organizations Funded:** Museums/historical societies; theaters/dance groups; libraries; public television/radio; arts councils; colleges; special education; libraries; medical research groups; counseling services; United Way; legal aid; multiservice centers; organizations for the elderly; organizations for the handicapped; organizations for women; organizations for drug abusers; organizations for youth; organizations for men; centers for children; housing agencies; organizations for offenders; organizations for minorities; neighborhood agencies; community centers

**Targeted Population Groups:** Aged; substance abusers; children/youth; criminal offenders/exoffenders; handicapped; men/boys; women/girls; blacks; Hispanics; native Americans

**Employee Matching Gift Programs:** Higher education

**Types of Support for Organizations:** Continuing support; general operating support; matching grants (education only); program development; research; federated fund drives

**Type of Support for Individuals:** Scholarship program for children of employees

**Sample Grants:**
Urban Coalition, Minneapolis—$4,000
Park Avenue Athletic Club, Minneapolis—$750
Learning Center for Economics, Minneapolis—$500

**Financial Data for Year Ending August 31, 1982:**
Contributions Paid: $50,000 to $99,999 range
Largest/Smallest: $10,000/$100

**Contact Made by:** Letter of inquiry

**Contributions Decisions Made:** Quarterly, in September, December, March, and June (minor contributions decisions made monthly)

**Applicants Notified:** Within two weeks of decision

# QUETICO SUPERIOR FOUNDATION

2200 First Bank Place East
Minneapolis, MN 55402

**Established:** October 1947

**Type:** Private foundation

**Program's Purpose:** To promote the "conservation, maintenance, protection, and restoration of...the Rainy Lake and Pigeon River watersheds and contiguous areas"

**Geographic Orientation:** Northeastern Minnesota

**Sample Grants:**
Project Environment Foundation—$3,500
Voyageurs National Park Association—$3,500

**Financial Data for Year Ending December 31, 1981:**
Assets: $300,183
Grants Paid: $7,000
Number of Grants: 2

**Directors/Trustees:** Frederick Winston, president; Charles A. Kelly, vice-president; Walter E. Pratt, secretary/treasurer

# • THE ELIZABETH C. QUINLAN FOUNDATION

417 Minnesota Federal Building
Minneapolis, MN 55402
(612) 333-8084

**Contact Person:** Richard A. Klein, president/treasurer

**Established:** November 1945

**Type:** Private foundation

**Program's Purpose:** To provide financial assistance to religious, educational, scientific, medical, surgical, social, or charitable organizations operating within Minnesota

**Geographic Orientation:** Minnesota

**Fields of Activity:** Arts/architecture; history/preservation; media/communications; music/opera; theater/dance; arts education; elementary/secondary education; higher education; medical research; medical care/treatment; religious education; advocacy; community affairs; family services; welfare

**Types of Organizations Funded:** Museums/historical societies; theaters/dance groups; music/opera groups; libraries; public television/radio; arts councils; historic preservation; cultural centers; secondary schools; colleges; universities; scholarship funds; libraries; hospitals; medical research groups; chemical dependency services; counseling services; churches/synagogues; religious service groups; religious schools; religious colleges; environmental agencies; United Way; organizations for the elderly; organizations for the handicapped; organizations for women; organizations for drug abusers; organizations for youth; organizations for offenders; organizations for minorities; neighborhood agencies

**Types of Support for Organizations:** Capital support; continuing support; general operating support; program development; research; federated fund drives

**Type of Support for Individuals:** Scholarships (through tax-exempt organizations)

**Sample Grants:**
Hospitality House—$25,000 (over five years)
Elder Friends—$1,000
Insight—$1,000

**Financial Data for Year Ending December 31, 1981:**
Assets: $1,700,000
Grants Paid: $88,920
Number of Grants: 50
Largest/Smallest: $10,120/$100

**Paid Professional Staff:** No

**Contact Made by:** Letter of inquiry; complete proposal

**Available by Request:** Proposal guidelines; application procedures; annual report

**Proposal Deadlines:** September 1

**Board Meetings:** Annual, in October

**Applicants Notified:** By November 15

**Directors/Trustees:** Richard A. Klein, president/treasurer; Eugene P. McCahill, vice-president; Mary Elizabeth Lahiff, secretary; Anne L. Klein; Lucia L. Crane; Alice M. Lahiff

# RAMY FOUNDATION

1229 North Front Street
Mankato, MN 56001

**Type:** Private foundation

**Geographic Orientation:** Minnesota

**Sample Grants:**
Ducks Unlimited—$1,530
Loyola Fitzgerald Development Camp—$1,000
Mankato Classic—$120

**Financial Data for Year Ending December 31, 1981:**
Assets: $34,962
Grants Paid: $4,189
Number of Grants: 17
Largest/Smallest: $1,530/$16

**Paid Professional Staff:** No

**Director/Trustee:** Michael Ramy

# THE RANGE FOUNDATION

First Bank of Hibbing
Hibbing, MN 55746

**Established:** September 1971

**Type:** Private foundation

**Geographic Orientation:** Northern Minnesota

**Sample Grants:**
Salvation Army—$10,000
Headwaters Area Boy Scouts—$5,500
Junior Achievement, Hibbing—$350

**Financial Data for Year Ending August 31, 1981:**
Assets: $995
Grants Paid: $57,110
Number of Grants: 25
Largest/Smallest: $10,000/$350

**Paid Professional Staff:** No

**Directors/Trustees:** Robert Carlson; John H. Hearding; Dwight Jamar

# GERALD RAUENHORST FAMILY FOUNDATION

c/o Rauenhorst Corporation
Box 150
Minneapolis, MN 55440

**Established:** March 1965

**Type:** Private foundation

**Geographic Orientation:** National

**Sample Grants:**
College of Saint Catherine—$50,400
Progress Valley—$36,000
Gonzaga University, Spokane, WA—$1,500

**Financial Data for Year Ending December 31, 1981:**
  Assets:  $5,528,054
  Grants Paid:  $205,100
  Number of Grants:  24
  Largest/Smallest:  $50,400/$500

**Paid Professional Staff:** No

**Directors/Trustees:** Gerald Rauenhorst, president; Henrietta Rauenhorst, executive vice-president; Judith Mahoney, secretary; Mark Rauenhorst, treasurer

## RAWLINGS FOUR-STAR FOUNDATION

1914 First National Bank Building
Minneapolis, MN 55402
(612) 338-7630

**Contact Person:** E. W. Rawlings, president

**Established:** July 1963

**Type:** Private foundation

**Program's Purpose:** To provide financial support for education and religion

**Geographic Orientation:** National

**Fields of Activity:** Elementary/secondary education; higher education; religious education; business/economic education

**Types of Organizations Funded:** Secondary schools; colleges; universities; medical schools; churches/synagogues

**Type of Support for Organizations:** General operating

**Sample Grants:**
  Hamline University—$1,000
  Miami University of Ohio—$1,000
  Harvard Business School—$500

**Financial Data for Year Ending March 31, 1982:**
  Assets:  $73,787
  Grants Paid:  $4,000
  Number of Grants:  6
  Largest:  $1,000

**Paid Professional Staff:** No

**Contact Made by:** Letter of inquiry

**Applicants Notified:** Within two weeks of decision

**Trustees:** E. W. Rawlings, president; T. R. Anderson

## ● RED WING SHOE COMPANY FOUNDATION

419 Bush Street
Red Wing, MN 55066
(612) 388-8211

**Contact Person:** Joseph P. Goggin

**Established:** 1954

**Type:** Corporate foundation

**Program's Interests:** Youth services; local agencies

**Geographic Orientation:** Red Wing area

**Fields of Activity:** Music/opera; environmental education; medical research; science; crime/law enforcement; recreation; consumer interests

**Types of Organizations Funded:** Museums/historical societies; music/opera groups; public television/radio; historic preservation; colleges; medical research groups; environmental agencies; conservation groups; United Way; organizations for youth

**Employee Matching Gift Programs:** No

**Types of Support for Organizations:** Capital support; general operating support

**Sample Grants:**
  Red Wing Environmental Learning Center—$71,300
  Red Wing YMCA (building fund)—$50,000
  United Way of Red Wing—$5,500

**Financial Data for Year Ending December 31, 1981:**
  Assets:  $419,956
  Grants Paid:  $174,515
  Number of Grants:  39
  Largest/Smallest:  $71,300/$45

**Contact Made by:** Letter of inquiry

**Available by Request:** Annual report on contributions

**Applicants Notified:** Within one week of decision

**Directors/Trustees:** W. D. Sweasy, president; Terrance G. Shelstad, vice-president; Joseph P. Goggin

## ROBERT AND ANNE REZNICK FAMILY FOUNDATION

4331 West Twenty-fifth Street
Minneapolis, MN 55416

**Established:** November 1978

**Type:** Private foundation

**Geographic Orientation:** Twin Cities

**Sample Grants:**
  Minneapolis Federation for Jewish Service—$8,500
  St. Louis Park Crime Prevention Fund—$1,500
  United Cerebral Palsy—$100

**Financial Data for Year Ending December 31, 1981:**
  Assets:  $259,400
  Grants Paid:  $19,386
  Number of Grants:  43
  Largest/Smallest:  $8,500/$26

**Paid Professional Staff:** No

**Directors/Trustees:** Robert Reznick, president; Anne Reznick, treasurer; Gerald E. Magnuson, secretary

# RING FOUNDATION

100 North Seventh Street
Minneapolis, MN 55403

**Established:** December 1950

**Type:** Private foundation

**Geographic Orientation:** Twin Cities

**Sample Grants:**
Minneapolis Federation for Jewish Service—$12,000
United Way of Minneapolis—$1,000
Junior Achievement—$50

**Financial Data for Year Ending December 31, 1980:**
Assets: $140,910
Grants Paid: $16,150
Number of Grants: 6
Largest/Smallest: $12,000/$50

**Paid Professional Staff:** No

**Directors/Trustees:** Martin Ring, president; Harold Ring; Maxwell Barr

# • RIPLEY MEMORIAL FOUNDATION

Northwestern National Bank Endowment/Foundation
  Division
Seventh and Marquette
Minneapolis, MN 55480

**Contact Person:** Elinor K. Ogden, president

**Established:** 1957

**Type:** Private foundation

**Program's Purpose:** To grant funds to agencies whose services primarily are directed to meet the needs of women and children

**Geographic Orientation:** Minnesota

**Fields of Activity:** Medical/health education; mental health; special population groups

**Types of Organizations Funded:** Family-planning agencies; counseling services; organizations for women; organizations for youth; centers for children; neighborhood agencies

**Targeted Population Group:** Women/girls

**Type of Support for Organizations:** General operating

**Type of Support for Individuals:** Emergency, short-term assistance through the foundation's rehabilitation fund

**Sample Grants:**
Minneapolis Children's Health Center (scholarship funds for preschool day-treatment center)—$5,050
Domestic Abuse Project (to fund women's therapy program)—$1,500
YWCA (to support Contact Plus suburban program)—$1,000

**Financial Data for Year Ending December 31, 1981:**
Assets: $507,142
Grants Paid: $32,931
Number of Grants: 13
Largest/Smallest: $5,050/$1,000

**Paid Professional Staff:** No

**Contact Made by:** Request for guidelines

**Available by Request:** Proposal guidelines; application procedures; annual report

**Proposal Deadlines:** One month prior to board meetings

**Board Meetings:** Quarterly, third weeks of January, April, July, and October

**Applicants Notified:** Within one week of decision

**Directors:** Elinor K. Ogden, president (1982) (officers and board members rotate off the board regularly)

# RITZ FOUNDATION

850 Baker Building
Minneapolis, MN 55402

**Established:** November 1979

**Type:** Private foundation

**Geographic Orientation:** Minnesota

**Sample Grant:**
The Nature Conservancy—$150

**Financial Data for Year Ending December 31, 1981:**
Assets: $25,131
Grants Paid: $150
Number of Grants: 1

**Paid Professional Staff:** No

**Directors/Trustees:** Gordon Ritz, president; Norma R. Phelps, secretary-treasurer

# MARGARET RIVERS FUND

c/o First National Bank
Stillwater, MN 55082

**Type:** Private foundation

**Geographic Orientation:** St. Croix River Valley

**Sample Grants:**
Hudson Memorial Hospital, Hudson, WI—$50,000
Ascension Church, Stillwater, MN—$25,000
Newsweek Talking Magazine Fund for the Blind—$500

**Financial Data for Year Ending December 31, 1981:**
Assets: $7,532,880
Grants Paid: $430,450
Number of Grants: 135
Largest/Smallest: $50,000/$500

**Paid Professional Staff:** No

**Directors/Trustees:** William Klapp, president; Winston Sandeen, treasurer; Karl Neumeier, vice-president; Helen Moelter, secretary

## ROBINS, DAVIS AND LYONS FOUNDATION

33 South Fifth Street
Minneapolis, MN 55402

**Established:** January 1957

**Type:** Corporate foundation

**Sample Grants:**
Minnesota Landmark—$500
St. Paul Humane Society—$200
Animal Humane Society—$150

**Financial Data for Year Ending December 31, 1981:**
Assets: $68,379
Grants Paid: $1,050
Number of Grants: 4
Largest/Smallest: $500/$150

**Paid Professional Staff:** No

**Directors/Trustees:** Stephen J. Davis, president; Dean E. Smith, secretary

## D. B. ROBINSON FOUNDATION

c/o Kem-Tex Corporation
First National Bank Building
Winona, MN 55987

**Established:** 1959

**Type:** Private foundation

**Geographic Orientation:** Winona

**Sample Grants:**
St. Paul's Church—$5,890
Hour of Power—$600
Lamberton Animal Shelter—$100

**Financial Data for Year Ending December 31, 1981:**
Assets: $105,907
Grants Paid: $13,070
Number of Grants: 38
Largest/Smallest: $5,890/$25

**Paid Professional Staff:** No

**Directors/Trustees:** Douglas B. Robinson, president; Ruth Robinson, vice-president (from 990-AR, 1980)

## • ROCHESTER AREA FOUNDATION

436 First Bank Building
Rochester, MN 55901
(507) 282-0203

**Contact Person:** Isabel Huizenga, chairman

**Established:** 1944

**Type:** Community foundation

**Program's Purpose:** "To establish, aid and promote activities of a social, moral, educational and benevolent nature" in Olmsted County, MN

**Program's Limits:** Capital grants to tax-exempt organizations; aid to innovative programs; local scholarships; partial payments of medical expenses for indigent handicapped persons; no budget support for travel projects

**Geographic Orientation:** Olmsted County, MN

**Fields of Activity:** Arts/architecture; music/opera; higher education; medical care/treatment; medical/health education; public health; mental health; business/economic education; community affairs; crime/law enforcement; drug-abuse programs; disaster relief; family services; recreation

**Types of Organizations Funded:** Museums/historical societies; music/opera groups; public television/radio; colleges; universities; scholarship funds; libraries; hospitals; chemical dependency services; counseling services; science/social science (e.g., partial support of planetarium); legal aid; multiservice centers; organizations for the elderly; organizations for the handicapped; organizations for women; organizations for drug abusers; organizations for youth; organizations for men; centers for children; organizations for offenders; day-care centers

**Types of Support for Organizations:** Capital support; matching grants; program development

**Type of Support for Individuals:** Scholarships

**Sample Grants:**
Hiawatha Home for Adults—$10,000
Salvation Army Capital Fund—$10,000
Oxbow Interpretive Nature Center—$5,000

**Financial Data for Year Ending December 31, 1981:**
Assets: $998,332
Grants Paid: $54,822
Number of Grants: 18
Largest/Smallest: $25,000/$400

**Paid Professional Staff:** No

**Contact Made by:** Telephone inquiry

**Available by Request:** Proposal guidelines; application procedures; annual report

**Board Meetings:** Quarterly, on third Mondays of February, May, August, and November

**Applicants Notified:** Within one week of decision

**Trustees:** Isabel C. Huizenga, chairman; Howard T. Stewart, vice-chairman; Herbert M. Stellner, Jr., vice-chairman; Robert S. Brown, secretary; Dr. Theodore G. Martens, treasurer; Vera Elgin; Ann Ferguson; John Herrell; Clifford Johnson; Alfred Schumann; Margaret Thompson; Curtis Taylor; Charles Von Wald; Howard West; Barbara Withers; Robert A. Bezoier, executive secretary

## VERNON J. ROCKLER FOUNDATION

1420 TCF Tower
Minneapolis, MN 55402

**Established:** June 1969

**Type:** Private foundation

**Geographic Orientation:** Twin Cities

**Sample Grants:**
Beth El Synagogue—$500
Minnesota Orchestral Association—$50
Variety Club Heart Hospital—$15

**Financial Data for Year Ending June 30, 1981:**
Assets: $21,061
Grants Paid: $590
Number of Grants: 4
Largest/Smallest: $500/$15

**Paid Professional Staff:** No

**Director/Trustee:** Vernon J. Rockler

## • THE RODMAN FOUNDATION

2100 First National Bank Building
St. Paul, MN 55101
(612) 228-0935

**Contact Person:** E. Rodman Titcomb, Jr., president

**Established:** May 1969

**Type:** Private foundation

**Geographic Orientation:** Twin Cities; national

**Sample Grants:**
University of Puget Sound, Tacoma, WA—$50,000
(over five years)
Union Gospel Mission, St. Paul—$2,250
Merriam Park Community Center, St. Paul—$350

**Financial Data for Year Ending December 31, 1981:**
Assets: $296,394
Grants Paid: $131,600
Number of Grants: 50
Largest/Smallest: $20,000/$100

**Paid Professional Staff:** No

**Contact Made by:** Letter of inquiry

**Board Meetings:** Annual, in April and on an ongoing basis to consider grants

**Applicants Notified:** Within two to three weeks of decision

**Directors:** E. Rodman Titcomb, Jr., president; Julie C. Titcomb, vice-president; J. S. Micallef, secretary; Gordon E. Hed, treasurer; E. R. Titcomb

## ROSE AND HARRY ROSENTHAL FOUNDATION

220 East Fifth Street
St. Paul, MN 55101
(612) 224-1355

**Contact Person:** H. Rosenthal, director

**Established:** December 1959

**Type:** Private foundation

**Program's Purpose:** To support charitable, religious, scientific, literary, and educational organizations

**Geographic Orientation:** International

**Sample Grants:**
Jerusalem Foundation—$25,000
St. Paul United Jewish Fund and Council—$7,500
Brandeis University, Massachusetts—$1,000

**Financial Data for Year Ending December 31, 1981:**
Assets: $171,307
Grants Paid: $36,156
Number of Grants: 12
Largest/Smallest: $25,000/$100

**Paid Professional Staff:** No

**Director/Trustee:** Harry Rosenthal

## ROYCRAFT FOUNDATION

400 First Avenue North
Minneapolis, MN 55401

**Established:** December 1947

**Type:** Private foundation

**Geographic Orientation:** Twin Cities

**Sample Grant:**
Maslon Nursing Scholarship—$1,000

**Financial Data for Year Ending December 31, 1981:**
Assets: $25,006
Grants Paid: $1,000
Number of Grants: 1

**Paid Professional Staff:** No

**Directors/Trustees:** Roy B. Corwin, president; Milton H. Corwin, vice-president; Burt H. Corwin, secretary-treasurer

## ST. CROIX FOUNDATION

c/o First Trust Company of St. Paul
W-555 First National Bank Building
St. Paul, MN 55101
(612) 291-5114

**Contact Person:** Jeffrey T. Peterson

**Established:** December 1950

**Type:** Private foundation

**Geographic Orientation:** Stillwater-St. Paul area

**Sample Grants:**
Ascension Episcopal Church—$5,500
Hope International Family Services—$1,700
Science Museum—$500

**Financial Data for Year Ending December 31, 1981:**
Assets: $425,199
Grants Paid: $29,800
Number of Grants: 15
Largest/Smallest: $5,500/$100

**Paid Professional Staff:** No

**Contact Made by:** Complete proposal

**Directors/Trustees:** Robert S. Davis, president; Ianthe B. Hardenbergh, vice-president/treasurer; Gabrielle Hardenbergh, secretary

## ST. JUDE MEDICAL

1 Lillehei Plaza
St. Paul, MN 55117
(612) 483-2000

**Contact Person:** Sharon A. Hansen, corporate relations manager

**Established:** 1981

**Type:** Charitable contributions program

**Program's Interests:** Education; culture; health care; community service

**Geographic Orientation:** Twin Cities; Minnesota; international

**Fields of Activity:** Music/opera; theater/dance; higher education; research; medical research; medical care/treatment; medical/health education; public health; mental health; life sciences; physical sciences; community affairs; drug-abuse programs; employment/job training; family services

**Types of Organizations Funded:** Museum/historical societies; theaters/dance groups; music/opera groups; cultural centers; special education; Junior Achievement; medical research groups; chemical dependency services; research/study institutes; United Way; organizations for the handicapped; organizations for drug abusers; organizations for youth; centers for children

**Employee Matching Gift Programs:** No

**Types of Support for Organizations:** Capital support; continuing support; product contributions

**Type of Support for Individuals:** Research support

**Sample Grants:**
Diabetes Education Exchange—$500
Granville House—$500
Washburn Child Guidance Center—$250

**Financial Data for Year Ending December 31, 1982:**
Contributions Paid: Under $15,000

**Contact Made by:** Letter of inquiry; request for guidelines

**Available by Request:** Proposal guidelines; application procedures

**Contributions Decisions Made:** Quarterly, in March, June, September, and December

## • THE ST. PAUL COMPANIES, INC.

385 Washington Street
St. Paul, MN 55102
(612) 221-7875

**Contact Persons:** Polly Nyberg, grants administrator; Iris Lewis, community relations administrator (education only)

**Type:** Charitable contributions program

**Program's Interests:** Education; health and social services; humanities; community development

**Program's Limits:** Support to United Way agencies restricted to management technical assistance (see company's guidelines)

**Geographic Orientation:** Twin Cities; Minnesota; cities where The St. Paul Companies have service centers

**Fields of Activity:** Arts/architecture; history/preservation; media/communications; music/opera; theater/dance; arts education; elementary/secondary education; vocational education; higher education; adult/continuing education; medical research; medical care/treatment; medical/health education; public health; mental health; advocacy; business/economic education; community affairs; crime/law enforcement; drug-abuse programs; economic development; employment/job training; equal rights/legal aid; family services; safety; special population groups; welfare; other welfare/social service activities

**Types of Organizations Funded:** Museums/historical societies; theaters/dance groups; music/opera groups; libraries; zoos; public television/radio; arts councils; historic preservation; cultural centers; elementary schools; secondary schools; vocational schools; colleges; universities; educational councils; scholarship funds; special education; adult education; hospitals; medical schools; medical research groups; clinics; chemical dependency services; family-planning agencies; counseling services; United Way; legal aid; multiservice centers; organizations for the elderly; organizations for the handicapped; organizations for women; organizations for veterans; organizations for drug abusers; organizations for youth; organizations for men; centers for children; housing agencies; organizations for offenders; organizations for minorities; neighborhood agencies; day-care centers; community centers

**Employee Matching Gift Programs:** Higher education; elementary/secondary education; many types of nonprofit organizations

**Types of Support for Organizations:** Capital support; continuing support; endowment; general operating support; matching grants; program development; research; federated fund drives; program-related investments

**Type of Support for Individuals:** Scholarship program for children of employees

**Sample Grants:**
Science Museum of Minnesota—$60,000
Twin Cities Neighborhood Housing Services—$54,000
CHART—$15,000

**Financial Data for Year Ending December 31, 1982:**
Contributions Paid: $3,056,759
Number of Contributions: 155
Largest/Smallest: $184,800/$400

**Contact Made by:** Letter of inquiry

**Available by Request:** Proposal guidelines; application procedures; annual report on contributions

**Proposal Deadlines:** Four months prior to contributions decision date

**Contributions Decisions Made:** Monthly (end of month)

**Applicants Notified:** Within four weeks of decision

## • THE SAINT PAUL FOUNDATION

1120 Northwestern National Bank Building
St. Paul, MN 55101
(612) 224-5463

**Contact Person:** Paul A. Verret, president

**Established:** 1940

**Type:** Community foundation

**Program's Purpose:** To provide support for educational, charitable, cultural, or benevolent purposes, preferably for those who live in the St. Paul area

**Geographic Orientation:** St. Paul area

**Fields of Activity:** Arts/architecture; history/preservation; language/literature; media/communications; music/opera; theater/dance; arts education; elementary/secondary education; vocational education; higher education; adult/continuing education; medical care/treatment; medical/health education; public health; mental health; social sciences; advocacy; community affairs; crime/law enforcement; drug-abuse programs; economic development; employment/job training; environment/energy; equal rights/legal aid; disaster relief; family services; recreation; safety; special population groups; welfare; other welfare/social service activities

**Types of Organizations Funded:** Museums/historical societies; theaters/dance groups; music/opera groups; libraries; zoos; public television/radio; arts councils; historic preservation; cultural centers; elementary schools; secondary schools; vocational schools; colleges; universities; scholarship funds; special education; adult education; libraries; other educational organizations; hospitals; medical research groups; clinics; chemical dependency services; family-planning agencies; counseling services; religious service groups; environmental agencies; energy agencies; conservation groups; United Way; legal aid; multiservice centers; organizations for the elderly; organizations for the handicapped; organizations for women; organizations for drug abusers; organizations for youth; centers for children; housing agencies; organizations for offenders; organizations for minorities; neighborhood agencies; day-care centers; community centers; other welfare/social service organizations

**Targeted Population Groups:** Refugees (limited duration programs); minorities

**Types of Support for Organizations:** Capital support; continuing support; matching grants; program development; federated fund drives; program-related investments; other

**Types of Support for Individuals:** Emergency health and welfare aid through Community Sharing Fund

**Sample Grants:**
Loa Family Community, Drivers' Training Program—$33,100
College of Saint Catherine, Hispanic Motivation Program—$25,000
Minnesota Composers Forum (to fund general manager)—$7,500

**Financial Data for Year Ending December 31, 1981:**
Assets: $45,312,391
Grants Paid: $3,939,632
Number of Grants: 263
Largest/Smallest: $975,000/$100

**Paid Professional Staff:** Yes

**Contact Made by:** Request for guidelines

**Available by Request:** Proposal guidelines; application procedures; annual report; newsletter

**Proposal Deadlines:** At least two months prior to meeting

**Board Meetings:** Five times per year

**Applicants Notified:** Within two weeks of decision

**Directors/Trustees:** Richard A. Moore, chairman; Sam Singer, vice-chairman; Jean V. West, treasurer; Benjamin G. Griggs, Jr.; Reuel D. Harmon; Ronald M. Hubbs; Richard A. Klingen; Richard H. Kyle; Norman M. Lorentzsen; Dr. Dwight L. Martin; Timothy P. Quinn; Charles L. Rafferty; James W. Reagan; J. Thomas Simonet

## SALEM FOUNDATION

445 Minnesota Street, #2120
St. Paul, MN 55101

**Established:** August 1967

**Type:** Private foundation

**Geographic Orientation:** Minnesota; Florida

**Sample Grants:**
D.E.A.F. Media—$7,950
United Fund of Collier County, Florida—$1,250
American Humanities Foundation—$250

**Financial Data for Year Ending May 31, 1981:**
Assets: $789,383
Grants Paid: $68,400
Number of Grants: 51
Largest/Smallest: $7,950/$100

**Paid Professional Staff:** No

**Directors/Trustees:** Elizabeth M. Parish, president; John C. Parish, vice-president/secretary; Michael Parish

## THE SALKIN FOUNDATION

7400 Excelsior Boulevard
Minneapolis, MN 55426

**Established:** January 1945

**Type:** Private foundation

**Geographic Orientation:** Twin Cities

**Sample Grants:**
First Unitarian Society—$3,500
Minnesota Orchestral Association—$1,000
American Association of Ethiopian Jews—$300

**Financial Data for Year Ending April 30, 1981:**
Assets: $167,816
Grants Paid: $11,175
Number of Grants: 10
Largest/Smallest: $3,500/$125

**Paid Professional Staff:** No

**Director/Trustee:** Morrey L. Salkin, president/treasurer

## CARL AND VERNA SCHMIDT FOUNDATION

Route 4
St. Peter, MN 56082

**Type:** Private foundation

**Geographic Orientation:** Minnesota

**Sample Grants:**
Master Eye Foundation—$1,000
Calvary Baptist Church—$1,000
Zurah Shrine Circus—$30

**Financial Data for Year Ending November 30, 1981:**
Assets: $76,875
Grants Paid: $6,575
Number of Grants: 18
Largest/Smallest: $1,000/$10

**Paid Professional Staff:** No

**Director/Trustee:** Carl Schmidt

## SCHMITT FOUNDATION

88 South Tenth Street
Minneapolis, MN 55403

**Established:** February 1960

**Type:** Corporate foundation

**Program's Purpose:** In part, to provide grants for "scientific and educational promotion, study, research, development and use of music therapy"

**Geographic Orientation:** Minnesota

**Sample Grants:**
Schubert Club—$6,000
Edina ABC—$1,500
Concentus Musicus—$250

**Financial Data for Year Ending December 31, 1981:**
Assets: $15,826
Grants Paid: $35,765
Number of Grants: 116
Largest/Smallest: $6,000/$15

**Paid Professional Staff:** No

**Directors/Trustees:** Robert A. Schmitt; Robert P. Schmitt; Margaret H. Schmitt; Elizabeth A. Gile (all from 990-AR, 1980)

## SCHOTT FOUNDATION

3140 Harbor Lane North
Plymouth, MN 55441

**Established:** December 1980

**Type:** Private foundation

**Geographic Orientation:** Minnesota

**Sample Grants:**
Scholarship—$1,000
Minnesota Corporation for Public Broadcasting—$800
Southwest Minnesota Arts Council—$50

**Financial Data for Year Ending March 31, 1982:**
Assets: $161,644
Grants Paid: $3,050
Number of Grants: 7
Largest/Smallest: $1,000/$50

**Paid Professional Staff:** No

**Directors/Trustees:** Owen W. Schott, president; Maurice J. Holzknecht, treasurer; D. James Nielsen, secretary

## MENDON F. SCHUTT FOUNDATION

2100 James Avenue South
Minneapolis, MN 55405

**Established:** November 1957

**Type:** Private foundation

**Geographic Orientation:** Twin Cities

**Sample Grants:**
Senior Citizen Center—$2,500
Neighborhood Involvement Program—$1,500
KTCA—$500

**Financial Data for Year Ending December 31, 1981:**
Assets: $18,738
Grants Paid: $16,700
Number of Grants: 24
Largest/Smallest: $2,500/$50

**Paid Professional Staff:** No

**Directors/Trustees:** Elizabeth Schutt, president/treasurer;
Eugene Larson, vice-president; Gertrude Priest; Robert
E. Larson

## SECURITY FINANCIAL ENTERPRISES

(Security Life Insurance Company of America)
1200 Second Avenue South
Minneapolis, MN 55403
(612) 333-1295

**Contact Person:** Orem Robbins, chairman of the board

**Established:** 1960

**Type:** Charitable contributions program

**Program's Interests:** Health research and education

**Program's Limits:** Matching employee contributions

**Fields of Activity:** Higher education; adult/continuing
education; medical research

**Types of Organizations Supported:** Colleges;
universities; adult education; medical research groups;
United Way

**Employee Matching Gift Programs:** Higher education;
elementary/secondary education

**Type of Support for Organizations:** Matching grants

**Financial Data for Year Ending December 31, 1982:**
Contributions Paid: Under $15,000

**Contact Made by:** Letter of inquiry to employee

## THE FRED M. SEED FOUNDATION

1235 Yale Place
Minneapolis, MN 55403

**Established:** November 1960

**Type:** Private foundation

**Geographic Orientation:** National

**Sample Grants:**
Blake School—$10,300
Mount Olivet Lutheran Church—$2,820
100 Club of Rhode Island—$100

**Financial Data for Year Ending December 31, 1981:**
Assets: $363,066
Grants Paid: $25,700
Number of Grants: 40
Largest/Smallest: $10,300/$10

**Paid Professional Staff:** No

**Directors/Trustees:** Grace M. Seed, president; John C.
Seed, vice-president; James M. Seed, secretary

## SEXTON FOUNDATION

504 First Street North
Sartell, MN 56377

**Established:** August 1977

**Type:** Private foundation

**Geographic Orientation:** Minnesota

**Sample Grants:**
College of Saint Benedict—$6,000
Camp Courage—$3,500
City of Sartell Wading Pool—$200

**Financial Data for Year Ending November 30, 1981:**
Assets: $383,067
Grants Paid: $38,210
Number of Grants: 21
Largest/Smallest: $6,000/$100

**Paid Professional Staff:** No

**Directors/Trustees:** Yvonne Sexton, president; James
Sexton, secretary-treasurer; Mary Kay Sexton, vice-
president

## SAM AND LORRAINE SHARK FOUNDATION

4805 James Avenue South
Minneapolis, MN 55409

**Established:** June 1978

**Type:** Private foundation

**Geographic Orientation:** Twin Cities

**Sample Grants:**
Minneapolis Federation for Jewish Service—$1,525
Temple Israel—$1,068
Salvation Army—$150

**Financial Data for Year Ending April 30, 1982:**
Assets: $206,345
Grants Paid: $6,817
Number of Grants: 21
Largest/Smallest: $1,525/$100

**Paid Professional Staff:** No

**Director/Trustee:** Lorraine Shark, president

## ROBERT E. SHORT FOUNDATION

803 Degree of Honor Building
St. Paul, MN 55101

**Established:** July 1965

**Type:** Private foundation

**Geographic Orientation:** National

**Sample Grants:**
  College of Saint Thomas—$100,000
  Notre Dame University—$100,000
  Order of Saint Lazarus, Illinois—$1,000

**Financial Data for Year Ending June 30, 1982:**
  Assets: $246,937
  Grants Paid: $222,000
  Number of Grants: 6
  Largest/Smallest: $100,000/$1,000

**Paid Professional Staff:** No

**Directors/Trustees:** Robert E. Short, president/treasurer; Marion D. Short, vice-president; William R. Busch, secretary (from 990-AR, 1980)

## SIEFF FAMILY FOUNDATION

Box 580
Minneapolis, MN 55440

**Established:** December 1967

**Type:** Private foundation

**Geographic Orientation:** Twin Cities

**Sample Grants:**
  Minneapolis Federation for Jewish Service—$14,000
  Salvation Army—$840
  North Country Adventure—$390

**Financial Data for Year Ending December 31, 1981:**
  Assets: $365,315
  Grants Paid: $22,851
  Number of Grants: 65
  Largest/Smallest: $14,000/$10

**Paid Professional Staff:** No

**Directors/Trustees:** Philip Sieff, president/treasurer; Maurice Sieff, vice-president; John Sieff, secretary

## WILLIAM WOOD SKINNER FOUNDATION

c/o First Trust Company of St. Paul
W-555 First National Bank Building
St. Paul, MN 55101

**Established:** November 1965

**Type:** Private foundation

**Geographic Orientation:** Illinois; Minnesota

**Sample Grants:**
  Chicago Educational Television Association—$6,000
  LaSalle Expedition II—$2,500
  Art and Science Fund, Minnesota—$1,000

**Financial Data for Year Ending September 30, 1981:**
  Assets: $514,726
  Grants Paid: $45,550
  Number of Grants: 28
  Largest/Smallest: $6,000/$300

**Paid Professional Staff:** No

**Directors/Trustees:** Paul W. Guenzel; Elizabeth S. Guenzel; First Trust Company of St. Paul

## HOWELL P. AND MARGARET H. SKOGLUND FOUNDATION

4930 IDS Center
Minneapolis, MN 55402

**Type:** Private foundation

**Geographic Orientation:** Twin Cities

**Sample Grants:**
  Saint Olaf College—$5,000
  Buffalo Bill Museum—$1,000
  Plymouth Christian Youth Center—$500

**Financial Data for Year Ending December 31, 1981:**
  Assets: $168,684
  Grants Paid: $19,800
  Number of Grants: 16
  Largest/Smallest: $5,000/$300

**Paid Professional Staff:** No

**Directors/Trustees:** Margaret H. Skoglund; John C. Skoglund; Carol Sperry

## THE SKIPPER SLAWIK FOUNDATION

1850 University Avenue
St. Paul, MN 55104
(612) 645-8111

**Contact Person:** Mrs. Harold J. Slawik

**Established:** August 1958

**Type:** Private foundation

**Program's Purpose:** Ninety percent of grants for scholarships; 10 percent for sports activities; scholarships for financially needy children to attend private or parochial secondary schools (renewable every year, from freshman year through completion)

**Program's Limits:** Only one child per family; family income less than $30,000 per year

**Geographic Orientation:** Ramsey County

**Types of Organizations Supported:** Religious schools; sports groups

**Financial Data for Year Ending December 31, 1981:**
  Assets: $284,515
  Grants Paid: $23,015
  Number of Grants: Two to organizations; twelve scholarships
  Largest/Smallest: $1,000/$15

**Paid Professional Staff:** No

**Contact Made by:** School principal

**Available by Visit:** Annual report

**Board Meetings:** Annual, in May

**Applicants Notified:** Within eight weeks of decision

**Trustees:** Mrs. Harold J. Slawik; Jerome O'Brien Slawik; John Larson; Selections committee: Judge of Ramsey County Juvenile Court; St. Paul Public Schools representative; Archdiocese of St. Paul School System representative

## SMITH FOUNDATION

2600 Niagara Lane North
Minneapolis, MN 55441

**Established:** December 1943

**Type:** Private foundation

**Geographic Orientation:** Twin Cities

**Sample Grants:**
  Challenge—$10,000
  Minnesota Private College Fund—$5,000
  Bridge for Runaway Youth—$200

**Financial Data for Year Ending December 31, 1981:**
  Assets: $352,657
  Grants Paid: $60,525
  Number of Grants: 72
  Largest/Smallest: $10,000/$100

**Paid Professional Staff:** No

**Directors/Trustees:** Peter J. Geier, president; M. J. Johnson, vice-president; G. J. Kunik, treasurer; B. I. Clabaugh, secretary

## SOMERSET FOUNDATION

c/o First Trust Company of St. Paul
W-555 First National Bank Building
St. Paul, MN 55101

**Contact Person:** Paul J. Kelly, secretary

**Established:** September 1960

**Type:** Private foundation

**Geographic Orientation:** Twin Cities

**Sample Grants:**
  YMCA—$5,000
  First Baptist Church—$3,690
  Campus Crusade for Christ, California—$900

**Financial Data for Year Ending December 31, 1981:**
  Assets: $675,637
  Grants Paid: $9,590
  Number of Grants: 3
  Largest/Smallest: $5,000/$900

**Paid Professional Staff:** No

**Contact Made by:** Complete proposal

**Directors/Trustees:** Hella L. Mears, president; William F. Hueg, Jr., vice-president; Paul J. Kelly, secretary-treasurer

## THE SOUTHWAYS FOUNDATION

930 Dain Tower
Minneapolis, MN 55402
(612) 338-3871

**Contact Person:** John S. Pillsbury, Jr., president

**Established:** December 1950

**Type:** Private foundation

**Program's Purpose:** To support charitable and cultural institutions in the Minneapolis-St. Paul area and educational institutions in which family members have a special interest

**Geographic Orientation:** Twin Cities; national (for educational institutions in which family members have a special interest)

**Sample Grants:**
  United Way of Minneapolis—$31,500
  Yale University (in part matching individual family gifts)—$11,950
  Walker Art Center—$10,000

**Financial Data for Year Ending December 31, 1981:**
  Assets: $3,505,430
  Grants Paid: $294,669
  Number of Grants: 39
  Largest/Smallest: $31,500/$100

**Paid Professional Staff:** No

**Board Meetings:** Biannual, in May/June and December

**Trustees:** John S. Pillsbury, Jr., president; John S. Pillsbury III, vice-president; George S. Pillsbury, secretary-treasurer; Mrs. Robert G. Mitchell, Jr., assistant treasurer; Mrs. John S. Pillsbury; Mrs. Thomas M. Crosby

## SPIEGEL FOUNDATION

5601 East River Road
Minneapolis, MN 55440

**Established:** November 1962

**Type:** Private foundation

**Geographic Orientation:** Twin Cities

**Sample Grants:**
Minneapolis Federation for Jewish Service—$85,500
Torah Academy—$170
KTCA—$35

**Financial Data for Year Ending October 31, 1981:**
Assets: $9,931
Grants Paid: $86,690
Number of Grants: 12
Largest/Smallest: $85,000/$35

**Paid Professional Staff:** No

**Directors/Trustees:** Maurice L. Spiegel, president/
treasurer; Minnie Spiegel, vice-president/assistant
secretary; Richard G. Spiegel, vice-president/secretary

# LELAND E. AND GRACE J. STARR
# FOUNDATION

3415 Glenarden Road
St. Paul, MN 55112

**Established:** December 1968

**Type:** Private foundation

**Geographic Orientation:** Twin Cities

**Sample Grants:**
Hearing Society of Minnesota—$500
Salvation Army—$300
H.E.A.R.T.—$200

**Financial Data for Year Ending December 31, 1981:**
Assets: $63,302
Grants Paid: $3,200
Number of Grants: 12
Largest/Smallest: $500/$100

**Paid Professional Staff:** No

**Directors/Trustees:** Leland E. Starr, president/treasurer;
Grace J. Starr, vice-president/secretary; William R.
Busch (from 990-AR, 1980)

# SUMMER FUND

444 Lafayette Road
St. Paul, MN 55101

**Established:** November 1966

**Type:** Private foundation

**Geographic Orientation:** National

**Sample Grants:**
Camping and Education Foundation—$500
Colorado College—$150
United Negro College Fund—$100

**Financial Data for Year Ending December 31, 1981:**
Assets: $19,026
Grants Paid: $1,175
Number of Grants: 6
Largest/Smallest: $500/$100

**Paid Professional Staff:** No

**Director/Trustee:** Harry G. NcNeely, Jr.

# SWEASY FOUNDATION

419 Bush Street
Red Wing, MN 55066
(612) 388-8211

**Contact Person:** W. D. Sweasy, president

**Established:** 1960

**Type:** Private foundation

**Program's Purpose:** To provide general support for
charitable, educational, and recreational activities,
primarily in the Red Wing-Twin Cities area

**Geographic Orientation:** Red Wing; Twin Cities;
national

**Fields of Activity:** Arts/architecture; history/preservation;
media/communications; community affairs

**Types of Organizations Funded:** Churches/synagogues;
United Way; organizations for youth

**Type of Support for Organizations:** Continuing support

**Sample Grants:**
United Way of Red Wing—$1,000
Red Wing YMCA—$600
KTCA—$250

**Financial Data for Year Ending December 31, 1981:**
Assets: $128,200
Grants Paid: $6,295
Number of Grants: 23
Largest/Smallest: $1,000/$40

**Paid Professional Staff:** No

**Contact Made by:** Letter of inquiry

**Available by Request:** Annual report

**Board Meetings:** Annual

**Applicants Notified:** Within one week of decision

**Directors/Trustees:** W. D. Sweasy, president; Joseph
Goggin, vice-president; Terrance Shelstad, vice-
president

# HAROLD W. SWEATT FOUNDATION

1560 Dain Tower
Minneapolis, MN 55402

**Established:** June 1968

**Type:** Private foundation

**Geographic Orientation:** National

**Sample Grants:**
Yale Graduate School Alumni Fund—$20,125
Minneapolis Society of Fine Arts—$2,000
Colonial Williamsburg Fund—$100

**Financial Data for Year Ending February 28, 1982:**
Assets: $1,160,032
Grants Paid: $57,195
Number of Grants: 44
Largest/Smallest: $20,125/$15

**Paid Professional Staff:** No

**Directors/Trustees:** Martha S. Reed; A. Lachlan Reed;
William S. Reed

## SWEITZER FOUNDATION

1424 Englewood Avenue
St. Paul, MN 55104

**Established:** January 1969

**Type:** Private foundation

**Geographic Orientation:** Twin Cities

**Sample Grants:**
Hamline University—$100
Salvation Army—$50

**Financial Data for Year Ending December 31, 1981:**
Assets: $1,087
Grants Paid: $150
Number of Grants: 2
Largest/Smallest: $100/$50

**Paid Professional Staff:** No

**Directors/Trustees:** J. R. Sweitzer, president/treasurer;
James A. Sweitzer, secretary; Herbert G. Henneman,
Jr.


## OTTO SWOBODA FOUNDATION

1667 Hartford Avenue
St. Paul, MN 55116

**Established:** December 1955 (originally D. W. Hickey &
Company Foundation)

**Type:** Private foundation

**Geographic Orientation:** Minnesota

**Sample Grants:** Edgecumbe Presbyterian Church Organ
Fund—$1,000
St. Paul Area Council of Churches—$200
Women's Resource, Winona—$100

**Financial Data for Year Ending December 31, 1981:**
Assets: $14,269
Grants Paid: $1,700
Number of Grants: 7
Largest/Smallest: $1,000/$100

**Paid Professional Staff:** No

**Director/Trustee:** Otto C. Swoboda


## NORMAN H. TALLAKSON
## CHARITABLE TRUST

Glen Oaks Nursing Home
New London, MN 56273

**Established:** November 1978

**Type:** Private foundation

**Geographic Orientation:** Minnesota

**Sample Grants:**
Vinje Congregation, Vinje Lutheran Church, Willmar,
MN—$900
Youth for Christ—$700
Waldorf College, Iowa—$200

**Financial Data for Year Ending December 31, 1981:**
Assets: $120,694
Grants Paid: $5,700
Number of Grants: 20
Largest/Smallest: $900/$50

**Paid Professional Staff:** No

**Directors/Trustees:** Norman H. Tallakson; Loyal E.
Tallakson


## TANG FOUNDATION

6016 Idylwood Drive
Edina, MN 55436

**Established:** December 1969

**Type:** Private foundation

**Geographic Orientation:** Twin Cities

**Sample Grants:**
Augustana Lutheran Church—$100
Little Brothers of the Poor—$100

**Financial Data for Year Ending December 31, 1981:**
Assets: $3,865
Grants Paid: $200
Number of Grants: 2
Largest/Smallest: $100/$100

**Paid Professional Staff:** No

**Directors/Trustees:** E. Palmer Tang; Carlyle Pohlman


## ALEX G. TANKENOFF FOUNDATION

Metro Square Building
St. Paul, MN 55101

**Established:** August 1944

**Type:** Private foundation

**Geographic Orientation:** Minnesota; Wisconsin

**Sample Grants:**
United Way of St. Paul—$824
Temple Israel—$625
Junior Achievement—$50

**Financial Data for Year Ending December 31, 1981:**
Assets: $224, 697
Grants Paid: $4,004
Number of Grants: 33
Largest/Smallest: $824/$5

**Paid Professional Staff:** No

**Directors/Trustees:** Gary Tankenoff; James Tankenoff;
Joyce Malmon

# TEBBEN FOUNDATION

4624 IDS Center
Minneapolis, MN 55402

**Established:** December 1977

**Type:** Private foundation

**Program's Purpose:** In part, to support "the missionary and evangelistic activities of the Bethany Reformed Church and the Billy Graham Evangelistic Association"

**Geographic Orientation:** National

**Sample Grants:**
Bethany Reformed Church—$5,500
Midwest Challenge—$3,000
Christian Helpers Ministries—$130

**Financial Data for Year Ending December 31, 1981:**
Assets: $17,124
Grants Paid: $18,937
Number of Grants: 15
Largest/Smallest: $5,500/$25

**Paid Professional Staff:** No

**Directors/Trustees:** Herman J. Ratelle; Mildred Tebben; Brian Hoffman; Dalen Caspers

# ● TENNANT COMPANY FOUNDATION

Box 1452
701 North Lilac Drive
Minneapolis, MN 55440

**Established:** December 1972

**Type:** Corporate foundation

**Geographic Orientation:** Twin Cities

**Sample Grants:**
Greater Minneapolis YMCA—$16,500
Washburn Child Guidance Center—$4,000
Minnesota Chorale—$200

**Financial Data for Year Ending December 31, 1981:**
Assets: $170,533
Grants Paid: $233,791
Number of Grants: 123
Largest/Smallest: $16,500/$50

**Paid Professional Staff:** No

**Directors/Trustees:** George T. Pennock, president; Martin N. Kellogg, treasurer; Robert D. Langford, secretary; Roger Hale

# R. E. THEEL FOUNDATION

Box 1031
Rochester, MN 55901

**Established:** December 1968

**Type:** Private foundation

**Geographic Orientation:** Minnesota

**Sample Grants:**
Calvary Episcopal Church—$390
Rochester Civic Music—$200
Minnesota Arboretum Foundation—$100

**Financial Data for Year Ending December 31, 1981:**
Assets: $33,560
Grants Paid: $1,690
Number of Grants: 8
Largest/Smallest: $390/$100

**Paid Professional Staff:** No

**Director/Trustee:** Robert E. Theel

# THERESE FOUNDATION

1400 Northwestern National Bank Building
St. Paul, MN 55101

**Established:** November 1979

**Type:** Private foundation

**Geographic Orientation:** National

**Sample Grants:**
Maryknoll Fathers, New York—$2,850
Medical Mission Sisters, Pennsylvania—$2,000
Our Lady of Good Counsel Free Cancer Home—$500

**Financial Data for Year Ending December 31, 1981:**
Assets: $80,223
Grants Paid: $8,850
Number of Grants: 8
Largest/Smallest: $2,850/$500

**Paid Professional Staff:** No

**Directors/Trustees:** Mary T. Quigley, president; John R. Quigley, vice-president; Marvin J. Pertzik, secretary-treasurer

# JAMES R. THORPE FOUNDATION

First National Bank of Minneapolis
Box A700
Minneapolis, MN 55480

**Established:** October 1974

**Type:** Private foundation

**Program's Purpose:** To contribute to "programs that would support a significant broad cross-cut section of our population"

**Program's Limits:** Rarely grants for capital funds, construction, operating budgets; restricted to organizations operating in Minnesota

**Geographic Orientation:** Minnesota

**Sample Grants:**
YMCA—$75,000
Episcopal Dioceses of Minnesota—$50,000
Minneapolis Indian Domiciliary Care Center—$1,000

**Financial Data for Year Ending November 30, 1981:**
Assets: $3,958,128
Grants Paid: $409,200
Number of Grants: 46
Largest/Smallest: $75,000/$900

**Paid Professional Staff:** No

**Contact Made by:** Request for guidelines

**Available by Request:** Proposal guidelines

**Proposal Deadlines:** September 15 of the year preceding the need for funding

**Board Meetings:** Annual, in October or November

**Directors/Trustees:** Frank A. Thorpe, president; Samuel A. Cote, vice-president; Mary C. Boos, secretary; Samuel S. Thorpe III, treasurer

# • 3M FOUNDATION

3M Center, Bldg. 220-2W
St. Paul, MN 55144
(612) 733-8335

**Contact Person:** D. W. Larson, director of community affairs

**Established:** 1953

**Type:** Corporate foundation

**Program's Interests:** Cultural, educational, medical, youth, and civic activities of broad public interest; strongest consideration given to organizations located in areas where 3M has facilities and in which 3M employees are active participants

**Geographic Orientation:** Locations where 3M has facilities

**Fields of Activity:** Arts/architecture; history/preservation; music/opera; theater/dance; higher education; research; medical research; medical care/treatment; mental health; business/economic education; community affairs; crime/law enforcement; drug-abuse programs; economic development; family services

**Types of Organizations Funded:** Museums/historical societies; theaters/dance groups; music/opera groups; libraries; public television/radio; cultural centers; vocational schools; colleges; universities; scholarship funds; libraries; hospitals; medical schools; medical research groups; chemical dependency services; counseling services; United Way; legal aid; organizations for the elderly; organizations for the handicapped; organizations for women; organizations for drug abusers; organizations for youth; organizations for minorities; community centers

**Types of Support for Organizations:** Continuing support; matching grants; research

**Sample Grants:**
Hamline University—$100,000
Knoxville Community Hospital—$20,000
Metropolitan Center, Boston—$5,000

**Financial Data for Year Ending December 31, 1981:**
Assets: $5,869,703
Grants Paid: $4,012,861
Number of Grants: 2,006
Largest/Smallest: $130,000/$25

**Paid Professional Staff:** Yes

**Contact Made by:** Telephone inquiry; letter of inquiry

**Available by Request:** Proposal guidelines; annual report

**Proposal Deadlines:** Six weeks prior to quarterly meetings

**Board Meetings:** Quarterly in March, June, September, and December

**Applicants Notified:** Within twelve weeks of decision

**Officers/Directors:** Donald E. Garretson, president; James A. Thwaits, vice-president; Carlos W. Luis, secretary; Donald W. Larson, assistant secretary; Ralph D. Ebbott, treasurer; Mary A. Ginther, recording secretary; Robert M. Adams; Richard W. Brust; Charlton Dietz; Gordon W. Engdahl; Lewis W. Lehr (chairman/chief executive officer of 3M Company); Jerry E. Robertson; Stanley W. Thiele

# T.I.H. FOUNDATION

1644 St. Croix Circle
Minneapolis, MN 55422

**Established:** December 1959

**Type:** Private foundation

**Program's Purpose:** "To the maximum extent possible shall promote and participate in the propagation of the fundamental evangelical message of Jesus Christ, and generally the corporation shall further the Christian ministry"

**Geographic Orientation:** Twin Cities

**Sample Grant:**
Executive Counseling—$500

**Financial Data for Year Ending December 31, 1981:**
Assets: $107,948
Grants Paid: $500
Number of Grants: 1

**Paid Professional Staff:** No

**Directors/Trustees:** J. J. Barnett, president; Marjorie Barnett, secretary-treasurer; Gene E. Denler, vice-president

## TOZER FOUNDATION

c/o First Trust Company of St. Paul
W-555 First National Bank Building
St. Paul, MN 55101
(612) 439-4330

**Contact Person:** G. T. Waldref, president

**Established:** June 1946

**Type:** Private foundation

**Program's Purpose:** To support charity, religion, science, education; 80 percent of funds designated for scholarships for students from Pine, Kanabec, and Washington Counties

**Geographic Orientation:** Minnesota

**Fields of Activity:** Higher education; United Way

**Types of Organizations Funded:** Colleges; scholarship funds; hospitals; United Way

**Targeted Population Group:** Youth

**Types of Support for Organizations:** Capital support; continuing support; general operating support

**Type of Support for Individuals:** Scholarships

**Sample Grants:**
St. Paul Area United Way—$20,000
Gustavus Adolphus College—$15,000
College scholarships to individuals—$1,100

**Financial Data for Year Ending October 31, 1981:**
Assets: $8,250,587
Grants Paid: $702,569
Number of Grants: 25; 470 scholarships
Largest/Smallest: $20,000/$100

**Paid Professional Staff:** No

**Contact Made by:** Letter of inquiry

**Board Meetings:** Monthly

**Applicants Notified:** Within two weeks of decision

**Directors:** G. T. Waldref, president; R. S. Davis, vice-president; Albert E. Ranum, secretary, scholarship committee; H. L. Holtz; J. R. Oppenheimer; T. Simonet; E. C. Swanson; J. F. Thoreen

## TRALARDEN FOUNDATION

1914 First Bank Place West
Minneapolis, MN 55402

**Established:** April 1961

**Type:** Private foundation

**Geographic Orientation:** Twin Cities

**Financial Data for Year Ending December 31, 1981:**
Assets: $10,486
Grants Paid: $0

**Paid Professional Staff:** No

**Directors/Trustees:** T. R. Anderson, president; M. LaJean Anderson, vice-president/treasurer; Judith I. Fennema, secretary

## THE VALSPAR FOUNDATION

Box 1461
Minneapolis, MN 55440
(612) 522-2731

**Contact Person:** Linda Shockley, employment manager

**Established:** 1979

**Type:** Corporate foundation

**Geographic Orientation:** Minnesota; locations of plants

**Fields of Activity:** Arts; restoration/architecture; history/preservation; music/opera; theater/dance; higher education; community affairs

**Types of Organizations Funded:** Museums/historical societies; theaters; arts councils; historic preservation; colleges; universities; United Way; organizations for youth; centers for children; neighborhood agencies

**Types of Support for Organizations:** Continuing support; general operating support; matching grants

**Sample Grants:**
Minneapolis Housing and Redevelopment Authority—$11,667
North Dakota State University—$1,500

**Financial Data for Year Ending September 30, 1981:**
Assets: $89,316
Grants Paid: $124,017
Number of Grants: 106
Largest/Smallest: $11,667/$100

**Paid Professional Staff:** No

**Contact Made by:** Complete proposal

**Available by Request:** Annual report for corporation

**Board Meetings:** Quarterly

**Applicants Notified:** Within three weeks of decision

**Directors/Trustees:** Sam Guerrera, vice-president for consumer affairs; Herbert Denker, secretary for corporate affairs

## VERHEY FAMILY FOUNDATION

1400 Northwestern National Bank Building
St. Paul, MN 55101

**Established:** August 1980

**Type:** Private foundation

**Geographic Orientation:** Twin Cities

**Sample Grants:**
St. Paul Academy and Summit School—$3,815
Landmark Center—$100
Minnesota Zoological Society—$100

**Financial Data for Year Ending March 31, 1982:**
Assets: $52,475
Grants Paid: $4,015
Number of Grants: 3
Largest/Smallest: $3,815/$100

**Paid Professional Staff:** No

**Directors/Trustees:** Jane W. Verhey; Frederick E. Verhey; Thomas W. Verhey

## ARMIN F. VETTER FOUNDATION

1600 Conway Street
St. Paul, MN 55106

**Type:** Private foundation

**Geographic Orientation:** National

**Sample Grants:**
St. Pascal Church, St. Paul—$475
Catholic Near East Welfare, New York—$360
Red Cloud Indian School, South Dakota—$25

**Financial Data for Year Ending April 30, 1981:**
Assets: $23,673
Grants Paid: $1,394
Number of Grants: 13
Largest/Smallest: $475/$15

**Paid Professional Staff:** No

**Director/Trustee:** Armin F. Vetter

## JOHN VICKERY FOUNDATION

Merchants National Bank of Winona
102 Plaza East
Winona, MN 55987

**Established:** May 1969

**Type:** Private foundation

**Geographic Orientation:** Minnesota

**Sample Grants:**
Northland Children's Oncology Service—$1,500
Robert Hornberg Fund—$200

**Financial Data for Year Ending May 30, 1981:**
Assets: $17,648
Grants Paid: $1,700
Number of Grants: 2

**Paid Professional Staff:** No

**Trustee:** Merchants National Bank of Winona

## JULIUS L. VILLAUME CHARITABLE TRUST

c/o First Trust Company of St. Paul
W-555 First National Bank Building
St. Paul, MN 55101

**Established:** 1975

**Type:** Private foundation

**Geographic Orientation:** Twin Cities

**Sample Grants:**
United Way of St. Paul—$700
Children's Hospital—$400
Salvation Army—$300

**Financial Data for Year Ending December 31, 1981:**
Assets: $30,770
Grants Paid: $1,800
Number of Grants: 4
Largest/Smallest: $700/$300

**Paid Professional Staff:** No

**Directors/Trustees:** Harold L. Rutchick; Elsie B. Villaume; First Trust Company of St. Paul

## ● ARCHIE D. AND BERTHA H. WALKER FOUNDATION

1121 Hennepin Avenue
Minneapolis, MN 55403
(612) 332-3556

**Contact Person:** Walter W. Walker, secretary

**Established:** August 1953

**Type:** Private foundation

**Program's Purpose:** To provide primarily grants dealing with chemical dependency (chiefly alcoholism), and the treatment of "white racism in the white community"; a limited number of minor grants committed to areas outside these two areas

**Program's Limits:** No grants to individuals or to private foundations

**Geographic Orientation:** Twin Cities; national

**Sample Grants:**
Chemical Dependency Action Committee, Indiana—$28,650
Greater Minneapolis Council of Churches, Tillman Seminars—$1,000
Legal Rights Center—$500

**Financial Data for Year Ending December 31, 1981:**
Assets: $3,135,614
Grants Paid: $217,690
Number of Grants: 56
Largest/Smallest: $28,650/$500

**Paid Professional Staff:** No

**Contact Made by:** Complete proposal

**Available by Request:** Proposal guidelines

**Proposal Deadlines:** Most grants made in February from requests received prior to December 1

**Directors/Trustees:** Louise W. McCannel, president; Walter W. Walker, secretary; Harriet W. Heron, treasurer; Colleen M. Walker, vice-president

## W. WALKER FUND

1121 Hennepin Avenue
Minneapolis, MN 55403

**Established:** March 1972 (originally Elva Fund)

**Type:** Private foundation

**Geographic Orientation:** Twin Cities

**Sample Grants:**
United Way of the Minneapolis Area—$1,000
Abbott-Northwestern Hospital—$500
Minnesota Opera Company—$100

**Financial Data for Year Ending December 31, 1981:**
  Assets:  $43,180
  Grants Paid:  $2,250
  Number of Grants:  8
  Largest/Smallest:  $1,000/$100

**Paid Professional Staff:** No

**Directors/Trustees:** Walter W. Walker, president/ treasurer; Louise W. McCannel, vice-president; Elaine B. Walker, secretary

## THE DOUGLAS AND MILDRED WARNER FOUNDATION

606 Binnacle Drive
Naples, FL 33940

**Established:** April 1963

**Type:** Private foundation

**Geographic Orientation:** Twin Cities

**Sample Grants:**
  Colonial Church—$405
  Ducks Unlimited—$150
  Famine Relief—$15

**Financial Data for Year Ending December 31, 1981:**
  Assets:  $3,678
  Grants Paid:  $678
  Number of Grants:  8
  Largest/Smallest:  $405/$8

**Paid Professional Staff:** No

**Director/Trustee:** Douglas Warner, Jr.

## LEE AND ROSE WARNER FOUNDATION

444 Lafayette Road
St. Paul, MN 55101

**Established:** January 1959

**Type:** Private foundation

**Geographic Orientation:** Twin Cities

**Sample Grants:**
  Science Museum of Minnesota—$70,100
  Union Gospel Mission—$5,000
  Gunnery School—$500

**Financial Data for Year Ending December 31, 1981:**
  Assets:  $4,165,117
  Grants Paid:  $104,100
  Number of Grants:  17
  Largest/Smallest:  $70,100/$500

**Paid Professional Staff:** No

**Directors/Trustees:** Donald G. McNeely; Adelaide F. McNeely; Frank A. Koscielak

## H. E. AND HELEN R. WARREN FOUNDATION

c/o First Trust Company of St. Paul
W-555 First National Bank Building
St. Paul, MN 55101
(612) 291-5061

**Contact Person:** Thomas H. Patterson

**Established:** December 1958

**Type:** Private foundation

**Program's Purpose:** To provide grants primarily to educational, cultural, youth, and community-support organizations in Minnesota

**Program's Limits:** No grants to individuals or to organizations that require expenditure responsibility

**Geographic Orientation:** Minnesota

**Sample Grants:**
  Our Lady of Good Counsel Free Cancer Home—$2,500
  KTCA—$1,500
  Restoration of Commandant's House, Fort Snelling—$250

**Financial Data for Year Ending December 31, 1981:**
  Assets:  $331,577
  Grants Paid:  $18,070
  Number of Grants:  18
  Largest/Smallest:  $2,500/$100

**Paid Professional Staff:** No

**Contact Made by:** Complete proposal

**Directors/Trustees:** George C. King; Russell H. Johnson; First Trust Company of St. Paul

## • THE WASIE FOUNDATION

909 Foshay Tower
Minneapolis, MN 55402
(612) 332-3883

**Contact Person:** David A. Odahowski, executive director

**Established:** 1966

**Type:** Private foundation

**Program's Purpose:** To support organizations in areas of health, mental health, children, children with handicaps, and education

**Geographic Orientation:** Twin Cities

**Fields of Activity:** Higher education; medical research; medical/health education; mental health; family services

**Types of Organizations Funded:** Public television/radio; colleges; universities; hospitals; medical research groups; counseling services; religious colleges; research/study institutes; organizations for the handicapped; organizations for youth; centers for children; animal centers

**Types of Support for Organizations:** Capital support; continuing support; general operating support; matching grants; program development; research

**Type of Support for Individuals:** Scholarships

**Sample Grants:**
Camp Friendship—$5,000
Family Networks—$5,000
Little Brothers of the Poor—$2,000

**Financial Data for Year Ending December 31, 1981:**
Assets:   $10,500,000
Grants Paid:   $515,283
Number of Grants:   68
Largest/Smallest:   $60,520/$235

**Paid Professional Staff:** Yes

**Contact Made by:** Telephone inquiry

**Available by Request:** Application procedures

**Board Meetings:** Quarterly

**Applicants Notified:** Within four weeks of decision

**Directors/Trustees:** Marie F. Wasie; Jerome J. Choromanski; Ina N. Reed; Andrew J. Leemhuis; David A. Odahowski; Thelma G. Haynes; Audrey D. Smith

# WATSON FOUNDATION

252 South Plaza Building
Minneapolis, MN 55416

**Established:** December 1942

**Type:** Private foundation

**Geographic Orientation:** National

**Sample Grants:**
Ducks Unlimited—$9,000
Williams Fund, University of Minnesota—$1,000
1981 Navy League—$50

**Financial Data for Year Ending December 31, 1981:**
Assets:   $93,452
Grants Paid:   $15,546
Number of Grants:   67
Largest/Smallest:   $9,000/$5

**Paid Professional Staff:** No

**Directors/Trustees:** Leone C. Watson, president; Frederick O. Watson, secretary-treasurer; Kathleen W. Adams, vice-president

# ● WCCO AM/FM/TV

50 South Ninth Street
Minneapolis, MN 55402
(612) 330-2655

**Contact Person:** Elna Campbell, secretary to the chairman

**Type:** Charitable contributions program

**Program's Interests:** Human services; education; arts

**Geographic Orientation:** WCCO viewing and listening area

**Fields of Activity:** Music/opera; theater/dance; elementary/secondary education; higher education; medical care/treatment; mental health; social sciences; advocacy; community affairs; drug-abuse programs; economic development; equal rights/legal aid

**Types of Organizations Funded:** Theaters/dance groups; music/opera groups; libraries; public television/radio; elementary schools; secondary schools; colleges; universities; scholarship funds; hospitals; chemical dependency services; environmental agencies; United Way; legal aid; organizations for the handicapped; organizations for women; organizations for drug abusers; organizations for youth; housing agencies; organizations for offenders; organizations for minorities

**Employee Matching Gift Programs:** Any nonprofit organization (except church or United Way)

**Types of Support for Organizations:** Capital support; continuing support; general operating support

**Type of Support for Individuals:** Scholarships

**Financial Data for Year Ending September 30, 1982:**
Contributions Paid:   $300,000
Number of Contributions:   100
Largest/Smallest:   $29,710/$50

**Contact Made by:** Letter of inquiry

**Proposal Deadline:** February 15

**Contributions Decisions Made:** Quarterly

# WEDUM FOUNDATION

Box 644
Alexandria, MN 56308

**Contact Person:** Mayo Johnson, president/treasurer

**Established:** January 1959

**Type:** Private foundation

**Program's Purpose:** Primarily to provide support to religious organizations and education (scholarships)

**Geographic Orientation:** Alexandria area

**Financial Data for Year Ending December 31, 1981:**
Assets:   $263,060
Grants Paid:   $16,885
Number of Grants:   38 (predominantly scholarships)
Largest/Smallest:   $3,000/$100

**Contact Made by:** Request for guidelines

**Available by Request:** Proposal guidelines

**Directors/Trustees:** Mayo Johnson, president/treasurer; John Wedum, vice-president/assistant secretary; Jon Rosengren, vice-president; Sidney Landeene, secretary

# THE WEIL FOUNDATION

815 First Bank Place West
Minneapolis, MN 55402
(612) 333-3121

**Contact Person:** Fred Weil, Jr.

**Established:** October 1967

**Type:** Private foundation

**Geographic Orientation:** Twin Cities

**Sample Grants:**
Minneapolis Federation for Jewish Service—$3,500
United Way—$1,200
Minnesota Composers Forum—$50

**Financial Data for Year Ending December 31, 1981:**
Assets: $93
Grants Paid: $8,494
Number of Grants: 42
Largest/Smallest: $3,500/$10

**Paid Professional Staff:** No

**Director/Trustee:** Fred Weil, Jr.


# MAURICE AND MINNIE WEISBERG FOUNDATION

989 Lombard Street
St. Paul, MN 55105

**Established:** December 1953

**Type:** Private foundation

**Geographic Orientation:** Twin Cities

**Sample Grants:**
Temple of Aaron—$1,188
United Jewish Fund—$1,100
St. Joseph Hospital Fund—$106

**Financial Data for Year Ending December 31, 1981:**
Assets: $59,211
Grants Paid: $4,232
Number of Grants: 37
Largest/Smallest: $1,188/$5

**Paid Professional Staff:** No


# ELMER M. WELTZ (TRUST)

Northwestern National Bank of Minneapolis Trust Tax
Division
Seventh and Marquette
Minneapolis, MN 55479

**Established:** September 1967

**Type:** Private foundation

**Geographic Orientation:** Minnesota

**Sample Grants:**
Hope Lutheran Church, Minneota—$800
Southwest State University Foundation—$500
Marshall Park and Recreation Department—$200

**Financial Data for Year Ending September 30, 1981:**
Assets: $31,202
Grants Paid: $2,101
Number of Grants: 5
Largest/Smallest: $800/$200

**Paid Professional Staff:** No

**Trustee:** Northwestern National Bank of Minneapolis


# THE WERNER FOUNDATION

3912 West Twenty-fifth Street
Minneapolis, MN 55416

**Established:** June 1965

**Type:** Private foundation

**Geographic Orientation:** Twin Cities

**Sample Grants:**
Minneapolis Federation for Jewish Service—$49,647
St. Mary's Hospital Building Fund—$5,000
Minneapolis Society of Fine Arts—$948

**Financial Data for Year Ending December 31, 1981:**
Assets: $594,500
Grants Paid: $72,727
Number of Grants: 30
Largest/Smallest: $49,647/$10

**Paid Professional Staff:** No

**Directors/Trustees:** Harvey L. Werner, president; Violet
M. Werner, secretary; Thomas Feinberg


# • WEYERHAEUSER FOUNDATION

2100 First National Bank Building
St. Paul, MN 55101
(612) 228-0935

**Contact Person:** Julie C. Titcomb, president

**Established:** January 1950

**Type:** Private foundation

**Program's Limits:** Primarily to support programs and
services of national and international significance that
attempt to identify and correct causes of
maladjustment in American society

**Geographic Orientation:** National; international

**Sample Grants:**
American Friends Service, Philadelphia—$13,000
International Peace Academy, New York—$12,720
Solar City Institute, Washington, D.C.—$10,000

**Financial Data for Year Ending December 31, 1981:**
Assets: $4,605,270
Grants Paid: $167,904
Number of Grants: 14
Largest/Smallest: $34,334/$400

**Paid Professional Staff:** No

**Contact Made by:** Letter of inquiry

**Available by Request:** Proposal guidelines; annual report

**Proposal Deadline:** August

**Board Meetings:** Biannual, in May and November

**Trustees:** Julie C. Titcomb, president; George F. Jewett, Jr., vice-president; Walter S. Rosenberry III, treasurer; J. S. Micallef, assistant secretary/assistant treasurer; Mary J. Greer; Sara T. Greer; Elizabeth S. Driscoll; Elizabeth W. Meadowcroft; Bette D. Moorman; Vivian W. Piasecki; Charles A. Weyerhaeuser; Nancy N. Weyerhaeuser; Ginnie Weyerhaeuser; William T. Weyerhaeuser

## • CHARLES A. WEYERHAEUSER MEMORIAL FOUNDATION

2100 First National Bank Building
St. Paul, MN 55101
(612) 228-0935

**Contact Person:** Walter S. Rosenberry III, president

**Established:** March 1959

**Type:** Private foundation

**Geographic Orientation:** Twin Cities; national

**Sample Grants:**
Science Museum of Minnesota—$100,000 (over two years)
Minnesota Historical Society—$49,500
Denver Art Museum—$10,000

**Financial Data for Year Ending February 28, 1982:**
Assets: $98,875
Grants Paid: $266,500
Number of Grants: 10
Largest/Smallest: $50,000/$1,000

**Paid Professional Staff:** No

**Contact Made by:** Letter of inquiry

**Board Meetings:** On an ongoing basis to consider grant proposals; annual, in June

**Applicants Notified:** Within two to three weeks of decision

**Directors:** Walter S. Rosenberry III, president; Robert J. Sivertsen, vice-president; J. S. Micallef, secretary/treasurer; Gordon E. Hed, assistant secretary/assistant treasurer; Richard E. Kyle; Lucy R. McCarthy; Elise R. Donohue

## • F. K. AND VIVIAN O'GARA WEYERHAEUSER FOUNDATION

2100 First National Bank Building
St. Paul, MN 55101
(612) 228-0935

**Contact Person:** Mrs. Vivian W. Piasecki, president

**Established:** November 1966

**Type:** Private foundation

**Geographic Orientation:** Twin Cities; national

**Sample Grants:**
Minnesota Landmarks, F. K. Weyerhaeuser Auditorium—$50,000 (over five years)
Forest History Society, Santa Cruz, CA—$20,000
Miss Porter's School, Farmington, CT—$10,000

**Financial Data for Year Ending December 31, 1981:**
Assets: $89,723
Grants Paid: $109,775
Number of Grants: 22
Largest/Smallest: $20,000/$900

**Paid Professional Staff:** No

**Contact Made by:** Letter of inquiry

**Board Meetings:** On an ongoing basis to consider grant requests; annual, in May or June

**Applicants Notified:** Within three to four weeks of decision

**Directors:** Vivian W. Piasecki, president; Lynn W. Day, vice-president; Stanley R. Day, treasurer; Frank N. Piasecki, secretary; J. S. Micallef, assistant secretary; Gordon E. Hed, assistant treasurer

## FREDERICK AND MARGARET L. WEYERHAEUSER FOUNDATION

2100 First National Bank Building
St. Paul, MN 55101
(612) 228-0935

**Contact Person:** F. T. Weyerhaeuser, president

**Established:** July 1963

**Type:** Private foundation

**Geographic Orientation:** Twin Cities; national

**Sample Grants:**
Macalester College—$450,000
Princeton Theological Seminary—$75,000
Presbyterian Homes, St. Paul—$50,000

**Financial Data for Year Ending June 30, 1981:**
Assets: $4,289
Grants Paid: $783,500
Number of Grants: 12
Largest/Smallest: $450,000/$500

**Paid Professional Staff:** No

**Contact Made by:** Letter of inquiry

**Board Meetings:** On an ongoing basis to review proposals; annual in May or June

**Applicants Notified:** Within two to three weeks of decision

**Directors:** Frederick T. Weyerhaeuser, president; Charles L. Weyerhaeuser, vice-president; J. S. Micallef, secretary/assistant treasurer; Gordon E. Hed, treasurer/assistant secretary

## • WHITNEY FOUNDATION

1535 Dain Tower
Minneapolis, MN 55402

**Established:** January 1959

**Type:** Private foundation

**Geographic Orientation:** Minnesota; national

**Sample Grants:**
Carleton College—$10,000
United Way of Minneapolis Area—$5,000
Rum River Citizens League—$50

**Financial Data for Year Ending December 31, 1981:**
Assets: $29,385
Grants Paid: $118,761
Number of Grants: 241
Largest/Smallest: $10,000/$7

**Paid Professional Staff:** No

**Directors/Trustees:** Wheelock Whitney, president; Joseph Whitney, secretary; John K. Whitney, vice-president/treasurer

## BEN WILENSKY FOUNDATION

2210 Cedar Lake Boulevard
Minneapolis, MN 55416

**Type:** Private foundation

**Geographic Orientation:** Twin Cities

**Financial Data for Year Ending December 31, 1981:**
Assets: $35,249
Grants Paid: $0

**Paid Professional Staff:** No

**Directors/Trustees:** Ben Wilensky, president/treasurer; Dorothy L. Cohen, vice-president; Alan Wilensky, secretary

## PHILLIP AND SARA WILENSKY FAMILY FOUNDATION

1226 Washington Avenue North
Minneapolis, MN 55401

**Established:** November 1951 (originally Phillip Wilensky Foundation)

**Type:** Private foundation

**Geographic Orientation:** Twin Cities

**Sample Grants:**
Minneapolis Federation for Jewish Service—$4,000
Beth El Synagogue—$1,400
Dakota Children's Association—$500

**Financial Data for Year Ending December 31, 1981:**
Assets: $108,133
Grants Paid: $9,900
Number of Grants: 22
Largest/Smallest: $4,000/$25

**Paid Professional Staff:** No

**Directors/Trustees:** Saul Kollins, president; Leo Kromick, vice-president; Ann Kollins, treasurer; Revaline Kromick, secretary-treasurer

## JAMES T. WILLIAMS, SR., FOUNDATION

6412 Mendelssohn Lane
Hopkins, MN 55343

**Established:** December 1952

**Type:** Private foundation

**Geographic Orientation:** Twin Cities

**Sample Grants:**
College of Saint Thomas—$2,500
Courage Center—$2,000
Oblate Fathers, Nett Lake Indian Mission—$600

**Financial Data for Year Ending December 31, 1981:**
Assets: $222,590
Grants Paid: $32,250
Number of Grants: 42
Largest/Smallest: $2,500/$100

**Paid Professional Staff:** No

**Directors/Trustees:** Margaret W. Linstroth, president/treasurer; R. H. Williams, vice-president/secretary; J. Thomas Linstroth

## • WILLIAMS STEEL AND HARDWARE

Box 540
Minneapolis, MN 55440
(612) 588-9826

**Contact Person:** Linda Harding, grants coordinator

**Type:** Charitable contributions program

**Geographic Orientation:** Area in which the company does business

**Fields of Activity:** Education; welfare/social services

**Types of Organizations Supported:** Educational organizations; United Way; legal aid; multiservice centers; organizations for the elderly; organizations for the handicapped; organizations for women; organizations for drug abusers; organizations for youth; organizations for men; centers for children; organizations for offenders; organizations for minorities; day-care centers; community centers

**Employee Matching Gift Programs:** No

**Types of Support for Organizations:** Capital support; endowment; general operating support; program development; federated fund drives

**Type of Support for Individuals:** Scholarship program for children of employees

**Financial Data for Year Ending December 31, 1981:**
Contributions Paid: $100,000 to $499,999 range
Largest/Smallest: $14,000/$25

**Contributions Decisions Made:** Biannually

## EDWARD H. WILLMUS FAMILY CHARITABLE TRUST

1260 Northwestern Bank Building
St. Paul, MN 55101

**Established:** December 1964

**Type:** Private foundation

**Geographic Orientation:** Twin Cities; Minnesota

**Sample Grant:**
St. Rita Catholic Church—$250

**Financial Data for Year Ending December 31, 1981:**
Assets: $53,936
Grants Paid: $250
Number of Grants: 1

**Paid Professional Staff:** No

**Directors/Trustees:** Thomas M. Willmus; Dorothy R. Willmus; Geraldine Willmus

## CHARLES J. AND HENRIETTA MCDONALD WINTON FUND

4308 IDS Center
Minneapolis, MN 55402

**Established:** December 1959 (originally Charles J. Winton, Jr. Foundation)

**Type:** Private foundation

**Geographic Orientation:** Twin Cities

**Sample Grants:**
Courage Center—$4,000
Fresh Water Foundation—$1,000
Minnesota Orchestra—$800

**Financial Data for Year Ending November 30, 1981:**
Assets: $80,767
Grants Paid: $8,800
Number of Grants: 6
Largest/Smallest: $4,000/$800

**Paid Professional Staff:** No

**Directors/Trustees:** H. McDonald Winton; McDonald Winton; H. W. Whitney

## WINTON COMPANIES FUND

4308 IDS Center
Minneapolis, MN 55402

**Established:** December 1953

**Type:** Corporate foundation

**Geographic Orientation:** California

**Sample Grant:**
Forest History Society, Santa Cruz, CA—$400

**Financial Data for Year Ending December 31, 1981:**
Assets: $6,477
Grants Paid: $400
Number of Grants: 1

**Paid Professional Staff:** No

**Directors/Trustees:** Clifford F. Anderson; Charles J. Winton, Jr.; David J. Winton; David M. Winton (from 990-AR, 1980)

## W M FOUNDATION

4900 IDS Center
Minneapolis, MN 55402

**Established:** November 1970

**Type:** Private foundation

**Geographic Orientation:** National

**Sample Grants:**
World Wildlife Fund, Washington, D.C.—$2,500
Nature Conservancy, Virginia—$1,000
Peregrine Fund, New York—$100

**Financial Data for Year Ending December 31, 1981:**
Assets: $15,563
Grants Paid: $4,200
Number of Grants: 5
Largest/Smallest: $2,500/$100

**Paid Professional Staff:** No

**Directors/Trustees:** Wallace C. Dayton, president/treasurer; Mary L. Dayton, vice-president/secretary; Sally D. Clement

## WOOD-RILL FOUNDATION

4900 IDS Center
Minneapolis, MN 55402

**Established:** December 1970

**Type:** Private foundation

**Program's Purpose:** "To encourage and promote the development of and public understanding, appreciation and enjoyment of painting, sculpture and other fine arts; and...to promote...the development of parks, playgrounds, museums, forest preserves...public recreation areas and the preservation of wildlife"

**Geographic Orientation:** National

**Sample Grants:**
The Minnesota Project—$50,000
Minneapolis Institute of Arts—$30,825
The Nature Conservancy, Virginia—$1,000

**Financial Data for Year Ending December 31, 1981:**
Assets: $394,737
Grants Paid: $216,135
Number of Grants: 42
Largest/Smallest: $50,000/$25

**Paid Professional Staff:** No

**Directors/Trustees:** Bruce B. Dayton, president; Virginia Y. Dayton, vice-president; Ronald N. Gross, secretary-treasurer

## GORDON A. YOCK CHARITABLE FOUNDATION

c/o First Trust Company of St. Paul
W-555 First National Bank Building
St. Paul, MN 55101

**Established:** December 1964

**Type:** Private foundation

**Geographic Orientation:** National

**Sample Grants:**
Golden Valley Lutheran College—$1,000
St. Paul's Lutheran Church, Florida—$850
World Vision, California—$150

**Financial Data for Year Ending December 31, 1981:**
Assets:  $49,288
Grants Paid:  $3,325
Number of Grants:  21
Largest/Smallest:  $1,000/$25

**Paid Professional Staff:** No

**Contact Made by:** Complete proposal

**Directors/Trustees:** Gordon Yock; Hedwig E. Yock; Laird G. Yock

## ZELLE CHARITABLE TRUST

c/o First National Bank of Minneapolis
120 South Sixth Street
Minneapolis, MN 55402

**Established:** December 1952

**Type:** Private foundation

**Geographic Orientation:** Twin Cities

**Sample Grant:**
Plymouth Congregational Church—$25,000

**Financial Data for Year Ending December 31, 1981:**
Assets:  $67,687
Grants Paid:  $25,000
Number of Grants:  1

**Paid Professional Staff:** No

**Trustee:** First National Bank of Minneapolis

## ZIFF FAMILY FOUNDATION

1055 East Seventy-ninth Street
Minneapolis, MN 55420

**Established:** December 1967

**Type:** Private foundation

**Geographic Orientation:** Twin Cities

**Sample Grants:**
Minneapolis Federation for Jewish Service—$5,500
St. Paul United Jewish Fund—$2,500
Multiple Sclerosis Society—$350

**Financial Data for Year Ending April 30, 1981:**
Assets:  $44,854
Grants Paid:  $13,054
Number of Grants:  20
Largest/Smallest:  $5,500/$25

**Paid Professional Staff:** No

**Directors/Trustees:** Louis Ziff, president; Joseph Ziff, vice-president/treasurer; Dennis Hymanson, secretary

# Appendixes

# Appendix 1

## INACTIVE FOUNDATIONS

These foundations file with the attorney general's office, but their files show
no grant making activity in the last three to five years.

Allen Foundation
Alpha Tau Omega Foundation of Minnesota
Mary C. Bartsh Scholarship Trust
Belford Foundation
Community Sharing Fund
Denada Foundation
Sarah Cowles Doering Fund
Edina Foundation
Futures Foundation
Garelick Foundation
Hibbs Family Foundation

Walter C. James Foundation
Jebco Foundation
Johnson Brothers Charitable Foundation
Manx Society of Minnesota
Metabolic Research
Florence Moline Trust
Peter C. and Hazel E. Neilsen Foundation
Owen Family Fund
Sweatt Foundation
Toro Foundation

# Appendix 2

## FOUNDATIONS WITH DESIGNATED RECIPIENTS

These foundations limit their grants to a selected list of organizations, which is usually determined
by the original trust instrument, or to scholarship funds for selected groups of students.

Adams Educational Fund
Marshall H. and Nellie Alworth Memorial Fund
American Finnish Workers Society Memorial
   Educational Trust
Arthur H. Anderson Charitable Trust
Ernest R. Anderson Residuary Trust
Charles W. Atkinson Trust
George G. Barnum
Gerrit Beckering
Alfred R. Bethke, et al., Family Charitable Trust
Victor and Muriel Bjorgo Foundation
Charles K. Blandin Cemetery Trust
Charles K. Blandin Residuary Trust
Vera D. Bliven Trust

Abe Bloomenson
Walter R. Bollinger Trust B
Charles L. Bonn Trust
Boy Scouts
B. H. Bracelin Trust
John F. and Myrtle V. Briggs Charitable Trust
Thea M. Brorby Charitable Trust
Gertrude E. Cammack Fund for Children
Irene M. Carlson Trust B
Catherine A. Casey Trust
Beryl W. Charlson Charitable Trust
Cloquet Cemeteries Trust
Elbridge C. Cooke Trust
William J. Cotter Trust

Dahlstrom Trust
John C. and Nettie V. David Memorial Trust
Joshua Hartwell Davis for Family and Children's
  Service
Frank M. Deforce Trust
Aniela Derus Trust for the Benefit of Order of St.
  Benedicts
Mary Lou and Adelaide E. Diether Charitable Trust
Lawrence S. Donaldson II
Peter M. Dougall
Roy A. Drew Residuary Trust
Duluth Community Trust
Hilma L. Eckstrand Trust
Economics Laboratory Foundation
Ely-Winton Hospital Association Scholarship Fund
E. J. Fairfield Trust
Lawrence T. Fallander Trust
Francis H. Fitzgerald Trust
Leonard Fried Educational Fund
Catherine A. Friedrich Trust
Louise D. Garvin Charitable Trust
Anthony L. and Ann B. Gaughan Charitable Trust
Clifford W. Gress Trust
George A. Guldan Testamentary Trust
Hallett Charitable Trust
Millard C. Hamer Trust
Minerva L. Hansen Trust
Charles M. Harrington Trusts (seventeen)
Fred W. Hase Trust
Brede Haugen Family Trust
George Healy Trust
Harold W. Healy Residuary Trust
Louise D. Heneman Trust
Hoerner Waldorf Corporation Charitable Foundation
Hormel Foundation
George A. Hormel Testamentary Trust
Robert J. Hughes, Jr. Trust
Hull Educational Foundation
James W. Hunt
Walter Hurlbut Book Fund Trust
Olive T. Jaffray Charitable Trust
Clem Jaunich Educational Trust
Edna M. Jencks
Anna H. Jenks
E. T. Johnson Trust
Gladys L. Johnson Scholarship Trust
Addie M. Jones
John Junell Trust
Michael J. Kamas Testamentary Trust
Rudy and Laura Kemske Scholarship Trust
Agustus H. Kennedy Memorial Trust Fund
Killen Scholarship Trust
James C. King Residuary Trust
Joseph Kitrick Charitable Trust
Charles H. Klein Trust A
Ralph R. Kriesel Trust B
Anna M. Kuhl Scholarship Trust
Helen Lang Charitable Trust
Betty W. Lawrence Trust

Laymen's Ministerial Endowment Fund
Frances V. Leach Charitable Trust
Elmer W. Lippmann Scholarship Trust
George R. Lorenz Residuary Trust
Mary Jane Lovell
Elmore Lowell Trust
Carol E. MacPherson Memorial Scholarship Fund
Tilly P. Manwaring Trust
Charles W. Mayo Trust
William McKerrow Scholarship Fund
Carl Meeske Residuary Trust
Melamed Scholarship Fund Charitable Trust
Reine H. Meyers Memorial Trust
Minnesota Hundred Club
Minnesota Surveyors and Engineers Society
National Distiller Distributors Foundation
Benjamin F. Nelson
E. G. Nethercott Medical Educational Foundation
Niels A. Nielsen Trust
Harold Frederick Oleson Trust
E. O. Olson Trust
Morten L. and Helen E. Olson Memorial Educational
  Association
Lena E. Oreck Trust
Margot L. Oreck
Edward M. Ozias Charitable Trust
George William and Mary Burnham Patton Scholarship
  Fund
Lulu R. Pellenz
Peter I. Peterson Residuary Trust
Hans and Thora Petraborg Educational Trust Fund
B. Harrison Pike Scholarship Memorial Fund
E. J. Raymond Trust
Dorothy N. Ribenack Trust
Richardson Foundation
Louis A. Roberg Endowment Trust
Emma E. Rogers Trust
Alexander J. M. Ross Trust
Russell Sabor Foundation
Saint John's Foundation Trust
Clement and Anastasia Scheurer Family Church Trust
  Fund
Vivian Fraser Schuh Residuary Trust
Benjamin Seifert American Legion Post Scholarship
  Foundation
Harold N. Simpson Trust
Fred Sims Memorial Trust
L. L. Skaggs Charitable Trust
Walter and Anna Soneson Scholarship Fund Trust
Sons of Jacob Trust
Albert L. Steinke Trust
Otto Stenberg Trust B
Benjamin W. Stephenson Trust
Walter E. Stremel Trust
Thief River Falls Foundation
Ellen P. Thomas Trust
Harlan R. Thurston Foundation
Flora Edith Torrance Trust
Josephine O. Towne Trust

Lillian Zenobia Turnblad Trust
E. M. Van Derlip Trust
Ethel M. Van Derlip Trust
J. B. Van Derlip Trust
John R. Van Derlip Trust
Fred C. Van Dusen Trust
Charles E. Voige Trust
Olga Walker Trust
George H. Warren Trust
George W. Warren Trust
Wayzata Memorial Education Foundation

Amie Webster Trust
Weesner Charitable Trust Fund
Ingeborg H. Wells Trust
Robert B. and Sophia Whiteside Scholarship Fund
Gomer Williams Trust
Emma Winkelmann Trust A
Emma Winkelmann Trust B
Flora Woodworth Trust
Thomas C. Wright Educational Trust
Berdie S. Yetter Charitable Trust
Florence M. Young Trust

# Appendix 3

## FOUNDATIONS MAKING GRANTS ONLY OUTSIDE MINNESOTA

These foundations are headquartered in Minnesota but do not make grants in Minnesota or to Minnesota organizations.

AHS Foundation
Bend Foundation
Circle Foundation
I. George Fischbein Foundation
George Frederick Jewett Foundation
Donald and Dorothy Leslie Foundation
Merci

# Appendix 4

## FOUNDATIONS NOT ACCEPTING APPLICATIONS

At the time of the survey, these foundations reported that they would not accept new applications for funding.

Adams-Mastrovich Family Foundation Trust
Morris Chalfen Foundation
Deinard Foundation
Malcolm J. Estrem Foundation
Hunter Foundation
Theodore H. Johansen Family Foundation
Johnson Foundation
Edgar and Ethel Johnson Fund
Everett R. and Ruth M. Johnson Fund
Marvin L. and Mildred L. Johnson Fund

Lund Family Charitable Foundation
Lundeen Foundation
William B. and Barbara D. McKinstry Foundation
Meadowood Foundation
Kingsley H. Murphy Family Foundation
Arthur J. Popehn Foundation
Carl Sharpe Foundation
Harold J. and Marie O'Brien Slawik Foundation
Charles B. Sweatt Foundation

# Appendix 5

## MINNESOTA COUNCIL ON FOUNDATIONS
## 1982 DIRECTORY QUESTIONNAIRE

Please return by August 20, 1982 to
Minnesota Council on Foundations.
1216 Foshay Tower,
Minneapolis, MN 55402.
Questions—call (612) 338-1989.

1. Foundation name:_____

2. Address:_____

3. Telephone number:_____

4. Contact person and title:_____

5. Date established:_____

6. Type of foundation: ☐ Private　　☐ Corporate　　☐ Community　　☐ Independent

7. Statement of purpose:_____

_____

_____

_____

8. Program limitations:_____

_____

_____

_____

9. Geographic orientation:　☐ Twin Cities　　☐ Minnesota　　☐ National
　　　　　　　　　　　　　　☐ International　　☐ Other (be specific)_____

10. Sample grants: Please list three typical grants, recipients, and amounts

_____

_____

_____

_____

# 1982 DIRECTORY FOUNDATION QUESTIONNAIRE

## 11. FIELDS OF ACTIVITY:

### ARTS AND HUMANITIES
- ☐ Arts/architecture
- ☐ History/preservation
- ☐ Language/literature
- ☐ Media/communications
- ☐ Music/opera
- ☐ Theater/dance
- ☐ Arts education
- ☐ Other

### EDUCATION
- ☐ Elementary/secondary
- ☐ Vocational
- ☐ Higher
- ☐ Adult/continuing
- ☐ Research
- ☐ Other

### HEALTH
- ☐ Medical research
- ☐ Medical care/treatment
- ☐ Medical/health education
- ☐ Public health
- ☐ Mental health
- ☐ Other

### RELIGION
- ☐ Religion
- ☐ Religious education
- ☐ Other

### SCIENCE
- ☐ Life sciences
- ☐ Physical sciences
- ☐ Other

### SOCIAL SCIENCES
- ☐ Social sciences
- ☐ Legal education
- ☐ Other

### WELFARE/SOCIAL SERVICES
- ☐ Advocacy
- ☐ Business/economic education
- ☐ Community affairs
- ☐ Crime/law enforcement
- ☐ Drug abuse programs
- ☐ Economic development
- ☐ Employment/job training
- ☐ Environment/energy
- ☐ Equal rights/legal aid
- ☐ Disaster relief
- ☐ Family services
- ☐ Recreation
- ☐ Safety
- ☐ Special population groups
- ☐ Welfare
- ☐ Consumer interests
- ☐ Other

## 12. TYPES OF ORGANIZATIONS SUPPORTED:

### ARTS AND HUMANITIES
- ☐ Museums/historical societies
- ☐ Theaters/dance groups
- ☐ Music/opera groups
- ☐ Libraries
- ☐ Zoos
- ☐ Public TV/radio
- ☐ Arts councils
- ☐ Historic preservation
- ☐ Cultural centers
- ☐ Other

### EDUCATION
- ☐ Elementary schools
- ☐ Secondary schools
- ☐ Vocational schools
- ☐ Colleges
- ☐ Universities
- ☐ Educational councils
- ☐ Scholarship funds
- ☐ Special education
- ☐ Adult education
- ☐ Junior colleges
- ☐ Libraries
- ☐ Other

### HEALTH
- ☐ Hospitals
- ☐ Medical schools
- ☐ Medical research groups
- ☐ Medical societies
- ☐ Medical libraries
- ☐ Clinics
- ☐ Chemical dependency services
- ☐ Family planning agencies
- ☐ Counseling services
- ☐ Other

### RELIGION
- ☐ Churches/synagogues
- ☐ Religious service groups
- ☐ Religious schools
- ☐ Religious colleges
- ☐ Other

### SCIENCE/SOCIAL SCIENCE
- ☐ Research/study institutes
- ☐ Environmental agencies
- ☐ Energy agencies
- ☐ Conservation groups
- ☐ Other

### WELFARE/SOCIAL SERVICES
- ☐ United Way
- ☐ Legal aid
- ☐ Multi-service centers
- ☐ Organizations: elderly
- ☐ Organizations: handicapped
- ☐ Organizations: women's
- ☐ Organizations: veterans'
- ☐ Organizations: drug abusers'
- ☐ Organizations: youth
- ☐ Organizations: men's
- ☐ Centers for children
- ☐ Housing agencies
- ☐ Organizations: offenders
- ☐ Organizations: minority
- ☐ Neighborhood agencies
- ☐ Day care centers
- ☐ Community centers
- ☐ Animal centers
- ☐ Other

# 1982 DIRECTORY FOUNDATION QUESTIONNAIRE

13. TYPES OF SUPPORT FOR ORGANIZATIONS:
    ☐ Capital support
    ☐ Continuing support
    ☐ Endowment
    ☐ General operating
    ☐ Matching grants
    ☐ Program development
    ☐ Research
    ☐ Federated fund drives
    ☐ Program related investments
    ☐ Other
    ☐ None

14. TYPES OF SUPPORT FOR INDIVIDUALS:
    ☐ Aid to needy persons
    ☐ Scholarships
    ☐ Fellowships
    ☐ Education loans
    ☐ Travel
    ☐ Research
    ☐ Other
    ☐ None

15. DO YOU TARGET SPECIFIC POPULATION GROUPS?    ☐ YES    ☐ NO
    IF YES, PLEASE SPECIFY
    ☐ Aged
    ☐ Substance abusers
    ☐ Children/youth
    ☐ Criminal offenders/ex-offenders
    ☐ Handicapped
    ☐ Men/boys
    ☐ Women/girls
    ☐ Refugees
    ☐ Minorities
          ☐ Asian Americans
          ☐ Blacks
          ☐ Hispanics
          ☐ Native Americans
    ☐ Veterans
    ☐ Other

# 1982 DIRECTORY FOUNDATION QUESTIONNAIRE

16. Financial data for fiscal year ending _____
    Day            Month          Year

17. Foundation assets: $_____

18. Grants paid:     Total .............$_____   Largest .......$_____

    Number of grants .. _____

    Average $ per grant .$_____   Smallest .......$_____

19. Paid professional staff:     ☐ Yes     ☐ No

20. Preferred form of initial contact:

    ☐ Telephone inquiry          ☐ Complete proposal
    ☐ Letter of inquiry          ☐ Other: _____
    ☐ Request for guidelines

21. Available public information (by request): Please check all appropriate items

    ☐ Proposal guidelines        ☐ Annual report
    ☐ Application procedures      ☐ Other: _____

22. Deadline for proposals to be submitted:

23. Board meets:     ☐ Annually
                     ☐ Biannually
                     ☐ Quarterly     ON (specify dates):_____
                     ☐ Monthly
                     ☐ Other

24. Applicants notified within _____ weeks of decision

25. Directors/trustees: Please list name and title

    _____

    _____

    _____

Survey completed by _____ Date_____

# Appendix 6

## MINNESOTA COUNCIL ON FOUNDATIONS
## 1982 DIRECTORY QUESTIONNAIRE

Please return by September 10, 1982 to
Minnesota Council on Foundations,
1216 Foshay Tower,
Minneapolis, MN 55402.
Questions—call (612) 338-1989

1. Corporation name:_____

2. Address:_____

3. Telephone number:_____

4. Does your company have a charitable contributions program? _____Yes _____No
   (If yes, please complete this questionnaire and return to the MCF. If no, or if you have
   a company-sponsored foundation for which you have previously completed a similar
   questionnaire, please so indicate and return this form to us.)_____

   _____

   _____

5. Contact person and title:_____

6. Date established:_____

7. What are your primary areas of interest for funding?_____

   _____

   _____

8. Funding limitations or restrictions:_____

   _____

   _____

9. Geographic orientation:  ☐ Twin Cities      ☐ Minnesota      ☐ National
   ☐ International      ☐ Other (be specific)_____

10. Sample grants: Please list three typical grants, recipients, and amounts

    _____

    _____

    _____

# 1982 DIRECTORY CORPORATE QUESTIONNAIRE

## 11. FIELDS OF ACTIVITY:

### ARTS AND HUMANITIES
- ☐ Arts/architecture
- ☐ History/preservation
- ☐ Language/literature
- ☐ Media/communications
- ☐ Music/opera
- ☐ Theater/dance
- ☐ Arts education
- ☐ Other

### EDUCATION
- ☐ Elementary/secondary
- ☐ Vocational
- ☐ Higher
- ☐ Adult/continuing
- ☐ Research
- ☐ Other

### HEALTH
- ☐ Medical research
- ☐ Medical care/treatment
- ☐ Medical/health education
- ☐ Public health
- ☐ Mental health
- ☐ Other

### RELIGION
- ☐ Religion
- ☐ Religious education
- ☐ Other

### SCIENCE
- ☐ Life sciences
- ☐ Physical sciences
- ☐ Other

### SOCIAL SCIENCES
- ☐ Social sciences
- ☐ Legal education
- ☐ Other

### WELFARE/SOCIAL SERVICES
- ☐ Advocacy
- ☐ Business/economic education
- ☐ Community affairs
- ☐ Crime/law enforcement
- ☐ Drug abuse programs
- ☐ Economic development
- ☐ Employment/job training
- ☐ Environment/energy
- ☐ Equal rights/legal aid
- ☐ Disaster relief
- ☐ Family services
- ☐ Recreation
- ☐ Safety
- ☐ Special population groups
- ☐ Welfare
- ☐ Consumer interests
- ☐ Other

## 12. TYPES OF ORGANIZATIONS SUPPORTED:

### ARTS AND HUMANITIES
- ☐ Museums/historical societies
- ☐ Theaters/dance groups
- ☐ Music/opera groups
- ☐ Libraries
- ☐ Zoos
- ☐ Public TV/radio
- ☐ Arts councils
- ☐ Historic preservation
- ☐ Cultural centers
- ☐ Other

### EDUCATION
- ☐ Elementary schools
- ☐ Secondary schools
- ☐ Vocational schools
- ☐ Colleges
- ☐ Universities
- ☐ Educational councils
- ☐ Scholarship funds
- ☐ Special education
- ☐ Adult education
- ☐ Junior colleges
- ☐ Libraries
- ☐ Other

### HEALTH
- ☐ Hospitals
- ☐ Medical schools
- ☐ Medical research groups
- ☐ Medical societies
- ☐ Medical libraries
- ☐ Clinics
- ☐ Chemical dependency services
- ☐ Family planning agencies
- ☐ Counseling services
- ☐ Other

### RELIGION
- ☐ Churches/synagogues
- ☐ Religious service groups
- ☐ Religious schools
- ☐ Religious colleges
- ☐ Other

### SCIENCE/SOCIAL SCIENCE
- ☐ Research/study institutes
- ☐ Environmental agencies
- ☐ Energy agencies
- ☐ Conservation groups
- ☐ Other

### WELFARE/SOCIAL SERVICES
- ☐ United Way
- ☐ Legal aid
- ☐ Multi-service centers
- ☐ Organizations: elderly
- ☐ Organizations: handicapped
- ☐ Organizations: women's
- ☐ Organizations: veterans'
- ☐ Organizations: drug abusers'
- ☐ Organizations: youth
- ☐ Organizations: men's
- ☐ Centers for children
- ☐ Housing agencies
- ☐ Organizations: offenders
- ☐ Organizations: minority
- ☐ Neighborhood agencies
- ☐ Day care centers
- ☐ Community centers
- ☐ Animal centers
- ☐ Other

# 1982 DIRECTORY CORPORATE QUESTIONNAIRE

13. TYPES OF SUPPORT FOR ORGANIZATIONS:
    - ☐ Capital support
    - ☐ Continuing support
    - ☐ Endowment
    - ☐ General operating
    - ☐ Matching grants
    - ☐ Program development
    - ☐ Research
    - ☐ Federated fund drives
    - ☐ Program related investments
    - ☐ Other
    - ☐ None

14. TYPES OF SUPPORT FOR INDIVIDUALS:
    - ☐ Aid to needy persons
    - ☐ Scholarships
    - ☐ Fellowships
    - ☐ Education loans
    - ☐ Travel
    - ☐ Research
    - ☐ Other
    - ☐ None

15. DO YOU TARGET SPECIFIC POPULATION GROUPS?   ☐ YES   ☐ NO
    IF YES, PLEASE SPECIFY
    - ☐ Aged
    - ☐ Substance abusers
    - ☐ Children/youth
    - ☐ Criminal offenders/ex-offenders
    - ☐ Handicapped
    - ☐ Men/boys
    - ☐ Women/girls
    - ☐ Refugees
    - ☐ Minorities
        - ☐ Asian Americans
        - ☐ Blacks
        - ☐ Hispanics
        - ☐ Native Americans
    - ☐ Veterans
    - ☐ Other

16. Do you have an employee matching gift program?   ☐ Yes   ☐ No
    If Yes, please specify:
    - ☐ Higher education
    - ☐ Elementary/Secondary education
    - ☐ Any non-profit organization
    - ☐ Other (please describe) _____

17. Do you have a scholarship program for children of employees?   ☐ Yes   ☐ No

# 1982 DIRECTORY CORPORATE QUESTIONNAIRE

18. Financial data for fiscal year ending_____
    Day                    Month                    Year

19. Contributions paid:

    Total ....................$_____ Largest ..............$_____

    Number of contributions...... _____

    Average $ per contribution ..$_____ Smallest .............$_____
    (If you do not wish to give the specific amount, please check below
    the appropriate range for your annual contributions program.)
    ☐ Under $15,000
    ☐ $15,000-$49,999
    ☐ $50,000-$99,999
    ☐ $100,000-$499,999
    ☐ $500,000-$999,999
    ☐ Over $1 million

20. Preferred form of initial contact:

    ☐ Telephone inquiry          ☐ Complete proposal
    ☐ Letter of inquiry          ☐ Other: _____
    ☐ Request for guidelines

21. Available public information (by request): Please check all appropriate items

    ☐ Proposal guidelines        ☐ Annual report on contributions
    ☐ Application procedures      ☐ Other: _____

22. Deadline for proposals to be submitted:

23. Contributions Decisions Made:

    ☐ Annually
    ☐ Biannually
    ☐ Quarterly      ON (specify dates):_____
    ☐ Monthly
    ☐ Other

24. Applicants notified within _____ weeks of decision

Survey completed by_____ Date_____

# Indexes

# Index of Foundations

# Index of
# Types of Organizations
# Funded by Specific Grant Makers

This index is based on responses to the MCF survey of grant makers. It includes only those funders that responded to the survey or that had a clear statement of purpose in the original trust instrument.

## ARTS AND HUMANITIES

EDUCATION

# Index of Grant Makers by Size

(According to Grants Paid)

The McKnight Foundation—$24,796,148  66
The Bush Foundation—$12,256,713  13
Dayton Hudson Foundation—$7,141,648  22
Northwest Area Foundation—$5,870,135  79
General Mills Foundation—$5,658,633  40
Honeywell Foundation—$4,500,581  50
C. K. Blandin Foundation—$4,136,956  9
3M Foundation—$4,012,861  106
The Saint Paul Foundation—$3,939,632  98
The St. Paul Companies, Inc.—$3,056,759  97
Charles and Ellora Alliss Educational
  Foundation—$2,877,400  1
The Phillips Foundation—$2,740,363  89
Burlington Northern Foundation—$2,646,176  12
The Pillsbury Company Foundation—$2,613,370  90
The Minneapolis Foundation—$2,417,664  70
Otto Bremer Foundation—$2,361,403  10
First Bank System Foundation—$1,909,773  33
Northern States Power Company—$1,400,000  79
I. A. O'Shaughnessy Foundation—$1,371,100  84
Deluxe Check Printers Foundation—$1,305,554  24
The Cargill Foundation—$1,251,963  15
First National Bank of Minneapolis
  Foundation—$1,138,153  35
Jerome Foundation—$1,094,002  54
Northwestern National Bank of
  Minneapolis—$1,087,000  80
Benjamin A. Miller Family Foundation—$1,029,000  69
Northwestern Bell Telephone Company—More than
  $1,000,000*  80
The Andreas Foundation—$988,681  3
General Service Foundation—$977,526  41
First Bank St. Paul—$947,000  33
Archer-Daniels-Midland Foundation—$858,313  3
F. R. Bigelow Foundation—$820,205  8
The Fingerhut Foundation—$802,408  32
Frederick and Margaret L. Weyerhaeuser
  Foundation—$783,500  112
Medtronic Foundation—$756,337  68
Investors Diversified Services (IDS)—$750,000  53

Tozer Foundation—$702,569  107
Andersen Foundation—$646,696  2
Mardag Foundation—$634,822  65
H. B. Fuller Company—$582,854  38
Carolyn Foundation—$565,864  15
Edwin W. and Catherine M. Davis
  Foundation—$558,680  22
Bemis Company Foundation—$549,442  6
Bayport Foundation—$538,648  5
Mary Livingston Griggs and Mary Griggs Burke
  Foundation—$518,032  45
The Wasie Foundation—$515,283  109
Edwards Memorial Trust—$505,100  30

Piper, Jaffray and Hopwood—$100,000 to $499,999
  range*  90
Williams Steel and Hardware—$100,000 to $499,999
  range*  113
The Gainey Foundation—$498,600  38
Groves Foundation—$486,211  46
Northwestern National Life Insurance
  Company—$462,072  81
The Hubbard Foundation—$446,647  51
Joseph Foundation—$437,680  56
Graco Foundation—$437,667  43
Margaret Rivers Fund—$430,450  94
Minneapolis Star and Tribune Foundation—$421,500  71
James R. Thorpe Foundation—$409,200  105
Ordean Foundation—$401,416  84
Hersey Foundation—$400,940  49
The Jostens Foundation—$377,000  57
International Multifoods Charitable
  Foundation—$364,580  52
Deluxe Check Printers—$362,556  23
Curtis L. Carlson Foundation—$337,507  15
Jostens Inc.—$322,900  56
Harris Foundation—$305,112  47
Northwest Bancorporation Foundation—$300,043  80
The Donaldson Foundation—$300,000  26
WCCO AM/FM/TV—$300,000  110

*Corporations with internal giving programs, rather than foundations, are not legally required to make public their contributions record. Corporations marked here with an asterisk gave the MCF the range in which their contributions fall, rather than a specific figure.

Minnesota Mutual Life Charitable Trust—*$297,927* 72
The Southways Foundation—*$294,669* 102
Baker Foundation—*$288,534* 4
Charles A. Weyerhaeuser Memorial
 Foundation—*$266,500* 112
Onan Family Foundation—*$265,615* 83
W. R. Hotchkiss Foundation—*$263,628* 50
Lewis and Annie F. Paper Foundation—*$259,985* 87
Cenex Foundation—*$251,100* 16
Marbrook Foundation—*$250,550* 65
The Gelco Foundation—*$246,948* 40
Charity, Inc.—*$245,978* 17
Grain Terminal Foundation—*$243,250* 43
Lieberman-Okinow Foundation—*$236,402* 62
Tennant Company Foundation—*$233,791* 105
Robert E. Short Foundation—*$222,000* 101
Richard Coyle Lilly Foundation—*$218,600* 62
Archie D. and Bertha H. Walker
 Foundation—*$217,690* 108
Wood-Rill Foundation—*$216,135* 114
Athwin Foundation—*$208,118* 4
Gerald Rauenhorst Family Foundation—*$205,100* 92
Northern Star Foundation—*$197,380* 78
Inter-Regional Financial Group Foundation—*$191,700* 53
Dye Family Foundation Trust—*$190,000* 29
Mary Andersen Hulings Foundation—*$178,660* 51
James F. Bell Foundation—*$177,413* 6
Ferndale Foundation—*$175,106* 32
Red Wing Shoe Company Foundation—*$174,515* 93
McQuay-Perfex Foundation of Minnesota—*$168,621* 68
Weyerhaeuser Foundation—*$167,904* 111
Sumner T. McKnight Foundation—*$166,850* 67
Land O'Lakes, Inc.—*$162,000* 61
The Jack and Bessie Fiterman Foundation—*$157,900* 36
Minnesota Foundation—*$157,879* 71
Patrick and Aimee Butler Family
 Foundation—*$151,790* 13
Conwed Foundation—*$148,990* 19
Elmer L. and Eleanor J. Andersen
 Foundation—*$147,481* 2
Chadwick Foundation—*$146,080* 16
Hartz Foundation—*$143,720* 47
Greystone Foundation—*$137,910* 44
Hawthorne Foundation—*$136,800* 48
The Rodman Foundation—*$131,600* 96
Alice M. O'Brien Foundation—*$126,878* 82
The Beim Foundation—*$125,000* 5
The Valspar Foundation—*$124,017* 107
Apache Foundation—*$122,296* 3
American Hoist and Derrick Foundation—*$122,075* 2
Helen Harrington Charitable Trust—*$119,078* 47
Whitney Foundation—*$118,761* 113
Sam Miller Foundation—*$118,689* 70
Joshua Foundation—*$116,077* 56
Menahem Heilicher Charitable Foundation—*$113,418* 48
Hugh J. Andersen Foundation—*$112,285* 2
Hartzell Foundation—*$112,109* 47
The Gladys and Rudolph Miller Foundation—*$111,929* 69

F. K. and Vivian O'Gara Weyerhaeuser
 Foundation—*$109,775* 112
Lee and Rose Warner Foundation—*$104,100* 109
Cray Research, Inc.—*$100,000* 21

MTS Systems Corporation—*$50,000 to $99,999 range** 74
Onan Corporation—*$50,000 to $99,999 range** 83
Pako Corporation—*$50,000 to $99,999 range** 86
Prudential Insurance Company—*$50,000 to $99,999
 range** 91
The McNeely Foundation—*$99,841* 67
Melamed Foundation—*$97,475* 69
Business Incentives Foundation—*$96,550* 13
Data Card Corporation—*$90,000* 21
Elizabeth C. Quinlan Foundation—*$88,920* 91
Albert T. O'Neil Foundation—*$86,900* 83
Spiegel Foundation—*$86,690* 102
S. B. Foot Tanning Company Foundation—*$84,650* 36
The Driscoll Foundation—*$84,032* 27
Deubener-Juenemann Foundation—*$80,150* 25
Dellwood Foundation—*$80,100* 23
Edward C. Congdon Memorial Trust—*$80,087* 19
John and Elizabeth Bates Cowles Foundation—*$78,900* 20
Malakoff Foundation—*$78,580* 64
Father Kasal Charitable Trust—*$78,250* 59
Caridad Gift Trust—*$76,900* 15
JNM 1966 Gift Trust—*$74,950* 55
The Werner Foundation—*$72,727* 111
The Ankeny Foundation—*$72,012* 3
Paulucci Family Foundation—*$70,143* 87
Grotto Foundation—*$69,000* 45
Salem Foundation—*$68,400* 99
George W. Neilson Foundation—*$66,500* 77
Maslon Foundation—*$66,499* 66
The Nash Foundation—*$65,000* 76
Myers Foundation—*$61,950* 75
Paul N. Myers, Jr. Foundation—*$60,903* 75
Smith Foundation—*$60,525* 102
Roger L. and Agnes C. Dell Charitable Trust
 II—*$59,500* 23
Jaeson H. Kline Foundation—*$58,848* 60
First Federal Savings of Minneapolis—*$58,088* 34
Federated Insurance Foundation—*$57,227* 32
Harold W. Sweatt Foundation—*$57,195* 103
The Range Foundation—*$57,110* 92
Russell T. Lund Charitable Trust—*$56,976* 63
The Cooperative Foundation—*$55,000* 19
Rochester Area Foundation—*$54,822* 95
The Eliza A. Drew Memorial Fund—*$53,036* 27
The Cherne Foundation—*$52,931* 17
Peerless Chain Foundation—*$52,000* 87
The Hanser Family Foundation—*$51,595* 46
MWVE Fund—*$51,273* 75
Numero-Steinfeldt Foundation—*$51,213* 82
Helen Lang Charitable Trust—*$50,000* 61

Charles D. Gilfillan Memorial—*$48,891* 41
Minnesota Title Foundation—*$47,259* 73

The Edward Fiterman Foundation—$46,925   36
National City Bank Foundation—$46,280   76
Hyman S. Kaplan Family Foundation—$46,000   58
William Wood Skinner Foundation—$45,550   101
Ingram Foundation—$45,335   52
George A. MacPherson Fund—$45,296   64
Martin and Esther Capp Foundation—$45,093   14
Joseph Paper Foundation—$44,865   87
The Harold and Florence Fischbein
   Foundation—$44,255   35
The Kahler Foundation—$43,659   57
The Hermundslie Foundation—$42,000   49
The Minnesota Rubber Foundation—$41,723   72
Bernard and Fern Badzin Foundation—$39,508   4
Mediclinics Educational Fund—$39,500   68
Minnesota State Bar Foundation—$38,597   73
Sexton Foundation—$38,210   100
George M. Palmer Foundation—$38,130   86
Buckbee-Mears Foundation—$37,933   12
Churchmen's Fellowship of Peace United Church of
   Christ—$37,500   18
Grace Overton Foundation—$37,298   85
Mankato Citizens Telephone Company
   Foundation—$37,046   64
Rose and Harry Rosenthal Foundation—$36,156   96
Schmitt Foundation—$35,765   99
George Kaplan Memorial Foundation—$35,500   58
MSI Foundation—$35,285   74
The Hannah Lips Foundation—$34,923   63
Fullerton Foundation—$34,525   38
Nadler Foundation—$33,750   76
Bronstien Family Foundation—$33,700   11
The Leavitt Foundation—$33,425   61
Ripley Memorial Foundation—$32,931   94
Doherty, Rumble & Butler Foundation—$32,850   25
James T. Williams, Sr. Foundation—$32,250   113
The Dyco Foundation—$31,566   29
Axel Newman Family Foundation—$30,064   77
Leisure Dynamics Foundation—$30,050   62
Laura and Walter Hudson Foundation—$29,980   51
The Galinson Foundation—$29,932   38
St. Croix Foundation—$29,800   96
The Pacific Foundation—$29,464   86
Mr. and Mrs. Edward F. Baker Foundation—$29,462   5
The Bentson Foundation—$29,373   7
Kelm Foundation—$28,650   59
Nevin N. Huested Foundation for Handicapped
   Children—$28,121   51
Sven and C. Emil Berglund Foundation—$27,380   7
The Jefferson Foundation—$27,200   54
Hendel Foundation—$26,349   48
The Fred M. Seed Foundation—$25,700   100
The Or Foundation—$25,416   84
Zelle Charitable Trust—$25,000   115

Arthur and David Cosgrove Memorial Fund—$24,969   20
Minneapolis Kiwanis Foundation—$24,898   71
David Winton Bell Foundation—$24,500   6

The Skipper Slawik Foundation—$23,015   101
Sieff Family Foundation—$22,851   101
Gandrud Foundation—$22,700   39
Alfred W. Erickson Foundation—$21,923   31
P.G.N. Foundation—$21,800   89
Manitou Fund—$21,125   64
The Harry V. Johnston Foundation—$20,826   55
Minnesota Natural Foundation—$20,415   72
W. R. Busch Foundation—$20,400   13
Howell P. and Margaret H. Skoglund
   Foundation—$19,800   101
The Sam and Irma Brown Family
   Foundation—$19,700   11
Robert and Anne Reznick Family Foundation—$19,386   93
William Boss Foundation—$19,191   10
Tebben Foundation—$18,937   105
Edelstein Family Foundation—$18,692   30
H. E. and Helen R. Warren Foundation—$18,070   109
William J. Benfield Testamentary Trust—$18,000   7
Lewis H. Johnson Family Foundation—$17,994   55
Burdick Grain Company Charitable
   Foundation—$17,665   12
Joseph C. and Lillian A. Duke Foundation—$17,650   28
Albert B. Cuppage Charitable Foundation—$17,500   21
Arthur T. Erickson Foundation—$16,950   31
Wedum Foundation—$16,885   110
Arthur and Constance Goodman Family
   Foundation—$16,851   42
Mendon F. Schutt Foundation—$16,700   100
Duluth Benevolence Foundation—$16,624   28
Ring Foundation—$16,150   94
Norling Brothers Foundation—$15,600   78
Watson Foundation—$15,546   110
Alexandra Foundation—$15,375   1
Roger L. and Agnes C. Dell Charitable Trust
   I—$15,120   23
Lerner Foundation—$15,043   62
The Frenzel Foundation—$15,000   37
M. J. Kennedy Foundation—$15,000   59
St. Jude Medical, Inc.—Under $15,000*   97
Security Financial Enterprises, Inc.—Under $15,000*   100
Samuel Cohen and Esther Cohen Foundation—$14,617   18
Douglas Foundation—$14,550   27
Dyson Family Foundation—$14,400   29
Malvin E. and Josephine D. Herz
   Foundation—$13,500   49
Duluth Improvement Trust—$13,250   29
D. B. Robinson Foundation—$13,070   95
Ziff Family Foundation—$13,054   115
Campbell Charitable Trust—$12,909   14
Granelda Foundation—$12,500   44
P & B Foundation—$12,000   86
Louis M. and Tess Cohen Family
   Foundation—$11,990   18
Adolph and Mildred Fine Fund—$11,207   32
The Salkin Foundation—$11,175   99
Duluth Clinic Education and Research
   Foundation—$10,899   28

Bing Foundation—*$400* 8
Winton Companies Fund—*$400* 114
Edward H. Willmus Family Charitable Trust—*$250* 114
Jane and William C. Norris Foundation—*$209* 78
Ernest C. Oberholtzer Foundation—*$200* 82
Tang Foundation—*$200* 104
Ritz Foundation—*$150* 94
Sweitzer Foundation—*$150* 104
Hartwell Foundation—*$100* 47
Big Game Club Special Projects Foundation—*$0* 8
Char-Lynn Foundation—*$0* 17
Oscar and Madge Hawkins Foundation—*$0* 48
Hubert H. Humphrey Foundation—*$0* 52
D. W. Jimmerson Foundation—*$0* 55
Joseph N. Larson Foundation—*$0* 61

George and Marion Levine Foundation—*$0* 62
Maleska Rothfork Family Foundation—*$0* 64
Navanod Foundation—*$0* 77
Oakleaf Foundation—*$0* 82
Owen Family Fund—*$0* 85
Tralarden Foundation—*$0* 107
Ben Wilensky Foundation—*$0* 113

NEW FOUNDATIONS (No Grants as of Publication
    Deadline)

Adducci Family Foundation—*$0* 1
B. C. Gamble and P. W. Skogmo Foundation—*$0* 39
North Star Research Foundation—*$0* 78